PLATO
and the
Question
of
Beauty

PLATO
and the
Question
of
Beauty

DREW A. HYLAND

Indiana University Press
Bloomington & Indianapolis

This book is a publication of

Indiana University Press
601 North Morton Street
Bloomington, IN 47404-3797 USA

http://iupress.indiana.edu

Telephone orders	800-842-6796
Fax orders	812-855-7931
Orders by e-mail	iuporder@indiana.edu

The paper used in this publication meets the minimum requirements of American National Standard for Information
Sciences—Permanence of Paper for Printed Library Materi-
als, ANSI Z39.48-1984.

Manufactured in the United States of America

Library of Congress Cataloging-in-Publication Data

Hyland, Drew A.
    Plato and the question of beauty / Drew A. Hyland.
        p.   cm. — (Studies in continental thought)
    Includes bibliographical references and index.
    ISBN-13: 978-0-253-35138-8 (cloth : alk. paper)
    ISBN-13: 978-0-253-21977-0 (pbk. : alk. paper) 1. Plato.
2. Aesthetics.   3. Plato. Phaedrus.   I. Title.
    B398.A4H95   2008
    111'.85092—dc22

                                        2007045005

1   2   3   4   5   13   12   11   10   09   08

A book on beauty, one that I would write, can have only one dedication:
For Anne

Walk in beauty.
Navajo farewell

Beauty is momentary in the mind—
The fitful tracing of a portal;
But in the flesh it is immortal.
Wallace Stevens, "Peter Quince at the Clavier"

But it's a beautiful thing to strive after the beautiful,
And to suffer whatever we have to suffer along the way.
Plato, Phaedrus, 274b

Contents

Preface and Acknowledgments

The question of beauty is the subject of lively discussion and debate today, particularly but not only as it pertains to the arts. Part of the intention of this book is to consider the extent to which Plato, as happens so often, was instrumental in setting the terms of the discussion and debate about beauty as it plays out in the history of western philosophy. In a sense, then, this book sets the stage for other studies of the question of beauty as it manifests itself in various periods of our history, certainly including the present. In this sense, I hope that the book has a certain timeliness.

When quoting Plato's texts as well as those of various commentators in the following pages, I have often used available translations as indicated in notes. However, in the majority of those citations, I have found it necessary to alter the translations somewhat, usually in order to make them as literal as possible. When the translations are entirely my own, I indicate that as well.

I have many people to thank for their help in the development of this book. First to be mentioned must be my students in seminars on Plato both at the New School for Social Research and at Trinity College. At both institutions I was privileged to be able to develop my ideas about the question of beauty in Plato in seminars full of engaged and engaging students. Their help in the development of my thoughts in this book is immeasurable.

A number of people at Indiana University Press have been of enormous help in seeing the project through. First among them is Dee Mortensen, senior editor for philosophy. I also wish to thank Laura MacLeod, assistant editor, and Miki Bird, managing editor. All have been not only helpful but good-humored and enjoyable to work with. John Sallis, the series editor, has encouraged me in this project from the start, and I am grateful for that encouragement. He along with Dennis Schmidt invited me to give a course at the Collegium Phenomeno-logicum in the summer of 2005 on "Memory and Responsibility," and the lectures I prepared for that course really formed the beginning of this project. I also want to especially thank my copy editor, David Dusenbury, for his very careful reading of and helpful improvements to my manuscript. In addition, my two anonymous referees offered astute comments that challenged me to im-prove the book as well.

Finally and as always, my wife Anne has been a constant source of support and encouragement. Especially on questions such as beauty, she is a wealth of wisdom and insight, and I thank her for all of these gifts.

PLATO
and the
Question
of
Beauty

Introduction

This will be a book about the question of beauty in the Platonic dialogues, but as Plato himself will make abundantly clear, the question of beauty cannot be adequately addressed except within a context of a whole host of other issues. Hegel may be the modern philosopher who best articulated the recognition that a consideration of any moderately rich issue as if it stood by itself, without a consideration of its connection to other issues that contribute to what it is, is the very meaning of "abstractness," but it was Plato who first exhibited that recognition in his dialogues. He did so in myriad ways, and certainly paradigmatically with the question of beauty. Indeed, we might begin our study with a reflection on one of the great mysteries of the dialogues: the question of what issues Plato decides to take up more or less explicitly, by contrast to those many other, no less crucial issues which are not addressed thematically, focally, but are allowed to arise in the context of other issues. Let us consider briefly some of the ways in which he does this.

Begin with those many dialogues that do seem to address an issue focally. They are of at least two sorts. The first and most explicit are those dialogues often referred to as "definitional" dialogues, where a given topic—courage, friendship, piety, knowledge—is pursued apparently with the goal of arriving at an unimpeachable "definition" of the topic in question. Such dialogues—the *Laches*, *Lysis*, *Euthyphro*, and *Theaetetus* among others—can give the impression that Plato, or rather the Platonic Socrates, believed that such issues could indeed be addressed atomically, by themselves, with minimal reference to other issues, and that such address could be literally definitive, resulting in an adequate definition. That these dialogues—and we shall have occasion to address one, the *Hippias Major*, in some detail—always fail of their apparent goal is by no means an unimportant consideration in this regard. And that failure, particularly in the case of the effort in the *Hippias Major* to adequately define *auto to kalon*, "beauty itself," will prove crucial to our understanding of how this theme is addressed in the other dialogues we shall consider in detail, the *Symposium* and *Phaedrus*.

There is a second way, however, in which issues such as eros, recollection, form, and beauty are addressed focally in dialogues. These issues *are* addressed in considerable depth and focally, each in several dialogues, but—and this is the crucial difference from the first set of focal issues—not (at least after the failure of the *Hippias Major*) with a goal of arriving at a definition. What is especially striking here is that one might argue that issues such as eros, recollection, form, and beauty are treated in even greater depth, in more dialogues, and in more ways than are the "definitional" issues—"justice" in the *Republic* would be an obvious and complicated exception—yet without the apparent goal of "defining" the issue in question in any strict sense. For no doubt complicated reasons that we will have to consider in detail, what knowledge we gain from these considerations concerning eros, recollection, or beauty is somehow other than that knowledge which could be articulated as a definition.

Third, however, there is a significant set of issues about which we learn much in the dialogues, issues such as truth (*aletheia*), trust (*pistis*), language (*logos*), or responsibility. These issues are never addressed thematically as the direct object of investigation, whether with the goal of definition or of focal knowledge. Yet who could deny that such issues are very much at play in the dialogues, and that we are given to think on them as we consider almost any dialogue?

One might add as a fourth set of issues those about which, in any explicit sense at all, the dialogues seem to be silent: what Heidegger liked to call the "unsaid" in the thinking of the dialogues. There are at least two modes of such silence with very different meanings. On the one hand, there is the silence of total absence, issues of philosophic importance that we might be tempted to say that Plato "failed to address" or "missed" in his writing. Given the thematic breadth of the dialogues, it is hard to name many examples here, but some have suggested various historically determined issues: there is no consideration of genocide, for example,[1] or even of the very significance of historical process itself. More important, however, are those issues about which the silence, given the issues addressed or the dramatic context, are *strikingly* absent: absent in such a way that we are invited to think that Plato *wanted us to be struck* by their very absence. Why, for example, in the *Theaetetus*—a dialogue devoted focally, even definitionally, to the question of knowledge—are the crucial Platonic "forms" or "ideas" never introduced? Or why, in the *Symposium*—a dialogue largely devoted to a magnificent elaboration of the problem of eros—when we finally *are* introduced to the notion of form by Diotima, are we not introduced to the "form of eros," which would give us, presumably, the knowledge we need of that notion, but instead introduced to the form of *auto to kalon*, beauty itself? Or why, to take a final example, is the question of the significance of silence never addressed even though again and again, silence plays a crucial *dramatic* role in the happening of a dialogue, as when Socrates falls largely silent before the Eleatic Stranger in the *Sophist* and *Statesman*, or in the *Timaeus*?

The mystery to which I earlier alluded, then, is this: why does Plato choose to address certain issues with the explicitness of an attempt at definition, others focally but without an eye to definition, and others in the various ways that I have set out? (There may be more ways than those I have indicated. My attempt here is not to be exhaustive but to note the broad array of modes in which Plato allows issues to arise for the consideration of the reader.) One thing is for sure: no adequate "Platonic epistemology" could be offered which did not take these various modes into account.

This mystery becomes especially acute with the question of *to kalon*, beauty. For it is addressed in at least three different ways in the three dialogues, the *Hippias Major, Symposium,* and *Phaedrus,* in which the thinking about beauty becomes focal. I emphasize the focal character of the address in these dialogues because there is probably not a single Platonic dialogue in which the issue of beauty is not in play in some way (an indication, surely, of the correctness of Nietzsche's insight about the profound importance of beauty for the ancient Greeks, if not for us as well).[2] In the *Hippias Major,* the address of beauty is at its most focal: it is one of those dialogues in which Socrates attempts with his interlocutor—in this case the sophist, Hippias—to achieve an unimpeachable definition of beauty, an attempt whose failure we shall have to observe with considerable care. Even in this dialogue, however, we witness that the issue cannot be addressed atomically and in isolation: almost a quarter of the dialogue goes by before the theme of beauty is explicitly taken up and an attempt at a definition made, though as we shall see, the theme is subtly in play literally from the first line of the dialogue. In the *Symposium,* no attempt at defining beauty is made—indeed, very good reasons are given why it cannot in principle be defined. Nevertheless, "beauty itself" becomes the object lesson by which Diotima tries to lead Socrates to an insight into a "Platonic form," in the culmination of her speech (the famous "ascent passage" at 210ff.). But beauty is not by any means introduced arbitrarily as that example, and we shall have to watch with care just how the movement of the dialogue takes us ineluctably to that theme. In the *Phaedrus,* the address of beauty makes yet another decisive shift. For in that dialogue, it is the *existential experience* of beauty—the beauty of a beloved and the affect of that beauty on the lover—which is the primary mode by which we are led to understand something of the significance of beauty for human life.

In all three dialogues, I shall claim, one crucial issue that will arise will be the *non-discursive* dimension of beauty, a dimension that will work in a crucial dialectic with the also inevitable discursive dimension, the dimension having to do with *logos*. The dialectic of the discursive and the non-discursive with regard to beauty, I hope to show, will be decisive to what understanding we can gain of the meaning and significance of beauty for human life, at least as the dialogues exhibit it.

But this dialectic, it will be shown, is not limited to the issue of beauty. Beauty, it will turn out, is just one example—the *Phaedrus* will indicate why it is the most dramatic and accessible example—of the dialectic of discursivity and non-discursivity in play in all modes of genuine knowing. That dialectic will also be operative with regard to the other "beings" as they are called in the *Phaedrus,* those beings that are elsewhere called "forms" or "ideas" and are so often regarded as definitive of Platonic philosophy. All "formal" knowledge will exhibit this dialectic, this play of discursive logos and silent, "noetic" vision.

Nor does it stop here. That dialectic will be shown to be decisively exhibited in philosophy itself. By the standards both of the ancient Greeks and of our own dominant conceptions of philosophy, this understanding will be controversial. It will amount to taking seriously what is too often reduced to a cliché, that for the Platonic Socrates, "philosophy is a way of life." To take this cliché seriously is to recognize that philosophy cannot then be simply "argument," or even logos in a broader sense alone. It must rather be what we might call "embodied logos": logos as weaved into a life lived. To see how Plato develops this notion, we shall turn to a consideration of his Second and Seventh Letters. As we shall see, these will very much have to do with a certain *critique*—in the Kantian sense—of logos, a critique that reveals both the absolute necessity of logos for a philosophic life but at the same time points to its limits. That, finally, will lead us to return to the concluding half of the *Phaedrus,* the famous critique of rhetoric and of writing itself. So the last thing we will have to consider is how what we have developed in the book might shed light on Platonic writing, the writing of the dialogues themselves.

The structure of the book will thus be as follows: chapter 1 will examine the attempt in the *Hippias Major* to achieve a definition of *to kalon* that will withstand Socrates' *elenchus.* With the failure of that effort, we shall turn in chapter 2 to the very different way in which beauty is addressed in the *Symposium,* culminating in the ascent to "beauty itself." In chapter 3, we shall turn to the powerfully "existential" portrayal of the actual effect of beauty on a lover when in the presence of a beautiful beloved in the *Phaedrus.* Chapter 4 will turn to the Letters in order to draw out how the dialectic we will have seen developed earlier of discursive and non-discursive experience plays out in the very character of Platonic philosophy itself, philosophy best understood as *philosophic living.* That will lead us, finally, to a return to the latter half of the *Phaedrus* and the question of Platonic writing in chapter 5.

Before beginning, we need to say a word about the complicated word *kalon* and its cognates in Greek. The word actually resembles the contemporary use of the English "beauty" in the enormous range of its meaning. To be sure, it means "beauty" in the fairly narrow and standard sense that we have come to call "aesthetic." But the Greek especially shades toward the sense of "nobility," as in the common Greek phrase *kalos k'agathos*, "noble and good," often ascribed to a fine man or "gentleman." In turn, the word can shade into the sense of "good" in an extra-moral sense, as in "that's a good idea" or "you speak well." Indeed, it is possible that the often deplored extended sense of the word "beauty" in common parlance today ("Let's go have a drink! Beautiful idea!" or "We won the game last night! Beautiful!") actually approaches something of the range of the Greek word. For this reason, some translators, especially in the case of the *Hippias Major*, prefer "fine" to "beauty" as the best translation of the word. However, for my purposes at least, that translation loses the connection to the more obvious cases, as in the *Symposium* and *Phaedrus*, where "beauty" is clearly the word called for. For that reason, even when the meaning of the word is stretched, I shall translate *to kalon* and its cognates as forms of "beauty," occasionally adding "and noble" when the term is clearly appropriate.

One final introductory point: three of the texts I shall consider in some detail, the *Hippias Major* and the Second and Seventh Letters, are still controversial as regards their authenticity as Platonic writings, although I think it is fair to say that the majority of scholarship on the issue these days leans toward their authenticity. I shall not be examining the question of "Platonic authenticity" in any depth, either in the case of the *Hippias Major* or the Letters, and in this introduction I want to at least indicate why. In brief, the reasons adduced for these judgments, both pro and con, strike me as usually at least as unstable as the judgments themselves.

Consider, as one instance, the work of Ludwig Edelstein, who devotes most of a careful and distinguished book to demonstrating the inauthenticity of the Seventh Letter.[3] The vast majority of Edelstein's arguments against the authenticity of the Seventh Letter, perhaps understandably, depend on perceived inconsistencies between the views expressed in the Letter and "Plato's views" as purportedly expressed in the dialogues. And how are "Plato's views" in the dialogues determined? By what Socrates, or Timaeus, or the Eleatic Stranger says in this or that dialogue. One example from Edelstein: in the crucial discussion of the need for a sustained philosophic education in the Seventh Letter, nothing is said of the need to study mathematics (though the circle is used as a guiding example) as the core beginning to an adequate philosophic education. Yet the *Republic* teaches us (does it not?) that the systematic study of mathematics is a crucial sine qua non to the possibility of educating philosopher-rulers who will rule the perfectly just city that the *Republic* is intended to establish (or is it?). Surely, assumes Edelstein, if Plato had written the Letter, he would not have forgotten his own teaching in the *Republic*![4] But notice the host of assumptions in this judgment (and indeed, in all such judgments regarding the consistency of

"Plato's views"). The most massive assumption is that what Plato has *Socrates* say to this particular group of people, in the context of the *Republic,* about the educational importance of mathematics to ruling, is what he (he being Plato) would *always* say about education. Judgments such as this forget, to name only one problem, that the vast majority of the Platonic dialogues—dialogues surely written to educate the reader—proceed with no references or only occasional references to mathematics. Indeed, the number of dialogues that actually employ mathematics—as opposed to having a character within the dialogue insist that mathematics *must* be employed—is remarkably small. The slave boy in the *Meno* is taught a lesson in geometry, but only as an example to illustrate the theme of recollection. Timaeus certainly employs geometry in the dialogue of his name, but as an account of the structure of the cosmos, not a theory of education. Are we to count the hilariously complicated nuptial number of *Republic* book 8 (546a ff.) then, which will tell us by a mathematical deduction whether we should have sex, with whom, and when, as an example of the educational importance of mathematics? In short, if we look not at what is said by this or that character within the dialogues but at the education *of the readers* of the dialogues, we see that mathematics is almost never employed as a sine qua non. Is it so surprising that the author of the Seventh Letter would not do so either?

The point of these few remarks is emphatically *not* to demonstrate the contrary thesis: that the Seventh Letter (or the Second, or the *Hippias Major*) is authentic. I prefer instead the considerations adduced by Leo Strauss.[5] He observed that in the history of Platonic scholarship, an article or book has been written at some point about every single dialogue purporting to "demonstrate" its inauthenticity. Fine, suggests Strauss, let us assume that *all* those articles or books are correct. Indeed, let us assume the most radical version of such a hypothesis: every single "Platonic" dialogue is written by a different author. That only means, suggests Strauss, that there are not one but thirty-five titanic geniuses of ancient Greece writing under the name of "Plato"! What then? Our task as readers, even on this most preposterously radical of hypotheses, remains the same: to understand the peculiar relations of sameness and difference that pervade all the dialogues, and the Letters as well. To this may be added the important destabilizing of the very question of the "author" that has been accomplished in the last century by so many continental thinkers and quite especially about Plato.[6] I wish to take very seriously the notion that authorial authority is *unstable.* That is not to say that it is *irrelevant*—that the very question of authorial intention and authorial consistency cannot and should not even be raised. I want only to insist that it is an unstable appeal, one not to be taken as decisive. With these considerations, then, let us turn to the "Platonic" texts in question in the hope that, whoever their author (and over a beer, as it were, I would say it is probably Plato), light might be shed therein on the questions that are gathered under the name of "Plato": questions of the Platonic understanding of beauty, of Platonic philosophy, and of Platonic writing.

ONE

The Question of Beauty in the *Hippias Major*

The *Hippias Major* appears to be one of those many dialogues, often called "Socratic" dialogues or, by a further leap of speculation, "early" dialogues, in which Socrates pursues a given topic with the apparent aim of achieving a definition of the relevant term. It is sometimes yet further speculated that such dialogues are more or less accurate accounts of the historical Socrates, and that these "early" dialogues and their definitional concerns are "later" superseded by the more "mature" Plato's interest in forms. This book will join any number of other recent books in calling this speculative set of interpretive principles into question, but this much is certainly the case: Socrates, for a good chunk of his life (at least as dramatically portrayed by Plato) seemed very interested in defining terms, especially terms designating what the Greeks considered virtues.

Now a definition, particularly of the sort that Socrates seems to seek, could be said to make a notably bold claim: to comprehend (in the literal sense, to take entirely together) the meaning of a term, and to do so fully and adequately. Socrates' procedure in these definitional dialogues clearly implies that he demands of such definitions that they be able to successfully withstand all putative counter-examples and other refutational arguments. It remains question-worthy whether Socrates, the great spokesman for aporia, is genuinely confident that any definition of the massive issues with which he concerns himself could in principle accomplish this bold feat. That is why I say that Socrates "seems" interested in definition, because it is hardly certain that the Platonic Socrates has as his serious goal in these dialogues to succeed in discovering an unimpeachable definition. If he did, then the portrayal of Socrates in the dialogues threatens to become not just comedy but farce: Socrates, going from conversation to conversation, whether with young men, pompous acquaintances, or sophists, always trying to define this or that quality, and never succeeding. But also, comically, never learning from his failures: he simply continues in the next dialogue, with his next partner, in the quixotic effort to finally get a definition of something right. If Socrates were that slow a learner, are we to take Plato to be teaching that we should be that slow as well? Or is the effect of this series of failures not rather to finally drive the reader to the recognition that the understanding of a virtue, whatever it may be, cannot be reduced to a definition, a logos in that highly focused sense? Indeed, the Platonic Socrates himself may have come to this recognition: there is ample enough evidence to suggest that his apparent concern with definitions may be a surface concern, one intended only to open up deeper issues. Socrates, and surely Plato, may have other, more complicated motives—motives in light of which such dialogues could hardly be called failures. We shall see this in the *Hippias Major.*

As we turn to that dialogue let us begin, as we must in every dialogue, with a consideration of the cast of characters. Surely one of the most striking features of the dialogues is that none of them addresses "everyman," as if the same issues could be discussed in the same way with anyone. Instead, in every dialogue in which a particular virtue or quality is addressed thematically, the specific topic of discussion is always occasioned by an existential situation. That is, one might say that the Platonic dialogues never present philosophy as "abstract," with no reference to an occasion out of which the given topic arises. (Though characters *within* a given dialogue may assert a conception of philosophy as abstract: one thinks here of Parmenides, or the Eleatic Stranger.) Socrates almost never picks a philosophic issue out of thin air, as it were, and says "let's talk about *x* today." Rather, the topic is always occasioned, sometimes even demanded, by the existential or dramatic situation. A few examples: in the *Charmides,* the young Charmides (who is of course the future tyrant) is troubled by "morning headaches" for which Socrates claims that the cure must be a cure both of the body and the soul, namely, *sophrosyne.* Socrates, that is, gleans from the fact that the headaches come "in the morning" that the cause of Charmides' headaches is precisely his lack of *sophrosyne.* Socrates, for his part as he tells us, gets a glimpse inside the beautiful young Charmides' cloak and is "inflamed with passion," and so needs to think about the importance of *sophrosyne* himself![1] In the *Republic,* Socrates is constrained, however playfully, to stay in the Peiraeus and go to the house of Cephalus and Polemarchus. He then engages them in a very long discussion of justice, one of whose central questions is that of the justice of constraining the philosophers to rule. In the *Euthyphro,* Socrates is on the way to the King Archon to answer the charge of impiety, and Euthyphro, about to prosecute his father in the name of piety, claims to be an expert on the topic which guides the dialogue. In the *Lysis*, the young boys Lysis and Menexenus claim at their young age to be friends, and Socrates laments, poignantly, that he has "never had a friend" (*Lysis* 212a). So friendship is the focal topic of that dialogue. In the *Laches* we find that two of the participants, Socrates and Laches, have distinguished themselves by courage whereas the third participant, Nicias, strikingly lacks that virtue. Yet both Nicias and Laches claim a certain expertise, and so the topic turns to courage. So—it will be crucial to reflect upon how and why the question of beauty becomes thematic in the *Hippias Major*. But first, again, let us consider the characters and dramatic situation.

Hippias is a well-known sophist from the city of Elis, near Sparta. He is one of the leading members of what we might consider the "second generation" of sophists, after such founding figures as Protagoras and Gorgias. He was, among other things, famous for his claim of making absolutely everything he ever used for himself—clothes, shoes, utensils, etc.—thereby demonstrating his independence from everyone. His acclaimed rhetorical ability made him one of the favorite "ambassadors" of his home city of Elis, as we see in the dialogue. So not surprisingly, his opening remark, in response to Socrates' own opening remark that it has been a long time since Hippias has been in Athens, is *ou gar schole:* he's a busy man with "no leisure." On his trips, he often made huge sums of money on the side, teaching his rhetorical ability—except in Sparta, as we will learn from this dialogue. So in many ways, Hippias is a prototypical sophist: very rich, very self-confident, and something of a blusterer who does not like to be refuted.

The other speaker is Socrates. Although the opening lines make it plausible to suppose that others are present, only Hippias and Socrates speak. Socrates, of course, has a very vexed and complicated relationship to sophistry. When he encounters sophists (as in the *Gorgias, Protagoras,* and book 1 of the *Republic*), his *elenchus* is often at its harshest. The basic reasons for Socrates' opposition to sophistry are clear enough. He is opposed to its fundamental premises regarding relativism of one form or another and the consequent emphasis on rhetoric understood as "making the weaker argument appear the stronger." At least as important, sophistry is a problem because sophistry and philosophy are very easily confused: both are centrally involved with argument; both often become agonistic; and both make (often conflicting) claims to insight regarding the human condition. A sign of the ease with which they are confused is that Socrates must in his own defense, in the *Apology,* take pains to separate himself from the sophists with whom he is obviously associated by the Athenians and his accusers. Socrates often responds to these apparent similarities by attempting to distance sophistry as far as possible—one might say exaggeratedly—from philosophy, and by attacking the sophists whenever he gets the chance. Given the encounter with Hippias that begins the dialogue, it is therefore hardly surprising that the first part of the dialogue would be a Socratic attack on the claims of the sophist Hippias to wisdom. More surprising by far is the eventual turn to the question of beauty, which we shall have to consider in due time.

The scene of the dialogue is fairly unspecific, relative to other dialogues. Clearly it takes place in Athens, where Hippias is on state business, and since he could not have traveled safely from Elis (near Sparta) during the active periods of the Peloponnesian War, most scholars put the dramatic date of the dialogue as between 421 and 416 BC, that is, during the famous "peace of Nicias." This is especially noteworthy when we compare it with the dramatic dates of the *Symposium* and *Phaedrus*. Especially if we push the date of Hippias' visit (and so this dialogue) toward its later range—that is, near to 416—it means that Plato has Socrates engage in three dialogues during this approximate period, each of which deals thematically with the question of *to kalon*. For the *Symposium* can be dramatically dated with some precision to February, 416 BC (the occasion of the festival where Agathon won his first prize for tragedy); and the *Phaedrus,* with less precision, as occurring between 418 and 416 BC.[2] The Platonic Socrates, it seems, was at this point in his life (in his middle fifties) very concerned with the question of beauty. We shall have to consider the significance of this in some detail, especially given the very different ways in which the question of beauty is addressed in each dialogue.

The opening line of the *Hippias Major* (Socrates says, "Hippias, beautiful and wise, what a long time it is since you have put in at Athens!") suggests that they bump into each other more or less by accident, and so that it probably occurs in a public place—perhaps the agora, where Socrates often spent time, or perhaps a gymnasium, also a favorite Socratic hangout. Although no other characters speak or are even mentioned, it is also at least plausible that others may be present, which perhaps explains in part Hippias's consternation when Socrates undercuts his claims to wisdom and subsequently his confident claims to be able to define beauty.

The first part of the dialogue, then, becomes a somewhat typical Socratic attack on the claims of sophistry, in this case, Hippias's confident claims to be wise—indeed, to be the wisest of the sophists—as evidence for which he adduces the vast sums he has made teaching his craft (282e). We will not have to examine these arguments in great detail, except to note how and why the topic of conversation gradually shifts to the question of beauty. Part of Socrates' calling Hippias's boasts into question involves his reminding Hippias that the Spartans, so close to Elis, refuse to pay him anything for his supposed wisdom and ability to teach (283c ff.). Socrates puts Hippias into the uncomfortable dilemma that either the Spartans don't know what they're doing (indeed, that they are even criminal!) by not paying Hippias to teach their youth (a charge Hippias does not want to make), or they are right in that Hippias *does not deserve* to be paid, to which he is even less willing to agree. The dénouement of this *elenchus,* and the occasion for the transition to beauty, is that when Socrates presses Hippias to say just what the Spartans *are* willing to hear from Hippias (without pay, of course), the best he can say is that they allow him to tell stories about the heroes of old and the foundations of ancient cities. Socrates bitingly concludes that the

Spartans "use you just as children use old women, to mythologize pleasantly" (286a). Hippias either is oblivious to or ignores Socrates' insult, and instead launches into an enthusiastic description of the wonderful story he told them recently, which he is going to rehearse again in Athens. The passage is worth quoting, since it is the occasion for the transition to the examination of beauty. Hippias says:

> And by Zeus, Socrates, I have just lately gained a reputation there by telling about noble and beautiful pursuits (*epitedeumaton kalon*), recounting what those of a young man should be. For I have a very beautiful discourse (*pagkalos logos*) composed about them, well arranged in its words and also in other respects. And the plan of the discourse, and the beginning, is something like this: After the fall of Troy, the story goes that Neoptolemus asked Nestor what the noble and beautiful pursuits were (*kala epitedeumata*), by following which a young man would become most famous; so after that we have Nestor speaking and suggesting to him very many lawful and most beautiful pursuits (*pampolla nomima kai pagkala*). That discourse, then, I delivered there and intend to deliver here the day after tomorrow in Pheidostratus' schoolroom, with many other things worth hearing; for Eudicus, the son of Apemantus, asked me to do so. Now be sure to be there yourself and to bring others who are able to judge of discourses that they hear. (286a–c; H. N. Fowler translation)

As I indicated in parentheses, four times in this brief speech Hippias uses various forms of *kalon,* the Greek word for "beauty." It is this repetition that is the immediate occasion for Socrates to introduce his troublesome "friend"— who turns out to be none other than Socrates himself—who, he says, challenges him whenever he speaks of the beautiful and asks him "hubristically" (286c9) to define the beautiful itself (*auto to kalon*—286e). This always puts Socrates in aporia (*eporoumen*—286d), and makes him resolve that the next time he sees "one of you wise men" (*humon to ton sophon*—286d7) he will ask him to define *to kalon.* So the definitional effort begins and sustains the rest of the dialogue.

One might at first think this is a rather thin justification for Socrates to seize on *to kalon* as a reason to change the course of the conversation toward a definition of beauty. But there are several good reasons for him to do so. First, the repetition of the term four times in a brief speech certainly does highlight the issue—it is certainly the dominant attribute in play in Hippias's remark. Moreover, Hippias's uses of the term point both to his claim to know what "beautiful pursuits" are for the young, and also to be able to articulate them "beautifully." So Hippias's uses of *kalon* embody two important sophist claims: to be wise—to know what beautiful pursuits are for the young—and to be able to speak beautifully about those pursuits. In this sense, the turn to the question of beauty simply focuses more precisely the *elenchus* of Hippias's sophistic claims to be wise and to be a beautiful speaker. The "beauty" of sophistry is very much in question here.

Perhaps more important, however, the term has in fact been in play literally from the first line of the dialogue. Recall Socrates' opening remark: "Hippias, beautiful and wise, what a long time . . ." Indeed, Socrates and Hippias have already used the term regularly and in perfectly intelligible ways in the dialogue so far, apparently without qualms or failure to understand each other. At 282b, when Hippias comments that he is in the habit of praising the ancients over present-day sophists, Socrates responds, "Beautiful (*kalos*) is your way of speaking and thinking, as it seems to me, O Hippias."[3] At 282d, after Socrates raises the issue that the wise men of old did not charge money for their wisdom whereas the present-day sophists do, Hippias responds, "Why Socrates, you know nothing of the beauties (*ton kalon*) of this." To Hippias's response that he makes more money than any of the other sophists, Socrates next responds, no doubt ironically, "That's a beautiful (*kalon*) thing you say, Hippias."[4] In fact, no doubt playfully and ironically, in Socrates' very response to the passage where Hippias uses "beauty" four times, and in introducing his troublesome "friend," Socrates yet again employs the term twice. "It's a beautiful thing (*eis kalon*— 286c3) you reminded me of," he says, and continues: "you come at a beautiful moment (*eis kalon hekeis*—286d)," in that Hippias will presumably be able to define the term for him. As we shall see, in the rest of the dialogue—in the very midst of trying unsuccessfully to define beauty—both Socrates and Hippias will continue to use the term, and in perfectly coherent ways.

There is an important lesson to be learned from this, one taught to us by the drama of the dialogue. If "to know" is reduced to something like "to be able to present and defend an unimpeachable definition," then we "know" very little indeed and next to nothing of enduring human importance. But the very movement of the dialogue demonstrates that in a less extreme sense, Socrates and Hippias already "know," and know quite well, what the term beauty means. They are able to employ it perfectly appropriately and even, in the case of Socrates, ironically. That is, if we move into the definitional effort thoughtfully, we should realize that we already "know" more than we can define. This, however, puts a larger question into play: perhaps, especially in the case of complicated issues such as beauty or the virtues, there is more than one legitimate sense of "knowing." Socrates' apparent demand for a rigorous definition implicitly claims that knowledge is homogeneous and to be very narrowly construed. But the dialogue itself—and we can easily see, all the dialogues—call into question this very claim made within its pages. The famous Wittgensteinian dictum, "Don't look for the meaning, look for the use" is already incipiently in play here. More important than the failure to adequately and rigorously define beauty will be the question raised by that failure in the midst of the regular and adequate "use" of the term: what are the relevant senses—and the plural should be emphasized here—in which we can be said to know or not know something like beauty? Surely the answer will not be limited to what we can define.

But there are yet other reasons why the introduction of the question of beauty may be appropriate. As we have already noted, Socrates, at least as he is portrayed by Plato, seems for some reason very concerned with the issue at this point in his life: the *Symposium* and *Phaedrus,* in addition to the *Hippias Major,* demonstrate this. It is perhaps worth reminding ourselves as well that Socrates is himself notoriously ugly, with his snub nose, bulging eyes, and stocky figure.[5] That beauty is very much on his mind is underscored when, by way of turning to the question of beauty thematically, Socrates introduces his troublesome "friend." For according to Socrates this friend, Socrates' double as it were, if he heard the discourse that Hippias had just uttered about the beauty of his mythological performance, would "speak about nothing else than the beautiful, for he has a habit of this": *eroit'an ou peri proteron e peri tou kalou, ethos gar to touto exhei* (287c). Recall that Hippias's speech in question was not thematically about the beautiful but about the story of Neoptolemus and Nestor. He simply *employed* one or another variants of the word for beauty in his discourse. Yet Socrates' "friend"—who is no one but Socrates himself—would seize upon "nothing else than the beautiful" because "he has a habit of this." This clearly underlines the abiding concern with the beautiful that informs Socrates' questioning, at least or especially at this time in his life. He does not here specify exactly why his friend would speak of nothing else but the beautiful. We shall have to watch through the rest of the dialogue—as well as the *Symposium* and *Phaedrus*—for the reason why. The question of beauty will have very much to do with philosophy itself.

So Socrates and Hippias turn to the attempt to define beauty itself. As always in the dialogues, the formulation of the question is itself of crucial significance. Socrates takes the trouble to be very clear that he is not asking for an *example* of a beautiful thing, but for what the beautiful itself is: *ti esti touto, to kalon* (287d). Hippias immediately confuses this with something that is beautiful: "Does the person asking this want to find out anything else than what is beautiful?" Socrates insists: "It doesn't seem so to me, Hippias, but rather what is the beautiful (*ti estin to kalon*)?" Hippias at last claims to understand the difference, but his first answer shows that he does not: "I understand, my good friend, and I will answer him what is the beautiful and I'll never be refuted. Know well, Socrates, if it is necessary to speak the truth, that a beautiful maiden is beautiful (*parthenos kale kalon*)" (287e).

At one level, this first answer repeats the mistaken first answer of many of Socrates' interlocutors in many dialogues of this sort. Charmides, in the dialogue of his name, first answers Socrates' query regarding *sophrosyne:* it is "doing everything in an orderly and quiet way, things like walking in the streets, and talking, and doing everything else in a similar fashion. So I think, he said, taking it all together that what you ask about is a kind of quietness" (*Charmides* 159b). Euthyphro, in his dialogue, answers first regarding piety: "I say that the pious is to do what I am doing now, to prosecute the wrongdoer, be it about murder or temple robbery or anything else, whether the wrongdoer is your father or your mother or anyone else" (*Euthyphro* 5e). Even the bright young

Theaetetus, in his dialogue, answers first that knowledge, which Socrates has asked him to define, is "what Theodorus teaches, I mean geometry and the subjects you enumerated just now. Then again there are crafts such as cobbling, whether you take them together or separately" (*Theaetetus* 146d). In these and other cases, the first answer points toward what we now call the denotation rather than the connotation that Socrates is looking for, and his first correction is to clarify this by drawing the distinction. Usually, one instance of this error is enough. In the case of the *Hippias Major,* two strange things happen. First, as we have seen, Socrates has *already,* in his very formulation of the question, pointed to the distinction between the two modes of definition and clarified what he seeks. Second, despite this and Socrates' refutation of the present definition, Hippias will continue for a while to point to denotative responses, until Socrates finally has to give him an explicit example (that is, a denotative instance!) of what he is looking for, "the appropriate" (293e). Nevertheless, here as usual, Socrates refutes the first definition by pointing out that "a beautiful maiden" is not *what beauty is* but one among many examples of beautiful things.

But in this particular case, something else is in play in Hippias's first response—something that, by the evidence of Plato's own texts, may not be wrong at all. For his first response seems to uphold the conviction that the first and most fundamental experience of beauty that we have is of *beautiful people.* Our experience of beauty typically (if not always) begins, Hippias seems to be assuming, with the experience of a beautiful person. He underlines this conviction by indicating first that it is correct because "it is what everyone thinks" (288a). The *Symposium* and the *Phaedrus,* it should be noted, will bear out this conviction. In her famous ascent passage in the *Symposium,* Diotima will insist that "it is necessary, if one rightly goes into erotic things, to begin with the love of a beautiful body" (210a ff.). To be sure, the ascent will take us beyond beautiful individual bodies, but it is striking that this is where we *must* begin according to Diotima. And in the *Phaedrus,* in Socrates' famous palinode, the core experience of beauty, the experience which Socrates will go into considerable detail analyzing, will again be the experience of a beautiful person (250d ff.). It is instructive that when we put these three texts together, the shared conviction that the original experience of beauty is the beauty of a person is "gendered" differently: Hippias says it will be a beautiful maiden; the *Phaedrus* teaches that it will be a beautiful boy; and in the *Symposium,* Diotima is neutral on the question (although the general context of the ascent tends to assume that the young Socrates is attracted to beautiful boys, Diotima's explicit remarks about the "necessary beginning" remain neutral). The larger point, then, seems not to be an issue of gender preference, but the more generic importance of beautiful people as the core experience of beauty.

The full implications of this apparently consistent teaching of the dialogues regarding the primacy of human beauty cannot be addressed in detail until we consider the *Symposium* and *Phaedrus,* but it is perhaps not too early to at least acknowledge the issue here. The Greeks, as Socrates' own subsequent examples of beautiful horses, lyres, pots, and other such things in this dialogue will show (288c ff.), were very aware that the range of potential objects of beauty is vast. That is neither surprising nor different from our own cultural norms. What seems to have changed, however, at least in "high" culture, is the assumption that the fundamental locus of beauty is the human body, and that from there the notion of beauty gets extended to its other potential objects. With the advent of the distinguishing in Kant and others of "aesthetics" as a separate discipline from other disciplines—and particularly from science/epistemology and morality/ethics—beauty as an issue comes to be located fundamentally in *aesthetics,* and so, most basically, in *art.* Once beauty becomes a fundamentally "aesthetic" term, it is in art that the core experience of beauty comes to be located for modernity.[6] But for the Greeks beauty begins, as it were, with the beauty of human bodies, and only from there radiates into art and elsewhere.[7] So although in Socrates' view Hippias cannot be right that a denotative instance of beauty captures what beauty is, nothing denies his insight that for the Greeks, beautiful humans is where the experience of beauty begins, at least for "almost everyone."

Hippias's first formulation of beauty, as we have seen, is that a beautiful maiden is beautiful. The Greek is formulated in such a way as to repeat a form of the word for beauty (*kalon*) twice in his concluding phrase: *parthenos kale kalon* (287e6). Socrates, in his reply, *also* begins with the word: "Beautifully answered, Hippias, by the dog, and notably": *Kalos ge, o Hippia, ne ton kuna kai eudoxos apekrino.* This is a complicated but sophisticated formulation. On the one hand it reminds us that, despite and in the midst of his claims to aporia about *to kalon,* Socrates is in fact perfectly capable of using the word appropriately. Yet on the other hand, this response actually begins the process of *elenchus:* in it Socrates exhibits an appropriate use of the term that has nothing to do with a maiden, but with a formulation in speech of a definition (however ironic his praise may be).

Socrates now continues with the refutation of Hippias's denotative formulation already adumbrated in his response to the sophist. Not just maidens but lots of other things are counted as beautiful. Socrates begins with examples that will easily elicit Hippias's agreement (horses, lyres—288b–c) and moves gradually to other instances that insult Hippias's sensibilities, but to which he must reluctantly agree (beautiful pots—288d–e). To this, Hippias tries to respond by asserting an implied hierarchy of beautiful things: "But I think it is like that, Socrates. This utensil is beautiful if beautifully made. But on the whole that's not worthy of judging beautiful compared to a horse and a maiden and all the other beautiful things" (288e). Such a hierarchy, of course, begs the question: what is the standard of beauty by which we might determine one thing to be "more beautiful" than another? Nevertheless, Hippias's use of the comparative allows Socrates to introduce yet another difficulty. If comparisons are appropriate, then compared to a goddess, even a beautiful maiden is ugly, and Hippias, in his example of the maiden, has pointed not even to something "beautiful in itself" but to something that is *both beautiful and ugly,* depending on the context (289a–c).

Socrates' formulation of his conclusion to this argument leads Hippias to his second formulation. Socrates says: "Do you still think that the beautiful itself, by which everything else is made beautiful, and appears as beautiful whenever that form (*eidos*) is added to it, that it is a maiden or horse or lyre?" (289d). Socrates' choice of the word *eidos* is of course pregnant. It gives an indication of what Socrates seeks as an answer, some "connotative" formulation, as we have been calling it, something that points to the "essence" of what beauty is. It also is an instance of the way Plato allows us to see how a reasonably common Greek word will gradually take on a specific, quasi-technical meaning in Plato's philosophical vocabulary. The use of the word here does not even come close to being "Plato's early theory of forms," but it does allow us to see how the notion of "form" begins to be important in the dialogues.

Hippias's second formulation is similarly complicated. "Gold," he says in response to Socrates' formulation above, is that which, when added to anything, will make it beautiful (289e). Hippias has taken a very narrow, literal sense of Socrates' "adding to," and declared that gold is precisely that which beautifies something when it is added to anything. In one sense, then, he *is* getting at something more general than his first answer. But the problem is, it is *still* some specific beautiful thing among others, and so a denotative instance of beauty and not the beautiful itself. Why does Hippias not catch on to the sort of definition Socrates wants as quickly as Socrates' other interlocutors? Is he stupid? That is dubious on the face of it. It is much more likely that Hippias is simply not *interested* in what he later disparaging calls Socrates' nit-picking distinctions that, Hippias believes, miss the point. And what is the point? As Hippias insisted in his first formulation as a "beautiful maiden," and as he will reiterate throughout, the point is to articulate a definition that "everyone will agree with." If everyone agrees, then no one will even try to refute him. Socrates' "friend," who keeps raising these objections, is regarded by Hippias not as someone who has a serious point to make but as a "boor" (288d) and an "ignoramus" (290e). That is, if Hippias can say something with which everyone or almost everyone will agree, he has in his opinion succeeded. At a telling point later in the dialogue, Socrates introduces the proposal that perhaps the beautiful is what is "pleasant through sight and hearing" (297e), and immediately raises *himself* the potential objection of his "friend" that beautiful activities and laws are pleasant—but not through sight and hearing. Hippias replies: "Perhaps, Socrates, these things will slip past the man" (298b). This points to a fundamental difference in Socrates' and Hippias's orientation. For Socrates, any objection that anyone can raise is relevant. For Hippias, it only becomes relevant if someone actually raises it—that is, if it becomes an issue in the present argument. Socrates thinks it relevant to raise *possible* objections. Hippias is interested only in objections that "most" people might have. If everyone or almost everyone agrees, that is tantamount (for him but not for Socrates) to its being true, and on this he is consistent with the convictions of sophistry. That is why he remains satisfied with his various "definitions" even when Socrates raises the objections he does.

Socrates now refutes Hippias's definition of the beautiful as "gold" by pointing out examples where gold, when added, would clearly not make something beautiful. Ivory, he gets Hippias to admit, is better than gold for making the face, feet, and hands of statues beautiful (290b), and even stone is better for making the eyes of statues beautiful (290c). It should be noted that Socrates thus turns the issue to the question of the beautiful in art, even if, almost immediately, to move beyond it. His example leads Hippias to at least gesture in the direction of a connotational definition: "We'll agree to this, whatever is appropriate (*prepe*) to each thing makes that thing beautiful" (290d). The problem is, this agreement vastly expands the range of the beautiful, and Socrates now performs what to the aesthete Hippias is the vulgar *reductio ad absurdam* of observing that when it comes to soup spoons, if the "appropriate" is the criterion, then figwood soup spoons are "more beautiful" than gold ones (290d–291c). The upshot is that "gold" still retains the defect of a denotational example: lots of things besides gold are beautiful, and given different contexts, many are beautiful whereas gold would not be.

Hippias's third effort shows that he still is not troubled by Socrates' demand that they move from a denotative to a connotative definition. Again, this cannot be stupidity on his part but a denial of the serious relevance of Socrates' distinctions, at least on the grounds that matter to Hippias. For he now almost exacerbates the problem with his early efforts by giving a *series* of beautiful things, again appealing to common agreement as the criterion: "I say, then, that for every man and everywhere it is most beautiful (*kalliston*) to be rich and healthy and honored by the Greeks, to reach old age, and, after providing a beautiful funeral for his deceased parents, to be beautifully and splendidly buried by his own children" (291d–e).

Hippias is troubled neither by the inclusion of the term to be defined in his definition nor by the fact that, by continuing to give specific instances of beauty, he will subject himself to the anticipated Socratic objections. Since, again, it is highly unlikely that Hippias is simply stupid, might there be a point to his persistence about which Plato is inviting us to wonder? Stated differently, what would be the conditions under which Hippias might be *right* to keep insisting on denotative examples rather than claims to articulating the "essence" of the beautiful? What if, as turns out to be the case, not only will the attempted essentialist definitions of beauty in this dialogue fail, but that the next two dialogues we shall study—the *Symposium* and *Phaedrus*—give us good reasons to conclude that there *cannot be* an adequate articulation of the "essence" of beauty itself? That there is something irreducibly non-discursive about it? Then how else *would* one begin a formulation regarding beauty than by giving a range of examples of beautiful things, the experience of which might lead us to "see" or "recollect" what beauty itself is? Perhaps, precisely in the light of what we are to learn in the subsequent dialogues, Hippias knows what he is doing and is right to persist in articulating "denotative" definitions of beauty.

But not according to Socrates. He begins his refutation of this, the third denotative characterization of the beautiful, by again appealing to his difficult "friend," who, he says, would berate him (and by implication, Hippias) for yet again not understanding that he is not looking for *instances* of beauty but for what the beautiful itself (*to kalon auto*—292d) is. Hippias's response is the same as he has insisted previously: "I know well that what is said is beautiful for everyone—everyone will think so" (292e). Plato is having Hippias persist, I suggest, in order to bring out the genuine impasse here between Socrates and Hippias, and to prepare the reader for the possibility that there may be at least a kernel of truth in Hippias's apparent stubbornness. He will not give in to this insistence on the "essence" of beauty that Socrates demands and, as we shall see in what follows, he never really does. For after Socrates refutes this third definition, it will not be Hippias but Socrates himself—still in the guise of his difficult friend—who explicitly moves the conversation to the "connotative" definitional attempts that will characterize the rest of the dialogue. Hippias, in fact, has now offered his last definition to be examined in the dialogue. The rest, the connotative definitions—the appropriate, the useful, the beneficial, and the pleasant through sight and hearing—will all be suggested and refuted by Socrates himself. Only at the very end of the dialogue, when Hippias rejects the force of Socrates' entire procedure, does Hippias offer one more definition of the beautiful—and it, once again, is definition by example. He says at 304b (and the dialogue ends at 304e):

> But now, Socrates, what do you think of all this? It is mere scrapings and shavings of discourse (*ton logon*), as I said before, divided into bits. But here is what is beautiful and worth much, being able to produce a discourse well and beautifully in a court of law or a council house or before any other public body before which the discourse may be delivered, to convince the audience and to carry off, not the smallest but the greatest of prizes, the saving of oneself, one's property, and one's friends. For these things, therefore, one must strive, renouncing these petty arguments (*smikrologias*), that one may not, by busying oneself, just as now, with mere talk and nonsense, appear to be a fool.

Socrates makes no attempt to refute this last set of examples but concludes the dialogue with a statement of his well-known aporia. Before we return to some details of Socrates' various "connotative" definitions and their refutations, I want to emphasize the steadfastness with which Hippias holds his ground in this dialogue. At the end, Hippias remains as convinced as he ever was that the best way to articulate "the beautiful" is to do so with good examples *that*

everyone will agree with. Moreover, he expresses his contempt for what he regards as the nit-picking attempts of Socrates to get at "the beautiful itself," which
have failed in any case. We shall have to see, in our subsequent study of other
dialogues, whether Hippias does not have a point.

Let us return to Socrates' refutation of Hippias's claim at 291e that the
beautiful has to do with being wealthy, healthy, well-honored, and able to bury
one's parents beautifully and have a beautiful funeral of one's own. Socrates (or
rather Socrates' troublesome friend) proceeds in the usual Socratic way, with a
counter-example—in this case, the gods. The beauty of living to bury one's
parents does not seem to fit, he suggests, with the gods and heroes, such as
Achilles and Heracles (293a–d). It would not be beautiful for them, and so the
case of burying one's parents can be either beautiful or ugly, depending on
context. Hippias's rejoinder that he was not talking about the gods (293b) is
passed over. It is noteworthy as well that the rest of Hippias's present formulation is not refuted either.

At 293e, and until the very end of the dialogue, Socrates takes over not just
the *elenchus* but the venturing of definitions as well. His first effort, still speaking
through his "friend," returns to a notion adumbrated in the discussion of "gold"
as an example—the "appropriate." His refutation of this, such as it is, depends on
the crucial disjunction—and as we shall see, the crucial ambiguity—between
"appearing" (*phainesthai*) and "being." Socrates says, "See then, do we say that
the appropriate is that which, when it is added, makes each of those things to
which it is added appear beautiful (*phainesthai kala*), or which makes them be
beautiful (*e ho einai poiei*), or neither?" (294a). Hippias answers, as any good
sophist should, that the beautiful is what makes things appear as beautiful (*ho
poiei phainesthai kala*—294a), but the example he gives in clarification gets him
into difficulty. For he adds as an example: "as when a man puts on clothes or
shoes that fit, even if he be ridiculous, he appears more beautiful." This example
opens the way for Socrates to argue that this would make the beautiful deceptive,
and something deceptive "would not be what we are looking for, would it
Hippias?" (294b). He goes on to insist that the beautiful must be not what makes
things appear beautiful, but be beautiful (294c).

At least three important issues are in play in this exchange. The first is
an ambiguity contained alike in the English word "appear" and the Greek *phainesthai.* Both can indeed mean "appear" in the sense of "merely seem to be"; but
both can also, more positively, mean "appear" in the sense of "shine forth,
appear on the scene, show itself" (as in "Socrates appeared in the agora yesterday"). Hippias's unfortunate example points to its deceptive sense, on the
basis of which Socrates rejects it (we shall address whether this is satisfactory in
a moment). But they pointedly do not consider the other possible sense of
phainesthai, that the beautiful might have something important to do with the
shining forth, the showing itself of things. It is noteworthy that such a connection

of beauty and appearance in this positive sense is passed over in this dialogue, as it will not be in the dialogues we shall subsequently study. It would hardly furnish an adequate "definition" of the beautiful. But surely the connection of beauty with the showing forth of things might well be an important element in a longer discussion of the experience of the beautiful. In the *Hippias Major,* such a possibility is only adumbrated, not adequately developed. This is one more sense in which this dialogue prepares the way, both positively and negatively, for the longer and more adequate discussions of beauty to follow.

Second, the distinction between "mere appearance" and being is, of course, a core disagreement between the Platonic Socrates and the sophists whom he encounters. From the sophistic standpoint, Hippias is right to reply that the appropriate would be what would make us "appear" beautiful, for from the sophist standpoint *to appear just is to be.* "Human being is the measure of all things, of what is, that it is, and of what is not, that it is not," said the first and greatest of all sophists. This debate between Socrates and Protagoras is played out in the section of the *Theaetetus* on knowledge as perception.[8] As a sophist, Hippias should not accept the distinction between being and appearance, but insist instead on something like the Protagorean thesis that what appears *just is,* at least for the person to whom it appears. Instead, his example of clothes and shoes making someone look good "even if he is ridiculous" tacitly acknowledges the difference between appearance and being that will enable Socrates to proceed with his *elenchus.*

Third, Socrates assumes that the fact that beauty might be deceptive on this definition is enough to refute it. He seems unwilling to accept that beauty *might very well,* at least some of the time, have something to do with deception or illusion. He does not argue against this impossibility but simply asserts it. Should we accept it without argument? That is hardly obvious. To say the least, the notion that beauty might have some interesting connection to illusion, either contingently or necessarily, hardly goes away in the subsequent philosophical history of the topic. There are all sorts of possibilities here that might have been considered: perhaps beauty *is necessarily* connected with illusion. If so, that would in fact be the understanding of beauty that we seek. Or, beauty may *sometimes* be illusory, sometimes not. Would not that too be an important dimension of an adequate understanding of what beauty is? Socrates' somewhat curious assumption in this passage seems to be that, based on the appearance/being distinction and his clear preference for being, beauty *must* be connected with what is as opposed to what "merely" appears. But that has hardly been demonstrated.

Putting these three points together, we might suggest that the present passage broaches this very important issue: perhaps, whatever beauty turns out to be, it has very much to do with *the shining forth of things, the way they appear to us,* whether that appearance turns out to be well or ill-founded.[9] Whether and under what conditions the mode of appearing that might be beauty devolves into illusion is a matter for thought regarding beauty, not a reason to reject a characterization of it. That issue is in play in the passage; it is not yet addressed in this dialogue, but again, the way is prepared.

Hippias's response to this argument of Socrates' suggests that he may glean something of all this, if through a glass darkly: "But Socrates, the appropriate makes things both be beautiful and be seen to be beautiful, when it is present" (294c). Socrates responds to this potentially promising if complicated response by shifting the sense of *phainesthai* (unannounced, of course) away from the sense of mere seeming to the more positive sense of appearance. He raises the question of whether it is possible that "things which are really beautiful not appear as beautiful, at any rate, when that is present which makes them appear" (294c). When Hippias assents to this loaded proposition, Socrates proceeds to show him that in fact, the two issues, being beautiful and appearing as such, do not necessarily go hand in hand—that many things that are in fact beautiful do not *appear* to everyone as such. Having pointed this out, he forces Hippias to a choice: is "the appropriate" that which makes things *be* beautiful or appear to be such? The necessity of this choice hardly follows from the fact that some beautiful things are not recognized as such by all; nevertheless, Hippias, still consistently maintaining his sophist principles, asserts that the appropriate is what makes things *appear* as beautiful (294e). Still playing on the ambiguity in the term *phainesthai,* Socrates concludes that "the appropriate" cannot then be what makes things *be* beautiful, and the definition appears to fail.

Socrates now suggests another alternative: perhaps the beautiful is "the useful" (*chresimon*). But since "the useful," as Socrates here understands it, is what *enables* us to do something, he quickly inflects "the useful" into "ability" or "power" (*dunamis*) and concludes somewhat startlingly: "Then power (*dunamis*) is beautiful and lack of power (*adunamia*) is ugly (*aischron*)?" (295e8).[10] We can pass over quickly the rather too easy slide from "the useful" to "power"— surely, while "enabling power" is *one* inflection of "the useful" it hardly exhausts the meaning of the latter term—in order to note that to say the least, the invocation of a connection between beauty and power is a Platonic provocation of the highest order.[11] As has already happened a number of times, Plato only allows the theme to be announced in this dialogue. In a moment, the notion of beauty as power will be all too easily refuted and we shall move on. It will remain for the *Symposium* and especially the *Phaedrus* to begin to speak in some detail of the genuine power of the beautiful, that is, of the beautiful beloved and the power that experience has on the lover. To put the point another way, perhaps "power" is indeed insufficient as a *definition* of the beautiful. It hardly follows that the issue of power is not a central feature of any adequate understanding of the beautiful. As with the other issues we have already addressed, the context of or the demand for a *definition* of a complex issue such as beauty seems more to close off than to open up an adequate understanding of the term. Is it any wonder, then, that the quest for definitions of such terms always fails, and that a different way of understanding them will be necessary?

Socrates' refutation of his own notion that the beautiful is power is so quick that it is easy to pass over the important issues implicitly raised by it. For he points out to Hippias that having the power or ability to do this or that is just as true of the bad and mistaken things we do as of the good and successful things, and one hardly wants to characterize the beautiful in terms of a power that might just as well lead us to bad acts and mistakes as the opposite (296b–d). Since the power or ability to make mistakes and do bad things is no less a power, power cannot be the beautiful. This of course will soon become a decisive question and not an easy conclusion in the next two dialogues and indeed, in the subsequent history of the subject: *is* there a kinship, or even a necessary connection, between beauty and the good, or even beauty and moral worth? Once again, the issue is only intimated here and passed over much too quickly. We must await the ascent passage of the *Symposium* for the issue to become thematic in a more appropriate way. But we should again notice that it is in play here, even if only implicitly.

Nevertheless, Socrates gains Hippias's acceptance of the straightforward unacceptability of the notion that power or ability to make mistakes and do bad things might be beautiful. Hippias then helpfully makes a proposed modification: the powerful might be the beautiful, "if they are powerful and useful for the good" (296d).

Yet again, a potentially decisive moment in an understanding of the beautiful is limned, but passed by too quickly. For Hippias now invokes a possible connection between the beautiful and the good—to say the least, a connection that has generated controversy throughout the history of the question. *Is* there a connection between the good and the beautiful, and if so, what is its nature? Or, is the beautiful somehow an issue that stands outside the question of the good, "beyond good and evil"? As we turn to Socrates' refutation of this formulation by Hippias, we need to be struck by how many decisive issues regarding the question of beauty are being raised in this dialogue—raised, but never adequately examined. It is as if the *Hippias Major* is a dialogue in which one decisive question regarding beauty after another is announced, but left for other dialogues (and the subsequent history of philosophy) to address more adequately.

Socrates' refutation is founded on at least two repetitions of the very same sort of fallacy of which he had earlier accused Hippias. Hippias, recall, had wanted to draw no distinction between *the beautiful* (*to kalon*) and something that *is beautiful;* and Socrates, in their earlier exchanges, had insisted on the distinction in moving from "denotational" to his preferred "connotational" definitions. Now, Hippias suggests that "if it is power to do good," the useful or powerful might be the beautiful (296d). Socrates first says of this power to do good things, "but that is beneficial, is it not?": *alla men touto ge ophelimon estin.*

E ou (296e). Upon getting Hippias's assent he moves quickly, against his earlier argument, to: "Then the beneficial seems to us to be the beautiful, Hippias": *To ophelimon ara eoiken hemin einai to kalon, o Hippia* (296e7). In this argument, moving from the claim that something "is *x*" to "then it is the *x*" seems to be legitimate! And as if to underline the contradiction to his earlier insistence that this sort of move is illegitimate, Socrates repeats it in the continuation of his *elenchus:* he now claims that this must mean that the beneficial is the *cause* (*aition*) of the good (296e9). And from there—insisting that the cause of something must be different from the thing caused[12]—he concludes not, as he should by his earlier argument, that the beautiful, as different from the good, cannot *be the good* (i.e., cannot be identical with it); but instead that *the beautiful cannot be good, nor the good beautiful!* (*Ma Di', o ariste, oude ara to kalon agathon estin, oude to agathon kalon*—297c3.)[13] Their shared dismay at this—unjustified—conclusion leads them to Socrates' next suggested definition which invokes pleasure. But the double employment of the very fallacy on the basis of which Socrates had refuted Hippias's earlier efforts should alert us that the connection—even the potential intimacy—of the beautiful and the good has by no means been refuted by Socrates here, and that the question of such a connection cries out for more adequate treatment.

Their mutual dismay at the conclusion that the beautiful cannot even be good[14] leads Socrates to invoke yet another crucial issue in regard to the beautiful, the issue of pleasure. Perhaps, he now suggests, the pleasures through sight and hearing constitute the beautiful (297e ff.). Once again, a feature of beauty that has proved to be of the highest importance (and controversy) is invoked, only to be summarily (and dubiously, yet again) dismissed. As all the talk of "aesthetic pleasure" attests, to this day we are inclined to include as one of the features of beauty a certain pleasure that is present in our experience of beauty. This is of course compatible with its also including, or at least sometimes including, a certain pain or frustration. Nevertheless, surely Socrates is insightful here in invoking the possibility of a decisive connection between beauty and pleasure.

In Socrates' formulation, however, he limits the range of that pleasure that would constitute beauty to sight and hearing. His reason, as he goes on to show Hippias, is the presumed vulgarity of the pleasures of smell, taste, and especially touch. Such vulgar pleasures could not possibly constitute the beautiful, and so Socrates limits the beautiful to the presumably more refined senses of sight and hearing (298e–299b). There are two problems to be noted immediately. First, if Socrates really did believe his just-completed refutation of the claim that the beautiful is the beneficial (which led to the conclusion that the beautiful is not good), then why should he now immediately express dismay at the potential vulgarity of some putative instances of beauty? Such instances can be rejected out of hand, as they are here, only on the assumption, against his last argument, that there *is* some sort of connection between the beautiful and the good after all. Second, having granted this, it is by no means obvious that by limiting the range of the beautiful to the pleasures of sight and hearing, we have avoided the vulgar instances of pleasure and so of beauty. Pleasant sights and pleasant sounds can be just as vulgar as pleasant tastes, smells, and physical experiences (as the case of pornography, to mention only one obvious example, shows easily). So the limitation of those pleasures that might constitute beauty to sight and sound is dubious on the face of it.

To this Socrates himself immediately adds a further complication. If beauty is pleasure through sight and sound, what of "beautiful activities and laws" (298b)? Hippias, throughout preserving a certain admirable (if anti-philosophic) sophistic consistency, suggests: "Perhaps, Socrates, these things might slip past the man" (298b). That is, Hippias continues to be interested here not in some abstract conception of "the truth," but in what will be accepted by most people. If a potential objection can slip by unnoticed, then it isn't an objection. To this, Socrates does two things. First, he denies that this objection would ever slip by his troublesome "friend," whom he now at last identifies as none other than "the son of Sophroniscus" (298c)—that is, Socrates himself. But second, he neverthe-less *accepts* Hippias's suggestion that they pass over the problem of beautiful laws and activities in order to pursue the definition of the beautiful (to which these instances would be clear counter-examples) as "pleasures of sight and hearing."

Socrates now proceeds to refute this definition by developing various logical and conceptual complications associated with the conjunction of the two dif-ferent senses, sight and hearing (299cff). What is refuted, then, is the conjunc-tion of sight and hearing as the pleasures that constitute the beautiful (which as we have seen was dubious in any case). What is strikingly *not* refuted is that the beautiful might have something importantly to do with pleasure. Perhaps this is what is hinted at in Socrates' final effort at a definition of the beautiful, after the conjunction of sight and hearing pleasures has been rejected: perhaps the beau-tiful is "beneficial pleasure." Not surprisingly, this possibility is summarily re-jected on the basis of the previously refuted notion that "the beneficial" might be what the beautiful is.

We have already had occasion to note the way the dialogue comes to a close. Hippias, portrayed in this dialogue as the more consistent of the two thinkers, responds to this last failure at an essentialist definition by trying one more time to characterize the beautiful in the only way he seems to believe it can be done. He offers one last formulation of what we may call some paradigm instances of beauty: being able to speak well in court and elsewhere, defending yourself, your property, and your friends (304a–b). This is, of course, precisely the "beautiful" trait that Hippias as a good sophist claims to have in abundance, and so there is here an ironic—at least partly ironic—return to the opening phrase of the dia-logue, "Hippias, beautiful and wise . . ." Perhaps, then, Hippias is right after all in this persistence—his rejection, in the end, of Socrates' characteristic insis-tence on a definitional formulation of the "essence" of the beautiful or of whatever term he addresses elsewhere. We can close our study of the *Hippias Major*, and point in the direction of the *Symposium*, by trying to understand the sense in which Hippias may indeed be right.[15]

As I indicated earlier in the chapter, a definition makes an extraordinarily bold claim; one that, epistemologically at least, borders on the hubristic: to comprehensively state the essence of the matter at issue *without remainder* (as we have seen, it is precisely these "remainders" that are often the basis of Socrates' refutations). The implicit claim, that is, is that the meaning and significance of such rich terms as the beautiful can be captured by logos, and indeed by a logos sufficiently concise to be called a definition. As we know, no dialogue of this sort genuinely succeeds in adequately defining such terms. When we put these efforts together, Socrates begins to look quixotic, a comic figure trying in this dialogue to define this term, failing—then bouncing to the next dialogue to try to define the next, failing there—trying yet again, etc. It is instructive that one of the leading translations of the *Hippias Major* is entitled, *Two Comic Dialogues: Ion and Hippias Major*.[16] Perhaps the real Platonic comedy is not in this or that particular dialogue but in the larger Socratic pursuit of definitions; and perhaps we are to see that it is comic through the constant failure of such efforts, yet Socrates' own persistence in continuing the effort. To say the least, it takes Socrates a very, very long time to learn the futility of such definitional efforts.

But that, surely is one of the lessons of this large group of dialogues, and there is no reason that we, the readers, should be as comically slow as Socrates in learning the lesson. Such definitional efforts would be plausible, the effort would be sensible, only if the premise on which they are founded were itself well-founded—that the essence of such terms as the beautiful might be accessible to a concise logos without remainder. If that premise is unsound, then the continued effort to "define our terms" becomes comically futile, as it in fact does in the dialogues.

It is this recognition that points us toward the *Symposium*, in at least two ways. First, very much will be said about the beautiful in that dialogue, by the early speakers and especially in the longer speech of Socrates and Diotima—much too much to be encapsulated in a concise definition. But second and more decisively, one of the things that will be *said*—at a crucial moment in Diotima's speech—is that there is something about "beauty itself" that is *not accessible to logos at all*. That is, no logos, and certainly not one concise enough to be called a definition, can capture the beautiful without remainder. This, as the *Phaedrus* will teach us, is not *only* true of beauty, but is *paradigmatically* true of this phenomenon: beauty is the best place to learn the larger lesson.

Perhaps this is why, in bringing the *Hippias Major* to a conclusion, Socrates returns, as he so often does, to his characteristic state of aporia. In response to Hippias's last denotative formulation at 304a–b, Socrates says: "Hippias, my friend, you are blessed because you know the things a man ought to practice, and have practiced them successfully, as you say. But I seem to be held by some daimonic fortune (*daimonia tis tuche*), so that I wander and am always in aporia, and exhibiting my aporia to you wise men, and in turn am reviled by you in speech whenever I exhibit it" (304b–c). By the end of his life, in the *Apology,* Socrates will have come to understand that this aporia is not just an occasional event in his life, but that it is more deeply a *stance toward the world:* a stance of questioning that is constitutive of his extraordinary self-knowledge. Perhaps, in the temporally close transition from the drama of the *Hippias Major* to the *Symposium* and *Phaedrus,* we are allowed to see this deeper recognition dawning on Socrates: the recognition that not everything can be defined, that not everything is logos.

Socrates finishes the dialogue by commenting that he thinks he knows the meaning of the proverb, "beautiful things are difficult": *chalepa ta kala* (304e9). The use of the plural ("beautiful things") as opposed to the singular ("the beautiful"—*to kalon*) is striking. Perhaps Socrates has truly learned the lesson from Hippias. For were he to have responded to this (his own) claim in his usual way, he would have taken "beautiful things are difficult" as a *definition* of the beautiful, which he would have then easily refuted. Instead, he concludes, he thinks he now knows its meaning. With this, we are prepared to move to the *Symposium.*

TWO

The Question of Beauty in the *Symposium*

We face a delicate task in turning now to the *Symposium* and *Phaedrus*. On the one hand, we want to pay particular attention to the way the question of *to kalon* emerges in these dialogues, since that is the focus of the present volume. But on the other, if we simply ignored everything but their references to beauty—jumping into each speech only when the term *to kalon* is mentioned—we would be ignoring the way Plato wrote. For as I emphasized in the introduction, beauty is one of those issues—in these dialogues at least—which Plato allows to emerge in the context of other issues with which, apparently, it is related. So we have to walk a fine interpretive line here. We have to be true to the dialogues and try to be open to the emergence of what happens in them as it happens, that is, we must read and interpret them as wholes; but this is not a *commentary* on either dialogue, and so our task is not to address every issue in them with more or less equal focus. We shall want to pay special attention to one particular emergence, that of the question of *to kalon*, for the manner of its emergence is extraordinary.

One thing at least we can say in this regard, for the *Symposium*: by the time of Agathon's speech (195a ff.), beauty has taken a place at the center of the discussion of eros. Agathon indicates this by characterizing eros as both beautiful itself and as loving the beautiful. It is that claim with which Socrates—perhaps strangely, given everything that has been said by the previous speakers—begins his speech. And by the time of Socrates' speech, we shall see the status of beauty in its relation to eros undergo a set of remarkable transformations that we shall have to follow with great care. But we cannot simply begin with Agathon's invocation of beauty or we would fail miserably to be true to the dialogue. So we must begin at the beginning, as it were, trying at once to understand something of the whole and to pay special attention to the emergence of the question of beauty.

The dramatic frame of the dialogue presents to us the character who will report what went on at the party at which the speeches on eros were given, signifying to us, in one of its most elaborate presentations in all the dialogues, that we are distanced from the actual event itself. Our interlocutor will be Apollodorus, whose most striking characteristic, we learn, is that he is a fanatical disciple of Socrates and who regards everyone as miserable except Socrates (173d). This becomes all the more important as we learn that even Apollodorus was not actually present at the discussion, but learned about it from yet another fanatical disciple of Socrates, Aristodemus (173b). That we learn of the discussion from two very biased interlocutors who share essentially the same biases prepares us to be wary of what, on first reading, surely looks to be the case: that the early speeches are merely a prelude to the real truth of the dialogue, which is contained in Socrates' speech. Of course that is the impression we would expect from these two highly prejudiced speakers! But we are invited to look to the early speeches to see if much more is not going on there than this biased impression would suggest.

The second feature of the dramatic frame of potential relevance to our reading is that, in passing and with no future relevance to the dialogue, Apollodorus mentions that the person to whom he is speaking is a certain Glaucon (172c). Whether or not this otherwise irrelevant fellow is the Glaucon of Plato's *Republic,* the name will inevitably call up to the reader that dialogue and is no doubt intended to do so. Why? One possible reason is that whereas the *Symposium* (and the *Phaedrus* as well) more or less praises eros, the *Republic* will present us with an almost relentless criticism of eros—beginning with Cephalus's expression of relief at being free of "that monster" (*Republic* 329c), to the Draconian rules regarding sex, to the final identification of eros with tyranny in book 8.[1] Each dialogue, it is thus indicated to us, must be qualified by the other; neither is the whole story, much less the "Platonic view" of eros.

Apollodorus begins his account of what happened at the party. Aristodemus, he says, happens upon Socrates and is surprised to see him bathed and wearing sandals (both unusual), and asks where he is going looking so *kalos.* Just as in the *Hippias Major,* the term is thus put into play almost immediately, and its employment, just as in the earlier dialogue, is initially tinged with irony. Socrates, recall, referred to the sophist Hippias as "beautiful and wise"; and now the notoriously ugly Socrates is described as "beautiful" by the biased Aristodemus, who is himself hardly beautiful. (Apollodorus describes him as *smikros,* "short," upon introducing him at 173b.) Socrates replies, no less ironically, that he is going to Agathon's party and is dressed up "so that beauty may go alongside

[handwritten marginal note: Beware of bias]

beauty": *hina kalos para kalon io* (174a9). It is worth noting immediately, in what will become an important word-play in the dialogue, that *agathon* is the Greek word for "good." That "beauty may go alongside beauty" already hints at the very claim Agathon will subsequently make, that eros is beautiful and loves the beautiful.

There follows the curious scene where Socrates invites Aristodemus to accompany him to Agathon's party uninvited, then rather rudely abandons the poor man to present himself at the party alone while Socrates lags behind thinking about something (174b–c). Only the *savoir faire* of Agathon, who upon Aristodemus's arrival pretends that he had been looking for him to invite him, mollifies this delicate situation engendered by Socrates' obvious disdain for convention.[2] When Socrates finally shows up, he and Agathon engage in some erotically loaded banter that concludes with Agathon saying, "You are hubristic (*Hybristes ei*), Socrates. We shall have a contest about wisdom, and Dionysus will be the judge" (175e). This is the first of a number of occasions in the dialogue where Socrates is accused of hubris. Alcibiades will level the same charge at 215b—one of several ways, as we shall see, in which his "praise" of Socrates will be tinged with criticism. That the speeches will be a *wisdom contest* is crucial. Despite the sophisticated air of gentility, these men are contestants over who is wisest regarding eros, on at least two levels: each will try to give the best speech personally, and each will represent a certain standpoint that might claim wisdom concerning eros.[3] The location in the order of Agathon's and Socrates' speeches will indicate that the primary disputants in the contest will be poetry or more broadly art, represented by Agathon, and philosophy, represented by Socrates. And of course, the beautiful Alcibiades, when he later enters the party—drunk and with a train of followers—is the very personification of Dionysus as he crowns first Agathon but then, when he sees him, Socrates as the winner of the contest.

After more banter in which it is decided to give speeches in praise of eros, Phaedrus begins his speech. One core of Phaedrus's teaching is that there is no better aid for living a *kalos* life (*kalos biosesthai*—178c) than for a beloved to have a "useful" (*chrestos*) lover, and a lover a beloved. His way of introducing this thesis is striking: "For I cannot say that there is a greater good right from youth than a useful lover or for a lover a beloved. What people who intend to live beautifully need is not provided by family, honors, wealth, or anything else, so well as by eros" (178c).

A number of important themes are announced here that play out in a complicated way in Phaedrus's speech. First, Phaedrus sees—and he is surely right in this—that there is an enormous stake for all of us in the character of our love lives, a stake precisely in terms of the possibility of our living "beautiful lives." Though the wrong kind of erotic relationship can be disastrous, the right sort of love relationship surely can be beneficial for living a "beautiful life." However tenuously, this would seem to be the first invocation of the connection between eros and beauty which will be such an enduring theme of the dialogue. As this theme gets played out, we shall have to consider it in the detail it deserves. For some reason, Plato seems insistently to raise for the reader a certain connection between two fundamental human experiences: that of eros, and that of beauty. We shall see the specific character of this connection evolve as the *Symposium* proceeds, and it will undergo further development in the *Phaedrus*. Here in Phaedrus's speech, it gets raised almost casually and in passing, but we should already be aware that something decisive is in play here. Second, Phaedrus states this theme precisely in terms of *usefulness* (*chrestos*). This is in fact one of the themes, if not the central theme, for Phaedrus. As is hinted in his earlier remark about the usefulness of salt (177b), he is deeply, indeed primarily, interested in usefulness, utility; and as the rest of his speech will show, the primary focus of this interest will be the usefulness of a lover to a beloved. This is because that is precisely Phaedrus's own erotic situation: he is the beloved of Eryximachus, and is convinced that his is the most "useful" erotic situation in which to be. But this raises a crucial question: just what is the nature of the right erotic relationship for living a beautiful life? That is what gets played out in the rest of his speech, and the results, if read with care, are striking.

Though for the rest of his speech, Phaedrus occasionally pays brief lip service to the benefit to a lover of having a beloved (he mentions it in passing twice at 178c, and again at 178e), he is primarily interested in the benefits to a beloved of having a lover, the culmination of which is that a lover will even be willing to die for his beloved (179b). In complicated ways, this is played out in the three examples he gives: those of Alcestis, Orpheus, and Achilles. For our purposes, the most important example is that of Achilles, where the truth of Phaedrus's understanding of eros comes to be revealed. Phaedrus begins by changing the story to suit his own erotic tastes and purposes. Achilles, he says, is the beloved of Patroclus (Homer does not characterize the relationship as erotic at all). Therefore, Phaedrus continues, when Achilles, the supposed beloved, is willing to die for his lover, the gods give him even greater praises and prizes than they would a lover who was willing to die for his beloved. Why? "Because the lover is inspired" (180b). Inspired by what? The answer could only be, by love! What then is the clear implication regarding the beloved? That he is *not inspired by love*! Phaedrus's position, I suggest, amounts to this: erotic relationships can be both dangerous and beneficial (he is surely right about this!). It is dangerous if you are a lover, that is, if you are inspired by love; this leads you, as Hesiod pointed out, to do all sorts of irrational things.[4] The benefits of eros accrue if you can be a beloved, like Phaedrus. For in this case, you get the benefits of the inspired if irrational loyalty of the lover, without suffering that irrationality yourself. The right relationship, that is, is to *stay out of love yourself but use the inspiration of a lover to gain all sorts of benefits.*[5] Phaedrus's "utilitarianism" is one of crass exploitation of what he takes to be the irrational inspiration of lovers.

Phaedrus sees, then, the large stake for human living in having the appropriate erotic relationship, and he also sees, if in a superficial way, that there is or ought to be a connection between eros and beauty, understood primarily in terms of living a beautiful life, living well. He also recognizes, however surreptitiously, the fact that eros is a doubled-edged sword: it can be a great benefit but also a great danger. His solution to this dilemma is to stay out of love himself—Phaedrus is, after all, a notably unerotic man—but to benefit from the inspiration of a lover. This will fail, as we shall see, because it assumes that the proper relationship to eros is to avoid it oneself. That is perverse, and the real question as we move to Pausanias's speech then becomes, what then is the right orientation toward love? Despite Phaedrus's surface claim that eros is useful in living a *kalos* life—one that is noble and beautiful—the core of his position is one of vulgar self-interest, and not at all beautiful. The appropriate relationship of eros and *to kalon*, then, will hardly be to keep them apart.[6]

It is therefore entirely appropriate that Pausanias, the next speaker whom Aristodemus remembers, should begin his speech in reference to Phaedrus's with the words, *Ou kalos moi dokei, o Phaidre:* "Not beautiful did it seem to me, O Phaedrus . . ." He goes on to explain that one cannot simply praise a single eros, since there is more than one (180c).

To explain what he means, Pausanias begins by developing the distinction in modes of eros, paralleling the mythical distinction between the "heavenly" (*ouranion*) Aphrodite and the "common" (*pandemion*) Aphrodite (180d–e). When, from 181b to 181e, he fills out the difference between these two eroses, it becomes clear that his real point is to associate as strongly as possible heterosexuality with common eros and pederasty with heavenly or noble eros. This is the first point he makes in his description of each kind of eros (181b, 181c). To be sure, Pausanias also tries to associate common love with other presumed negatives: it is merely of the body, not of the soul (as is heavenly love); and it is not concerned with intelligence but merely with gratification. But a moment's reflection will indicate that the difference between love of the body and love of the soul will hardly be measured by whether it is heterosexual or homosexual love![7] The real point of his distinction, then, is to identify homosexuality with "heavenly" love and heterosexuality with "common" love.

Along with this claim Pausanias, who is a sophist, virtually at the same time introduces his version of Protagorean relativism, and does so precisely with the issue of *to kalon* in mind:

> It is true of every action that doing it is in itself neither beautiful nor ugly (*oute kale oute aischra*).[8] For example, nothing of what we are doing now, whether drinking, singing, or conversing, is beautiful in itself. In activities, it is the manner in which it is done that determines its quality. When an action is done beautifully and rightly, it becomes beautiful, but if it is not done rightly, it becomes shameful (*kalos men gar prattomenon kai orthos kalon gignetai, me orthos de aischron*). So loving and love are not always beautiful and worthy of praise, but only the love that points toward beauty. (181a)

The decisive point is this: eros is neither beautiful nor shameful in itself. This is phenomenologically true, surely, and its truth will be preserved as we move forward and into Socrates' speech. However, as Pausanias understands it, eros will *become* beautiful or shameful according to the manner in which it is "done" (various forms of *prattein*). Even though eros is not inherently beautiful, then, the issue of beauty is very much at stake in our erotic lives. But this begs the critical question: everything depends on what *counts* as a "beautifully" (or "shamefully") performed action. We shall have to look later in his speech for what Pausanias takes as the measure, and later still, for what Socrates and Diotima take as the measure.

Here in Pausanias's speech the connection of eros and beauty is raised in some detail for the first time, and it is important to be mindful of the nature of the connection. Eros is, or can be, either *kalos* or *aischros*—either beautiful or shameful. It is neither in itself. We shall have to recall Pausanias's formulation when later we see Socrates, speaking for Diotima, present his version of this point: eros, he will say, is "in the middle" (*metaxu*) between a number of qualities, including beauty and ugliness (201e ff.). In both cases, the *criterion* of what counts as beautiful or ugly will be decisive.

Pausanias's speech, for all its insight, is already in trouble, at least as staged by Plato. On the one hand, he wants to affirm his own version of sophistic relativism (eros is neither beautiful nor shameful in itself, etc.). On the other hand, he wants to claim what amounts to the inherent superiority of homosexual to heterosexual eros. The two are incompatible. By the standards of his relativism, he should be claiming of *both* homosexuality and heterosexuality that "neither is beautiful or shameful in itself but becomes beautiful or shameful according to the manner in which it is performed." And is something like this not phenomenologically true? Pausanias cannot have both his relativism and his conviction that homosexuality is somehow inherently beautiful, heterosexuality inherently base. It should be added immediately that it hardly follows that the converse is true.

Pausanias now turns, much more explicitly than did Phaedrus, to his recognition that there are also dangers to eros. His proposal for dealing with these dangers will be *law* (*nomos*). "There oughtta be a law," he says in effect. But we begin to see another way in which Plato has Pausanias's speech begin to break down when we note who Pausanias's law is designed to protect. He begins, "Actually, there should be a law (*nomos*) against loving young boys, so that a lot of effort will not be squandered on an uncertain prospect. It is unclear how young boys will turn out, whether their souls and bodies will end up being bad or virtuous" (181e). Pausanias's version of the law regarding pederasty will be for the protection of the pederasts!

This leads him to a discussion of the various laws regarding pederasty (181e–184a). Not surprisingly, Pausanias is dismayed at those cities which straightforwardly outlaw pederasty. More interestingly, he also does not like those cities where pederasty is simply affirmed, and for an interesting reason: in such cities, rhetorical ability will not be necessary to seduce beloveds, and that will eliminate Pausanias's advantage. For as a sophist, Pausanias is nothing if not an able rhetorician. What he appreciates, he goes on to say, is those cities where the situation is more complex, such as in Athens. Here, he explains, on the one hand, lovers are praised and encouraged, yet on the other, parents do their best to keep their children from pederasts, and young boys who submit easily to the sexual advances of older lovers are chastised.

It is in introducing this complexity that Pausanias subtly indicates for the first time what his crucial criterion will be by which to distinguish beautifully performed erotic actions from basely performed ones. He says concisely and apparently in passing, "It is considered beautiful to succeed in this matter and shameful to fail" (182e). Pausanias's criterion for whether eros is beautiful or shameful is whether or not the lover succeeds! What is happening to the distinction between beautiful and shameful eros here? Pausanias is getting so carried away by his own erotic desires that, as we shall now see, he will allow to the lover *any behavior, beautiful or shameful,* if only he can succeed. In pursuit of the beloved, he says, the lover can beg, plead, sleep in the beloved's doorway, be a slave worse than any slave, even lie (183a–c). In Pausanias's erotic rapture here, the distinction between beautiful and shameful love with which he began is collapsing before our eyes.

At the rhetorical peak of his speech, Pausanias concludes his account of the complicated situation in Athens by characterizing the pederastic situation as the convergence of two "laws" (*nomoi*). It will be useful to hear the rhetorical flourish with which he develops his conclusion, then try to cut through the rhetoric to see what he is really talking about.

> When a lover and his beloved come together, each has a law (*nomon*). The lover is justified in performing any services he can for his beloved who gratifies him, and the beloved in turn is justified in providing whatever services he can for the one who is making him wise and good—assuming the former is able to introduce the other to prudence and other virtues, and the latter does want to acquire an education and other skills. When these two laws come together as one, then and only then does it happen that a beloved's gratifying a lover is something beautiful. Otherwise not at all. (184d–e)

The speech certainly sounds "noble" enough, but think about the actual situation he is describing: he is advocating that the beloved trade sex for wisdom![9] What we are seeing here as the speech reaches its peak is that the important distinction with which Pausanias began, that there is both beautiful (or noble) and base love, and that love itself is thus inherently neither beautiful nor base, is collapsing as Pausanias gives absolutely free rein to the lover to do anything he can to succeed. It is a reflection of Pausanias's sophistic rhetorical ability that he hides this vulgarity behind beautiful-sounding rhetoric.

What has Plato done, then, with Pausanias's speech? On the one hand, it contains crucial insights. First, and decisively for our own purposes, there is here established for the first time a clear connection between eros and beauty: eros *can* be beautiful. But it can also be shameful. Therefore it is neither beautiful nor base "in itself." Surely Pausanias is right here. But then everything will depend on the criterion by which we will distinguish beautiful from shameful loves. Pausanias first tried to make the distinction rest on sexual orientation: homosexual love is beautiful or noble, heterosexual love is base. That collapsed on his own relativist principle. But then, as he himself seemed to be carried away by his own erotic desires, he dissolved the very distinction between beautiful and base love into vulgarity: the "noble" lover can in fact conduct himself in every disgraceful manner so long as he succeeds. Then it is "beautiful." Pausanias cannot sustain his own important insights because of his erotic passion to seduce his beloveds. As we leave his speech, our guiding question must then be, what after all *is* the criterion by which we might distinguish beautiful from shameful love?

Aristophanes is scheduled to speak next, but during Pausanias's speech he has developed a case of hiccups (the Greek word can also mean "belching"), no doubt a symbol of his disgust at the import of Pausanias's speech. The direct effect of the incident is that Eryximachus the doctor both proposes three cures for Aristophanes' distress and agrees to speak in his stead while he is undergoing the cures. In a full commentary on the *Symposium,* the meaning of the hiccups and the cures would have to be taken up in detail, but they are not, I think, directly relevant to the question of beauty in the dialogue, and so we will pass quickly to the speech of Eryximachus.

Eryximachus is a doctor, a man of science, and his speech will ingeniously portray eros in such a way that, if successful, he, and therefore science, will win the wisdom contest regarding eros. Eryximachus begins by showing that he recognizes full well the import of Pausanias's speech which we have just drawn out. Pausanias, he says, "began his speech beautifully but did not adequately finish it, so I must try to put a conclusion to his speech" (186a). But as we shall see, what Eryximachus in fact does is totally transform Pausanias's position.

Both Phaedrus and Pausanias understood eros as primarily a personal, romantic phenomenon. That is, their paradigm of eros—indeed, the only genre that apparently interests them—is personal love between two humans. Therefore, insofar as they both tie the issue of beauty to eros, their understanding of beauty was also primarily confined to the beauty—or its lack—in this personal love. Eryximachus's first step (186a) is to radically expand the domain of eros. From the exclusive emphasis on individual, personal love assumed by Phaedrus and Pausanias, Eryximachus extends it to all animals, plants—indeed, to virtually everything there is! And he will surely be right to expand the realm of eros beyond that of personal love. Though personal love may be paradigmatic of erotic experience, it is surely not the only—nor even, quite possibly, the most philosophically important—manifestation of eros. Eryximachus here takes an important step in recognizing that eros is a much more pervasive phenomenon. However, whether the direction of Eryximachus's expansion is appropriate remains to be seen. For he expands the realm of eros throughout the *physical* cosmos. As we shall see, he has his own reasons for doing so. But will he be right, or is the appropriate direction of expansion, as Socrates will argue, to other modes of *psychic* eros, such as creativity and philosophy? And what is likely to happen to beauty with the relegation of eros on Eryximachus's part to the realm of the physical?

Eryximachus begins with a decisive transformation of Pausanias's distinction between the heavenly and common, the beautiful and shameful eros. He changes it to the distinction between healthy and diseased eros and, no less strikingly, explicitly limits the distinction to the body. "Respect for my *techne* leads me to begin with the medical art. This double love belongs to the nature of all bodies, for between health and sickness of bodies there is an agreed dissimilarity, and what is dissimilar desires and loves dissimilar things. Hence the love in a healthy body and the love in a sick body are different" (186b).

What is the basis of this change? In one step, Eryximachus changes the issue from what Pausanias understood to be largely the *psychic* distinction between beauty or nobility and baseness to the *physical* distinction between health and disease.[10] If Eryximachus can sustain this insistence that the question of eros is a question of the *body*—that is, a *physical* question—then who will win this wisdom contest? Science, of course, as embodied in his speech.

Eryximachus's move here is in fact brilliant. He recognizes that the only way he can make science authoritative is to insist that the understanding of eros is largely or exclusively a question of knowledge of the body, or more generally, of the contending physical forces in the universe that he names the two eroses. If he can sustain this claim, he wins the contest. As we shall see, his central failing will be that he himself will not be able to resist making claims—about beauty (or nobility) and shamefulness, about piety and impiety—that cannot be founded in the body. But let us not get ahead of ourselves.

Next, Eryximachus adds a second crucial factor. He begins, he says, with his own *techne*, medicine (186b–e). His point is that his medical *techne* can *control* the healthy and diseased eroses of the body for our pleasure. Note the important principle here that Eryximachus will soon expand: he is not only or even primarily interested in expanding the realm of eros throughout the cosmos. He is at least as interested in expanding the control by human *techne* of the healthy and diseased eroses in all their manifestations. Eryximachus's real intent is the control of the cosmos by human *techne*: "knowledge is power." He sees that the real point of scientific explanation, exemplified in his own medical practice, is human technical control.

In this regard it is striking that in his account of the medical *techne*, Eryximachus still pays lip service to the Pausanian distinction between noble or beautiful and base eros that he has in fact undercut.

As Pausanias just said, to gratify those human beings who are good is a beautiful thing, but to gratify those who are immoral is shameful. So also in the case of bodies, it is beautiful and noble to gratify what is good and healthy in each body and should be done (this is what is called the medical *techne*), but it is shameful to gratify what is bad and sick, and one should not do so if one wants to be a medical technician (*technikos*). (186b–c)

We should, he says here, avoid the shameful and diseased eroses. However, in little over a page, thanks presumably to the power of human *techne*, things change. By 187e, Eryximachus is saying (he has been speaking of music and poetry):

For the old account comes back: one should gratify decent men, *as well as those who, though they are not decent, might become more so,* and one should defend the love of these men—this is the beautiful love, the heavenly love of Urania. In the case of the common love, that of Polyhymnia, *one must be cautious about whom one engages in it with, so that one may gain pleasure for oneself without sickness.* (187d–e; my emphasis)

No longer do we have to avoid the diseased (or shameful) eros! Human *techne* will enable us to indulge in it without getting sick. Such is its power. Just as happened with Pausanias, so here with Eryximachus, his initial distinction and exhortation to pursue the healthy—and so "beautiful"—and avoid the diseased eros is collapsing. But in the case of Eryximachus, the collapse is due to his excessive confidence in the remarkable power of *techne*. What is truly "beautiful" to Eryximachus is *techne*.

Eryximachus now begins his expansion of the realm of eros—and the control of human *techne*—throughout the physical realm. In addition to medicine, he says, the double eros (and its control by *techne*) holds in music, gymnastics, agriculture and (as his enthusiasm for this double expansion gains steam) for the weather, the seasons of the year, and even the stars (188b)! But at this point we can see that Eryximachus's enthusiasm for science is carrying him away. For in his effort to expand the realm of *techne* throughout the physical cosmos—to enable us, in the words of a later thinker (Descartes), to become "the masters and possessors of nature"—Eryximachus extends the realm of the double eros beyond any possible human control.[11] The effort to master eros in all its manifestations by human *techne*, Plato may be quietly telling us, is doomed to fail.

But as Eryximachus concludes his speech, it fails in another way: for in his peroration he returns to Pausanias's psychic or ethical language of beauty, piety, *sophrosyne,* and justice (188c–d). Yet given his reduction of eros to the physical, on what basis can he still appeal to such notions? Can Eryximachus sustain such ethical/aesthetic judgments regarding beauty or nobility, piety, or justice, on the basis of the purely physical distinction between health and disease?

What I believe Plato presents us with in Eryximachus's speech is the kernel of a critique, in the Kantian sense, of the claim of science to be able to account

for the entirety of human experience, certainly including the realm of the beautiful. He shows Eryximachus correctly insisting that the realm of eros extends
beyond the narrow domain of personal love to which Phaedrus and Pausanias
confined it. He has him expand it in the only way possible if science is to be
authoritative: throughout the physical cosmos. But in a number of ways that I
have tried to draw out, and pointedly regarding the question of beauty, Plato has
that very attempt break down. If eros and its intimate connection with the
beautiful is at least in part psychic, and especially if it is *decisively* psychic, then
science cannot be the authoritative account of eros. Eryximachus's "physicalist"
position can, in principle, only explain *physical* beauty; but no one believes that
beauty is an exclusively physical phenomenon. The question we are left with as
we move to Aristophanes' speech, then, is this: in what direction *should* eros
be expanded, if not simply to the physical? Beauty, as we shall see, will have
everything to do with the response of the subsequent speakers, but only after
Aristophanes' speech.

After a long history of interpretation where Aristophanes' speech was not
taken seriously as a part of the *Symposium* that contained important teachings,[12]
nearly all interpreters now recognize that very important things are happening
in the comic poet's speech. As with the previous speeches, I shall not here
offer anything like a comprehensive reading, but concentrate on those aspects
that will prove germane to our theme as we move further along in the dialogue.
It is worth reminding ourselves as we begin that Aristophanes is the famous
and quite conservative comic poet who is already in a rather complicated and
strained relationship with the two leading symposiasts, Socrates and Agathon,
whom he has roundly and even viciously satirized in his plays.[13] It is therefore
not surprising, then, that in contrast to Pausanias and Eryximachus, both of
whom began their speeches with reference to the previous speech and in an
effort to correct or complete it, Aristophanes begins by asserting that he "has it
in mind to speak in a different way" than either Pausanias or Eryximachus
(189c; he simply ignores Phaedrus). Conservative thinker that he is, he is no
doubt particularly opposed to Pausanias's defense of pederasty—and the vulgarity into which it sinks—and to Eryximachus's "materialist" account of eros.[14]
Instead, as he now indicates, he will present a predominantly *religious* account,
which asserts first that if we understood the power of Eros we would build great
temples and altars to him, for he is the "most philanthropic" of the gods—
literally the god who loves human beings the most (189d). As it turns out, by the
standards of Aristophanes' subsequent account, Eros is not just the god who
loves us the most, he would seem to be the *only* one who loves us; the other gods
care about us, as we will soon learn, only for the sacrifices we give to them.

Aristophanes now begins his hilarious account, but we must note exactly
how he begins, for he does not begin directly with an account of *Eros,* but with
an account of *anthropinen physin kai to pathemata autes:* "human nature and its
sufferings" (189d). This will be crucial: the account of Eros given by Aris-

tophanes will not be an account of an isolated human phenomenon in which we occasionally indulge (today I fall in love, tomorrow I fall out of it), but an account of our very nature as it is now. This is our first clue as to Aristophanes' way of recognizing that Eros extends much further than just our love affairs (though for reasons that we shall soon understand, Aristophanes "officially" limits it to such personal relations). Indeed, it will hardly be an exaggeration to say that for Aristophanes, Eros is human nature as it is now (as opposed to our "original position").[15]

So Aristophanes begins his account of Eros/human nature. We should note first how akin it is to so many traditional religious accounts, including the biblical one. First, our original condition was superior to the one we are in now: we were once the hilarious "double people"—with four legs, four arms, two heads, etc.—that Aristophanes describes, and as such we were extraordinarily powerful (189e–190b). But, second, we had a fatal flaw, an "original sin": we were so hubristic as to try to overthrow the gods (190c). So, consequently, third, we experienced a "fall from grace": we had to be punished by the gods, who did so by reducing us to our present, inferior status (190c ff.). As a result of that, fourth: we must now continue to be pious toward the gods out of fear that they will punish us again if we are not (190d). It is remarkable the extent to which Plato has Aristophanes set out the core convictions of so many religious standpoints.

However, there are important differences as well that make Aristophanes' account, to say the least, unorthodox even by pagan standards. First, we learn that we are in fact cosmic creatures—progeny of the sun, moon, and earth respectively, and not of the Olympian gods (190b). Second, the gods themselves are portrayed as in aporia (190c)! Aristophanes comes close to portraying the gods, no less than us, as comic fools. We are to imagine them scratching their heads in aporia about what to do with us. Zeus finally comes up with the idea to split us, which is almost a disaster, so they have to try a second operation that finally makes the situation better (191b–c)! Third, the gods do not love us! They refrain from killing us off only out of self-interest: they want our sacrifices (190d). What they like about Zeus's solution is that, by doubling our number, they will double our sacrifices to them, as well as making us less of a threat. Eros is the *only god* who loves humans.

Zeus's first effort is nearly disastrous, as we spend all our time trying to join with our original half once we are split. So we were dying off after all, which would not serve the gods' purposes. By the second operation—which changed the location of our genitals and enabled us to procreate as we join each other— the race is saved (191c). But notice: the race is only saved by what we now call heterosexuals. He says of the formerly double men (now homosexuals) that they will now at least satisfy themselves "and stop" (191c)! This will be in tension with the apparent praise of homosexuality in which Aristophanes will soon indulge. Nevertheless, Aristophanes' account of the three sexual orientations as a result of the splitting of double males, double females, and the androgynous beings respectively, is remarkable. It represents one of the first accounts that what we now call "sexual orientation" is "by nature." It is, as we now say, "genetic." For Aristophanes, our sexual orientation is not a "lifestyle choice," but the way we are after our fall from grace.

And now, at 191d, we are at last told just what Eros is: "It is out of this situation, then, that the natural love (*ho eros emphutos*) for each other arose in human beings; it collects the halves of our original nature and tries to make a single thing out of the two parts so as to restore human nature." At 193a this is glossed as: "So the desire and pursuit of wholeness is called love." Eros is the desire to return to our original wholeness out of our present incompleteness. About this remarkable account a number of things must be said.

First, we should note the intimacy between Eros and human nature in this account. Eros is in fact a triadic phenomenon. It is, first, our incompleteness: our present ontological condition as incomplete beings. Human beings now *are* as incomplete; incompleteness is our very being. But second, Eros is our *recognition or experience* of our incompleteness. Stones and all sorts of things might be incomplete, but that of itself does not yet make them erotic, for they must also experience and recognize their incompleteness. Third and decisively, Eros is our desire to overcome our experienced incompleteness, to achieve our longed-for wholeness. So understood, Eros obviously extends way beyond sexual or even personal love, though for his own reasons, Aristophanes will not want to call attention to the wider expressions of Eros. For this is just as well an account of the erotic basis of all human aspiration—of the desire for wealth or political power or, crucially, of philosophy itself understood precisely in the Socratic sense of aporia. (*Aporia* is not being wise, recognizing that lack, and striving for wisdom.) It is no wonder, in this light, that Aristophanes does not want to explicitly indicate these other manifestations of Eros—about which, in his plays, he is so skeptical—but confines it to the relatively "safe" one of personal love. Even so confined, however, it should be noted that Aristophanes' account of human Eros has a remarkable feature: it is reciprocal! Apparently the erotic desire of a given pair to join together is entirely reciprocal: *both* desire this.[16]

But also, this account quietly indicates that Eros is not a god at all! Eros is our *human situation*, once we are rendered split or incomplete. At the beginning and end of his speech, Aristophanes asks us to worship Eros as the god who loves humans the most. But the core of his speech teaches something quite different, what we may call a certain humanism: that Eros is our human nature in our present condition. But this means that in fact, *none of the gods love humans.*

Aristophanes now discusses the three sexual orientations (191d–192c). Before his audience composed largely of homosexual men, he *seems* to somewhat denigrate lesbianism and especially heterosexuality (he mentions adulterers and adulteresses among this class, but not the good heterosexual couples of whom he approves in his plays and whom he has just described as the saviors of the

Agathon effeminate

human race), and to praise what we now/call homosexuals. But there are at least two jokes here. First, with Agathon sitting near him, whose notorious effeminacy he himself has mocked in the *Thesmophoriazusae,* he emphasizes repeatedly how "most manly" (*andreiotatoi*) the homosexuals are. Second, the "great proof" of this, says Aristophanes (192b), is that when these homosexual youths grow up they enter into politics (*eis ta politika*). But of course, Aristophanes makes it clear in his plays that he detests politicians almost as much as philosophers! The joke here, of course, is that Plato has Aristophanes behave true to form: he ironically praises the homosexual men present whose real "values" the conservative poet detests.[17]

Aristophanes now turns to a most serious consequence of our erotic condition as split, incomplete beings (192c–192e): we do not know ourselves. Commenting on those "original halves" that come together, immediately fall in love, and want to spend their lives together, and denying that this could be explained merely by sexual passion, Aristophanes says: "On the contrary, it is clear that there is something else that the soul of each wants but it cannot say what it is, so it prophesizes (*manteueai*) and speaks in riddles (*ainitetai*)" (192d). Human beings, for Aristophanes, do not know what they want. We need religion to make sense of our deepest desires (in this case, Hephaestus, who volunteers to meld us together into one forever). Our fallen human condition, then, is this: we do not understand the real meaning of our deepest desires, and in fact, we desire what we cannot have. After the first generation we are born split and *do not truly have* another "original" half, as Aristophanes will quietly make clear in his peroration. Human life is thus a striving after something at which we are fated by nature to fail. But this is the classic tragic situation. The comic poet is presenting a tragic view of the human situation.

Aristophanes is thus profoundly pessimistic about the possibility of self-knowledge—much more so, as we shall see, than is Socrates. For Aristophanes, we cannot know ourselves—in particular the nature of our erotic desires—and we need religion as a substitute. For Socrates, a *certain* self-knowledge—knowing what I know and what I do not know—is at least possible or worth striving for. This Aristophanic pessimism about the human erotic situation will prove a decisive difference between him and Socrates.

In his peroration (193a–e), Aristophanes returns to what we now recognize as the lip service he is paying to religion—the notion that Eros is a god whom we should revere. It is clear by now that his reasons for doing so are not that *he* believes what he is saying—the interior of his speech indicates quite the reverse—but that he thinks it best that *humans* believe this.

In doing so, however, he indicates once again the basis of his pessimistic and tragic position. "This is how the human race can become happy: we must perfect love and every man must find his own beloved, thereby returning to our original nature. *If this is what is best, then the nearest thing to that is necessarily the best in the present circumstances,* and that is to happen upon a beloved who is suited by nature to one's mind" (193c; my emphasis). Our "present circumstances" are that we are now born split and have no "natural" other half. We cannot attain what we desire most deeply, the real object of our eros. We must fail. Our consolation, at least in Aristophanes' eyes, should be to find a compatible mate whom we "happen upon" (*tuchoi*), and live peacefully and religiously with them.

As we shall see, Socrates will in a decisive way accept the core of Aristophanes' position as *part* of the "truth" about eros that he will teach. But only a part! Aristophanes, as we shall see, is literally half right—as Agathon will be. His excessive pessimism will have to be moderated by the truth of what we shall now see is the excessive optimism of Agathon's speech, to which we shall turn next.

The problem with Aristophanes' position is perhaps symbolized by a striking fact that I hope has quietly emerged in the course of this discussion of his speech: it is devoid of the issue of beauty! Aristophanes' is the only speech in the *Symposium* that does not so much as mention *to kalon* or its derivatives even once. Quite literally, there is nothing beautiful (or noble) about Aristophanes' position. His view of the human situation, far from being beautiful in any way, is that we are sad fools. This defect will be overcome in spades by Agathon, to whom we can now turn. And, as Socrates' later speech will show (and as will be exhibited even more powerfully in his palinode in the *Phaedrus*), it is Agathon who will be right on this point at least. There *is*, or can be, something beautiful about the human situation, and its beauty will be intimately tied to our eros. Aristophanes' profound pessimism leads him to miss this, but Agathon will correct this fault.

Aristophanes the comic poet has presented a tragic account of eros, developing it in terms of eros's inevitable incompleteness. Agathon, the tragic poet, will now present eros's comedy. Eros will be complete in every way: he is beautiful, young (he here confutes Phaedrus), delicate, just, courageous, *sophron*, and wise. He resembles, in short, the happy cherub of mythical accounts (not to mention Agathon himself!). At the very conclusion of the *Symposium*, Socrates is portrayed as convincing Aristophanes and Agathon that the tragic poet can write comedy and vice versa. Plato the philosopher is doing so before our eyes.

Agathon now proceeds to portray eros in his own image: young, beautiful, delicate, and with a wisdom that is demonstrated by his poetic ability. This gesture, as we shall see, will be repeated in Socrates' speech, where eros will look like Socrates! Agathon begins with precisely what Aristophanes ignored—eros's beauty. For the first time in the dialogue, beauty becomes genuinely thematic in its connection with eros. Eros, says Agathon, is beautiful and loves the beautiful.[18] In the midst of all the important things that have been said about eros in the various speeches, this is the point with which Socrates will begin his speech, even if to radically alter Agathon's straightforward assertion. This surely signals the crucial importance of Agathon's claim regarding the beauty of eros. Yet its importance, as we see in Socrates' subsequent *elenchus* of it, is not that the claim

[handwritten marginalia: "assumption foundation"]

that eros is beautiful and loves the beautiful is simply true. If not that, then what is the importance of Agathon's claim regarding the intimate link between eros and beauty?

First and foremost, Agathon invokes the close kinship of eros and beauty. Even if the particular way he formulates the kinship (eros is beautiful and loves the beautiful) is wrong, as it will be seen to be, he is surely right in correcting Aristophanes on this point. Eros cannot be adequately understood without invoking its kinship with beauty and taking steps to understand that kinship.

Second, one thing that the invocation of beauty will enable Agathon to do in principle is to join Eryximachus's emphasis on the body with the concentration of the other speeches on the soul. Eros has both physical and psychic manifestations, and both must be accounted for. How are we to make sense of eros in both its physical and psychic manifestations? Through beauty. Beauty is perhaps the paradigm case of a phenomenon that has both physical and psychic manifestations; we can speak of beautiful bodies, and we can speak of beautiful souls. Beauty can thus be the bridge by which all the manifestations of eros can be connected. We shall see that this is exactly what Socrates, speaking as Diotima, will do in the famous "ascent" passage at 210a ff.—which is an ascent, after all, of the love of beauty. Agathon may not be correct in the details of his formulation regarding eros and beauty, then, but he is surely insightful to see that the two are intimately connected in some way and that the articulation of this connection is critical to any adequate account of either. This is no doubt why Socrates will soon begin his speech from this claim of Agathon's.

Agathon then turns to eros's virtue (196b ff.). In a series of laughably invalid arguments, he proclaims eros's justice, *sophrosyne*, courage, and wisdom. To say the least, it is not always obvious that love is just, *sophron*, courageous, or wise! The crucial part of his claim, however, and the one that I suspect is the reason Plato placed his speech next to Socrates' and why the "wisdom contest" is decisively between Agathon and Socrates—between poetry and philosophy—is Agathon's claim regarding eros's wisdom. The sign and proof of eros's wisdom, says Agathon, is that eros is a poet and makes others poets (196d–e). The larger claim here is that the sign or criterion of wisdom is creativity. Agathon here puts into play, even if implicitly, the connection between eros, beauty, and creativity that, one might say, has never gone away. Indeed, it has even become more crucial with the modern advent of "aesthetics" as an independent discipline, wherein beauty becomes a largely "aesthetic" issue and so one primarily or paradigmatically connected with art. We still tend today to see the primary or at least the highest instances of beauty in art, and Agathon here puts that connection into play. Whether that primacy is something that the dialogues sustain, however, is another question—one that will have to await our study of the *Phaedrus* to respond to adequately.

If Agathon could sustain this claim that the sign of wisdom is creativity (*poiesis*), he would win the wisdom contest on behalf of poetry, win it quite particularly over philosophy (in the person of Socrates). The decisive issue will thus be: what is the highest human possibility, the sign of wisdom among humans? Creativity or understanding, poetry or philosophy? Now, this is stated too starkly. Though Agathon, in his complete lack of interest in conceptual logic, does not sustain the point, creativity certainly can and must embody understanding just as, as Socrates will show, there is a creative element, at least to a point, in philosophy. Nevertheless, in the end, the claim of philosophy will be that the ultimate thing at stake is understanding. Creativity, on Socrates' view, will be second—very high, but still second. This is no doubt one basis of the "longstanding quarrel between poetry and philosophy" of which Agathon's and Socrates' speeches are an instance. However poorly Agathon may defend his position, then, it remains the case—or so the *Symposium* seems to teach—that the standpoint of art is the decisive challenge to the claim that the philosophic life, one dedicated primarily to understanding, to truth, is the highest human possibility. No wonder, then, that Socrates will begin his speech by confronting Agathon's position.

Aristodemus reports that everyone applauded Agathon's speech.[19] If so, Socrates' applause seems ironic, for he now rudely dismisses all the previous speeches, but especially Agathon's, claiming sarcastically that he had no idea that praising something meant saying absolutely anything about it whether or not it was true. He refuses, he says, to participate in such a contest. But he will, he boldly asserts, tell them the truth about eros if they want to hear it (199b)! This dismissal will prove to be an enormous rhetorical overstatement on Socrates' part. As we shall see, far from rejecting all the previous speeches, he lifts up something from each of them as part of the "truth" about eros that he will deliver. Far from a blanket rejection of the previous speeches, what we are about to read is a proto-Hegelian *Aufhebung* of them. We can turn now to Socrates' speech.

Agathon has thematized (as opposed to merely mentioning) the issue of beauty in its connection with eros for the first time in the dialogue. Socrates will now criticize his specific formulation of this relation, but emphatically *not* criticize the importance of the connection itself. Moreover, as we are about to see, this criticism is invalid and Socrates knows very well that it is invalid. We shall have to look carefully, then, at exactly what is refuted and what is not in this little *elenchus* of Socrates.

The first point that Socrates sets forth with Agathon is that love is always love *of* something (199d). This establishes what we have learned from phenomenology to call the "intentional" character of eros. But the point is important: it shows that eros is *relational* in its very being. It is directed, that is, *out of itself, toward* an other which it is not. This means, among other things, that to the extent that Aristophanes was right—and he will prove very right indeed on this—in his claim that eros is intimately connected with human being, then our erotic character means that we as human are relational in our very being.[20]

The second point to be established begins at 200a and extends to 200e: that love is of something that it *lacks*. This is clearly Socrates' conceptual *Aufhebung* of the insight presented mythically by Aristophanes, that eros is always a manifestation of our lack, our incompleteness as split beings. But in Socrates' argument here, just what eros lacks is exceedingly complicated and requires the most careful reading. I will try simply to summarize accurately the argument here.[21] Whatever object love loves, it both desires and loves. But it desires and loves it when it does *not* have it. Socrates clarifies with some apparent counter examples (200b–d). We can say that someone *is* strong, fast, healthy, or wealthy and yet that they nevertheless *love* strength, speed, health, or wealth. What we really mean in those cases however, is that they really want to have those qualities *in the future*, something that they do not at present possess. So even here, we love what we lack. If, then, love is always of something that it lacks, and as Agathon has insisted, eros loves the beautiful, then eros must *lack* the beautiful—and so not be beautiful, as Agathon claimed. So Socrates gets Agathon to admit that eros cannot both love the beautiful and be beautiful (201b).

It is not just that the argument is manifestly invalid; Socrates *furnishes the means* by which Agathon, if he had a logical bone in his body, could have challenged it. Socrates has just established that one could *be* strong, fast, healthy, or wealthy *now*, but still *love it* in the sense of desiring to have it in the future. Agathon could easily reply that such is exactly the case with beauty: eros *is* beautiful now, and *loves* beauty in the sense that it desires to have it in the future; hence eros in this sense both is beautiful and loves the beautiful.

Note the complexity here: these examples establish—though Agathon is oblivious to this—that eros *could*, in a way, be beautiful and love the beautiful. This would not, of course, be an argument that it *is* both, only that it could in principle be so. Nevertheless, it would still exhibit a lack of a sort, to wit, the lack of possessing beauty in the future. This entails, however, that the element of lack or incompleteness in eros—and so in human being—is inseparable from *temporality*. This was implicit in Aristophanes' speech and Socrates now makes it explicit. In a remarkable prefiguration of the Heideggerian account of Dasein's temporality, we carry with us in our very being our past (our original wholeness, our having been rendered incomplete) into what we are now (our present experience of that incompleteness and desire for wholeness), and that very present situation (our being now) leads us to project ourselves onto the future (where we hope to overcome our lack). We cannot dwell on this issue at length, but I would just say this, that if there is an account of time in the dialogues— especially of what we now, thanks to Heidegger, call temporality—it is less where most people claim to find it, in the cryptic remark in the *Timaeus* that "time is the moving image of eternity,"[22] and more in the "existential" temporality of eros as it is developed in the *Symposium* and *Phaedrus*.

In any case, Socrates' two crucial premises by which he will refute Agathon are established: eros is of something, and of something that it lacks. From here *problematic but not completely wrong, half beautiful*

(200a–b), Socrates easily establishes that Agathon's formulation was problematic. As we have seen, it is problematic, not necessarily wrong! Its problematic character derived from Agathon's failure to recognize the crucial Aristophanic element of lack or incompleteness in eros. For Agathon, eros was total fullness; it was complete in every way, exhibiting every virtue, lacking nothing.

Socrates now adds one more point, but a crucial one (201c–d). He introduces now the intimacy of the issue of beauty and the good: "Isn't the good also beautiful?" he asks Agathon, who quickly assents. If so, then in lacking the beautiful, eros would also lack the good. Agathon replies that he cannot refute Socrates, but Socrates insists that he cannot refute the truth. The situation is in fact considerably more complicated. For one thing, the connection between beauty and the good is famously perplexing, and the various discussions in the Platonic dialogues of the kinship surely are a primary locus of the perplexity. That there is such a kinship seems a widely exhibited view in the dialogues. But the two are hardly identical, as a much younger Socrates will soon recognize in his conversation with Diotima (204e). Socrates at first here simply raises the issue as an issue; it is neither developed nor resolved. But we shall now have to watch how this connection plays out.

As Socrates turns to what he supposedly learned about eros from the priestess, Diotima, I remind the reader that the point of our study is not a comprehensive interpretation of the *Symposium*. We shall concentrate only on those aspects of Diotima's teaching which are directly or indirectly germane to the question of beauty in its relation to eros. The first of these aspects is surely Diotima herself. Socrates now rather generously lets Agathon off the hook, explaining that he too, when he was young, believed as Agathon did that eros was beautiful and loved the beautiful; and that just as Socrates now did with Agathon, Diotima showed the then young Socrates that he was wrong. Socrates now alters the character of his speech while preserving its structure as dialogue: he switches from the dialogue between himself and Agathon to his report of the dialogue between him and Diotima. Who, we must first ask, is Diotima?[23]

Three things, I think, are striking regarding Socrates' introduction of Diotima. First and surely most striking is that she is a woman. Socrates, in effect, says to the mostly homosexual male audience,[24] "I don't know about you guys, but I learned about eros from a woman!" At the very beginning of the dialogue, women—in this case the flute girls—were dismissed from the party so that the men could talk together (176e). True to that symbolic gesture, the dialogue has so far proceeded on the unspoken assumption that eros among males is the paradigm of love, and even more strongly, that eros could be accounted for *without the invocation of feminine erotic experience*. Socrates now corrects this by in effect reintroducing women—in the person of Diotima—into the dialogue. An understanding of eros *requires* an understanding of feminine erotic experience, and this is just what Diotima supplies. She introduces the significance of pregnancy, giving birth, and nurturing as well as, mythically, the significance of eros's mother and grandmother (Penia and Metis—203b). The very introduction of the woman, Diotima, then, is an implicit critique and rejection of the assumption of the previous speakers that eros could be accounted for without invocation of the feminine.[25]

Second, Diotima is a priestess: Socrates does not learn eros from "the philosopher Diotima." Coming from a priestess, this "philosophic" account of eros will be one that is highly inflected by the standpoint of religion. We see this in the repeated use of religious language and imagery throughout her speech, culminating in her attempt to introduce Socrates into the "higher mysteries" of eros (210a ff.). This presents the reader with an interpretive problem that is too often ignored by interpreters. Although religion and philosophy are no doubt related in complex ways, they are surely not identical. This means that we will have to "demythologize" Diotima's religious language to the more secular discourse of philosophy if we are to gain a sense of the philosophic import of what she is saying. At very least, we cannot take the straightforwardly religious language and imagery Diotima employs as "Plato's teaching" on eros.

Third, Diotima is a stranger or foreigner, the only non-Athenian introduced into the *Symposium*. Socrates emphasizes this throughout, often addressing her, "O stranger" (e.g., 204c, 211d). I suspect that this is meant to underline her otherness from those present, and so to introduce the importance of otherness—the problem of otherness, or what we now call "difference"—into the issue of eros.

Diotima begins by reformulating the issue (already established by Aristophanes and Socrates) of eros's *lack* of beauty in a way that establishes more adequately the ontological condition of eros vis-à-vis beauty and other qualities. Eros's ontological condition is not quite one of simple *lacking*, but rather that of the *metaxu*: eros is *the in-between.* She begins with beauty: Socrates at this young age was what we now call a "Platonist," a "dualist" of sorts who seemed to think always and only in binaries, and Diotima has an extremely difficult time freeing him from this binary thinking, or what we now also call "metaphysics." If eros isn't beautiful, he asks, must it not be ugly (201e)? Diotima shows him that such binaries are not necessary. Instead, eros is *in the middle* between beauty and ugliness, and also between goodness and evil, and also between knowledge and ignorance (202a ff.). Several things about this intermediary status need to be noted.

First, this is Diotima's *Aufhebung* of Pausanias's point that eros is not inherently either beautiful or ugly, noble or base. What Pausanias lacked, recall, was an adequate criterion for distinguishing noble or beautiful from base eros. As we shall see, Diotima will develop that on the basis of the hierarchical character of the various possible objects of eros. Eros directed exclusively on "lower" objects (wealth, power, the body) will be less beautiful or noble than eros directed on "higher" objects (creativity, knowledge, and philosophy).

Second, in another way, given the intimacy of eros and human nature, this constitutes an important correction of Aristophanes' version of "original sin," that we are somehow inherently flawed, or fools by nature. Eros, and so human being, is neither inherently sinful nor (prefiguring the romantic tradition) inherently good. It is *in the middle,* as Aristotle will later insist early in book 2 of his *Nicomachean Ethics,* capable of becoming one or the other.

At this point, third, the connection between eros and beauty now seems to be this: eros *can* be beautiful or ugly, just as Pausanias said. In *this* sense, it does not strictly or simply "lack" beauty. But its inherent status is to be neither one. It has instead this intermediate, in-between status, capable of gaining access to, and of becoming, either beautiful or ugly. It is then inherently neither beautiful nor ugly, and in *this* sense it does indeed "lack" beauty. But as we shall see, this is only the beginning of the story. *Eros lacks beauty as not inherent*

Fourthly, it should be noted that our intermediate status between wisdom and ignorance cannot fail to remind us of Socratic philosophy as aporia, indeed, Socratic "wisdom" as self-knowledge, as "knowing what I know and what I do not know." We see here a prefiguration of what will become more thematic later, that philosophy itself is a manifestation—one of the highest or most "beautiful" manifestations—of eros.

Socrates portrays himself to be a very slow learner. At 202d, he asserts that surely eros is a god! Diotima easily shows him that since eros lacks beauty and goodness, it cannot be a god. Socrates, yet again, goes for the binary: what then, he asks, is it mortal? This precipitates the important passage at 202e where the intermediate, *metaxu,* character of eros gets formulated in terms of its *daimonic* character. In a perfect example of a passage whose highly religious language would have to be demythologized to see its philosophic importance, Diotima speaks of the daimon eros as "carrying messages" and sacrifices back and forth between the gods and humans, and in a formulation whose religious obscurity fairly cries out for philosophic interpretation, she tells us that eros the daimon "binds the two (the divine and the mortal) together into a whole" (202e).[26]

Socrates, strangely, does not pursue this amazing statement of Diotima's further, but instead asks another question: who is eros's father, and who is its mother?[27] Diotima's answer is remarkable and again needs to be demythologized. Eros is the child of Poros (Resource, or Plenty), whose own mother is Metis (Wisdom, Craft), and of Penia (Poverty, Lack). Like most kids, as Diotima explains at length, eros takes after both its parents. Before we look at the specific characteristics, however, several things need to be said about this parentage.

First, this represents a clear criticism of Pausanias's claim that heterosexual eros was "common" or "vulgar," and that it was exclusively male love that is "beautiful" or noble. Eros, the *whole* of eros, says Diotima, derives from a combination of the masculine and the feminine. To understand eros's "origins," then, both the feminine and masculine elements need to be taken seriously. Moreover, it is noteworthy that two women are mentioned (eros's mother, Penia, and paternal grandmother, Metis) while only one man appears (the father, Poros). And this father, Poros, clearly gets his own fundamental character—

fullness or resource—from Metis, his mother. This means that the feminine cannot merely represent "lack" or incompleteness, as an exclusive attention to eros's mother, Penia, might suggest.[28] In any case, the double presence of the feminine in eros's parentage clearly emphasizes the decisiveness of the feminine for an understanding of eros.

Second, the mythical parentage makes some sense of a certain paradoxical character to eros. From its mother eros derives a kind of lack or incompleteness. From its father (and Poros' mother) eros derives an overfullness or wholeness. Paradoxically, then, eros manifests both an incompleteness and an overfullness. Aristophanes and Agathon were both literally half right! Eros *is* incomplete (Aristophanes' insight) and overfull (Agathon's insight).

Third, the Poros/Metis dimension—eros's overflowing overfullness—will soon be seen to be decisive in understanding the erotic basis of creativity, when we come to Diotima's famous "all humans are pregnant" passage at 206c.

Diotima now goes into considerable detail regarding what characteristics eros derives from each parent (203c ff.). Throughout, she continues to exhibit the in-between nature of eros, this time as in between the qualities of both parents. One crucial dimension of this being-in-between, for our purposes, is that eros is a "philosopher all its life" (203d). This prepares the way for what will soon become explicit—the erotic basis of philosophy. Diotima expands on this at 204a: the gods are not philosophers (for they are wise, and so do not lack wisdom), nor are the ignorant, who "think they know what they do not know." Philosophers, erotic at the core in this sense, are in-between. This conforms exactly to what will become the adult Socrates' own sense of philosophy as loving, and therefore lacking, wisdom, yet as being higher than those who "think they know what they do not know."

This leads Socrates, at 204b, to ask explicitly about philosophy: "Who are the philosophers, Diotima, if they are neither the wise nor the ignorant?" And Diotima now teaches Socrates what philosophy is. This is important: Socrates gets his very conception of philosophy from a woman. In the *Theaetetus,* Socrates gives a different account of his roots as a philosopher, but *still* locates the source of his philosophy in a woman: his mother, Phaenarete, the midwife.

As Diotima explains (204c), the intermediary character of eros clarifies Socrates' earlier confusion regarding the relation of eros to beauty. It is not eros itself that is beautiful, but the *object* of love, the beloved, that is regarded as beautiful. Socrates had confused love itself with the beloved, and so had mistakenly called love itself beautiful. We see here the next step in the relationship of beauty and eros. The object of eros, the beloved, is, apparently, always taken to be beautiful by the lover—a phenomenon whose significance we shall see played out in great detail in the *Phaedrus.*

Socrates next asks Diotima, what is the *use* (*chreian*) of eros to human beings (204c)? This leads Diotima to an interesting substitution that will constitute yet another inflection regarding the question of the beautiful; the substitution of the good for the beautiful as the ultimate object of eros. Diotima asks Socrates what the one who possesses the beautiful as object of eros will gain, and Socrates cannot answer (204d). So Diotima asks, "Suppose one were to replace 'beautiful' with 'good' and then ask, 'Come, Socrates, the one who loves, loves good things, but for what does he love them?'" Socrates replies, as he had for the beautiful, "For them to become his own." Diotima again asks what the person will have, if good things become his own, and Socrates now can answer: "That I am better prepared to answer. That person will be happy." The ultimate object of eros, it now seems, is less beauty than the good. But that now renders again unstable the question of the relation of beauty to eros, since it is, for the time being at least, no longer the primary object of eros. The good is the genuine *telos* of eros, and so of all human aspiration.[29] We shall have to watch for the next inflection in what is becoming the long, winding course of beauty in the *Symposium.*

Diotima's substitution of the good for the beautiful again raises for us the question of their connection. That Socrates can answer the question of what one has when one possesses the good—happiness—but could not do so with the same question regarding the possession of beauty suggests once again that the two are surely not identical. At the same time, the substitution itself puts them into clear relation to each other. As has happened already so often in this dialogue, the question is here simply put into play, not developed in detail, much less answered.[30] At the same time, we are not left entirely without resources. As happened in the *Hippias Major* and now for at least the second time in the *Symposium,* we see that one cannot think about the beautiful for very long without wondering about its connection to the good. Thinking about beauty, that is, inevitably seems literally to *invoke* the question of the good and its relation to beauty. We have also seen clues in each instance that the relationship will not be one of identity. The beautiful and the good are not identical, but it may surely be the case that the beautiful is good and the good beautiful. Or at least, that they *can* be so. This much we can say with confidence: thinking about the beautiful leads us to think about the good; one might say that each puts the other *in question.*

At 206b, Diotima now asks Socrates a crucial question, which he of course cannot answer: what is the *ergon,* the function, of eros? Diotima gives a brief, straightforward answer: "It is giving birth in beauty, both in body and in soul." The relation of beauty and eros now gets complicated yet again. It is not just that beauty is one object of our eros; in addition, eros has a certain creative or generative urge, and we seek to generate "in the beautiful." We are about to be informed of the erotic basis of all creativity, of the creative urge itself as erotic. And that creative urge, Diotima says, seeks always to create in the beautiful. This is yet another indication of the assumption, made apparently by Plato as well as virtually all of Greek culture, that creativity is somehow essentially tied to the beautiful. It will remain for modern "aesthetics" to disjoin that connection. Just what "in the beautiful" means here is not, I think, sufficiently developed in the *Symposium,* but must await Socrates' palinode in the *Phaedrus* for its more adequate development.[31] But Diotima importantly insists that the creative urge that seeks to generate in the beautiful does so *both in the body and in the soul.* This is the "truth" of Agathon's insistence on the connection of eros and beauty. Beauty "happens" both at the bodily and the psychic level. It will therefore be the bridge by which we can connect and make sense of both the bodily and the psychic manifestations of eros.

But Socrates claims not to have the slightest idea what Diotima is talking about. "A prophet is necessary to explain what you're saying, I said, for I do not understand" (206b).[32] Diotima must clarify this relation for him at length in a remarkable passage that constitutes something of a "minor" ascent to the more famous "major" ascent that begins at 210a. This minor ascent will begin at 206e with the famous "all humans are pregnant" passage, and continue to 209e, just prior to the "major" ascent. It is important to recognize that the two ascents are very different. The major ascent to which we shall turn presently is the ascent of the eros for beauty as it is directed on increasingly "higher" objects. This first ascent, however, is also quite complicated: it is an ascent of the desire to create in the beautiful, in quest of immortality. Though it is related to the major ascent in important ways, we shall have to notice the important differences as well.

Both ascents begin at the level of the body. Diotima begins this ascent of creativity in the beautiful in this way:

> All humans are pregnant, Socrates, both in body and in soul, and when we come of age, our nature is to desire to give birth. But it is impossible to give birth in ugliness (*en men aischro*), but only in beauty (*en de to kalo*). The union (*sunousia*) of a man and a woman is birth. This is a divine matter (*theion to pragma*), and this pregnancy and generation (*genesis*) instill immortality in a living, mortal being. (206c)

So much, one might say, for Plato's supposed "hatred of the body"! The physical union of man and woman that results in physical childbirth, this "lowest" level of the ascent of creativity, is *already* "something divine" (*theion to pragma*). It is important to notice the complicated moments in this first instance of creativity, all of which will be repeated in the following levels. First, this is an ascent of the desire for creativity: we are talking about the erotic basis of the creative urge, and that creative urge, contrary to Plato's supposed "hatred of art," is important indeed. Second, this urge only takes place "in the beautiful"; indeed, Diotima denies that it can take place in ugliness. This is the next stage in the evolution of the relation of beauty to eros. Beauty, as it were, is the "locus" of the creative urge. I take the phenomenological point of Diotima's claim here to be that we always *believe* that the object of our love and desire is beautiful, whatever others may think. Even if we acknowledge that our beloved is not physically beautiful, we insist that he or she has "inner beauty." No one ever says,

[margin handwriting:] kalos already divine

[bottom handwriting:] agathos, gathos, kai aischros

"My beloved is ugly in every possible way, but I love her still." Third, says Diotima, this desire to create in the beautiful is in quest of immortality. As she goes on to clarify in a truly remarkable claim for a priestess to make, this leaving-behind something of ourselves, in any of its forms, is the *only* kind of immortality possible for us mortals (208b). Diotima the priestess denies the possibility of personal immortality in anything like the usual sense, which, she says, is the prerogative only of the gods (208b).

Diotima now expands the ascent of creativity. In addition to this "divine" bodily creativity, there are also "soul pregnancies." Diotima names two types and gives two examples of each. There are the soul pregnancies of poets, which lead to the generation of poems—she names Homer and Hesiod as examples—and the soul pregnancies of law givers—she mentions Solon, the giver of Athenian law, and Lycurgus, the giver of Spartan law (209d–e). Presumably the reason why these "soul pregnancies" are "higher" than bodily ones is because the immortality gained from them lasts longer. The "immortality" gained by Homer, Hesiod, Solon, and Lycurgus has already lasted thousands of years! The names of their physical children are long forgotten.

A few more comments regarding these "higher" pregnancies are necessary. First, it is interesting that at 209c, Diotima seems to assume that creations of the sort exemplified by the four famous figures she mentions are done in the context of a love of a particular person, beautiful in soul and/or body, and that their artistic and constitutional creations are the "offspring" of such relationships. One might wonder, however, whether the "beautiful beloved" has to be an individual, or might not as well be a city, or even a people. It is at least as plausible, for example, that the "beautiful beloved" for whom and with whom Solon generated his "children" was Athens as that it was some individual person, male or female. Second, it is striking by contrast to the major ascent to follow that *philosophy is missing from this ascent.* The highest level of *this* ascent, assuming that poetry and laws are mentioned in lexical rather than an incidental order, is the creation of laws and institutions. As we shall see, this manifestation occupies only an intermediate level in the major ascent, where philosophy itself *will* be mentioned as the penultimate level of the ascent (210d). Why, we need to ask, is philosophy not even mentioned in this first ascent? I think the answer is that, although to be sure the ascent of philosophy will involve some creativity, the desire for creativity in quest of immortality is not the motivating origin of philosophy. The relations of similarity and difference between the two ascents testify to the relations of similarity and difference between philosophy and the other creative enterprises, especially poetry.

In the midst of this account of the human, erotic desire for creativity, Diotima points to a crucial implication for the human condition itself. For, as she says in a passage of striking significance (207d–208b), this constant creating of something new and leaving behind of the old is not just something we occasionally do, but the human situation itself. Our bodies, she points out, are constantly changing—becoming new and leaving behind something of the old—even though we are called the same individual. And the same is true of the soul, which, she says, constantly changes in every way, from its habits, characteristics, opinions, desires, pleasures, pains, and fears even to its knowledge, in which new knowledge is constantly replacing the old. What is especially striking about this passage is that it implies a remarkably Heraclitean conception of self-identity and individuality. It amounts to a non-substantial characterization of the soul. The soul here is in no sense a permanent soul-substance that remains the same through time, much less is it immortal in any usual sense. To the contrary, not just the body but, as Diotima insists, the soul itself is in constant flux, changing so constantly that one could almost say with Sartre that the soul "is what it is not and is not what it is." Or, less anachronistically, with Heraclitus: "the soul has a logos, which increases itself" (fragment 115). Such an account of the soul and human self-identity, of course, radically destabilizes the orthodox "Platonic" conception of a permanent soul-substance that is immortal.

but qualified?

At this point, after completing her discussion of the erotic basis of our creative urges, Diotima changes her tone and expresses a well-founded skepticism that Socrates, who has had difficulties enough understanding what she has said so far, will be able to follow her as she attempts to introduce him to what she calls "the higher mysteries" of eros (210a). As we shall see, her skepticism may indeed be well-founded; Alcibiades' speech will raise serious questions about whether Socrates understood Diotima's speech in an appropriately philosophic way. We are ready to begin our consideration of the famous "ascent" passage of the various stages of the eros for beauty, culminating in our insight into "Beauty itself," and the consequences of that insight. Before we look at the details of the ascent, however, we should consider some general points about it. First, it is striking that the ascent takes us up to "Beauty itself." One might expect, on the basis of an orthodox "Platonism," that in a dialogue whose guiding theme is eros, a speech that claims to and indeed has shed light on the nature of eros would culminate in an ascent to "Eros itself," the Platonic "form of Eros." Yet we get a very different but obviously related ascent, one to Beauty itself. Why do we not ascend to Eros itself? The answer has already been given by Diotima. If there were a "form of Eros," then Eros, like the other forms, would have the character of permanence, changelessness, perfection—all the characteristics of the Platonic "divine." But we have already been told by Diotima that eros is *not* divine but "in the middle" between the mortal and the divine. Eros's ontological status as intermediary between the mortal and the divine means that it cannot be "divine" in the Platonic sense, and so is not a form. We do not ascend to the "form of Eros" because there is not and cannot be such a form. This has crucial implications for any account of the nature of "knowledge" in the dialogues. For it implies that knowledge is irreducibly *heterogeneous*. That is, we gain *some* of our knowledge through the usual "Platonic" path of insight into a relevant form or idea. But, we here learn, not everything about which we have knowledge *has* a

I have some objections (?)

form—eros, for one, or the soul for another. So the kind of knowledge we might have of these is simply *different in kind* from the "formal" knowledge we have of some other objects of knowledge.

Second general point: this ascent continues, in a somewhat revised way, the point made in the earlier ascent regarding beauty. This ascent is one of various stages in the *love of a beautiful object,* whether of beautiful bodies, souls, laws and institutions, or knowledge. But in this second ascent, the creative dimension is no longer the guiding intent but, as it were, an epiphenomenon of this love. The lover will at each stage (until the highest) generate "beautiful speeches" (*kaloi logoi*—210a) in response to the beautiful object of his love. But such creative responses will no longer be the *point* of each stage—and indeed, as we shall see, at the highest stage it will simply die out. We are ready to begin to consider the details of this ascent passage.

Like the earlier ascent, this ascent too begins at the level of the body. This is an important similarity, one that underlines what could be called a general thesis of the dialogues themselves: to be sure, the body must be transcended philo- sophically, but just as surely, philosophy *begins* with the body—and "transcen- dence" of the body does not necessarily mean a "leaving-behind." But in this second, the "major" ascent, Diotima is strikingly emphatic, in a way that no translation of the passage that I have read adequately captures. She does not say something like, "One way to begin the ascent to philosophy . . ." or "An appro- priate way to begin . . ." or "Most people begin . . ." Instead, and most strikingly, her first word is *Dei:* the emphatic Greek for "it is necessary." "It is necessary," she begins, "for one rightly going into these matters to begin, when young, by turning toward beautiful bodies, and first, if his leader leads him correctly, to love a single body and to generate beautiful speeches (*kalous logous*) therein" (210a). Why, we must ask first, is it *necessary* to begin what will become the ascent to philosophic insight with the love of a beautiful body? What kind of "Platonism" is this? I think there are several responses. One possibility is that there is what we might anachronistically call a "phenomenological" necessity of beginning with the body. As the palinode in the *Phaedrus* will emphasize with great force, the experience of bodily beauty simply *is* the first immensely power- ful erotic attraction that humans experience. This may be true, but does not yet fully explain the *necessity.* The experience of and erotic attraction to bodily beauty is necessary, I suspect, because, as we are about to see, the whole point of the ascent to "Beauty itself" is to understand beauty *in all its manifestations,* and if we leave out the first and most fundamental of these, we will hardly under- stand the human significance of beauty. As Diotima will make explicitly clear (211a–b), the point of achieving insight into "Beauty itself" is not that it gives us yet another beautiful object to love, but that it enables us to understand beauty in all its manifestations. But to do so, we cannot ignore the first and most fundamental of these.

Second, we should note that in this ascent, the theme of generation or creativity is lifted up from the previous ascent, but inflected in a different way. For this time, the erotic attraction to a beautiful body leads to the generation not of human children but of "beautiful speeches." This testifies at once to a similarity in the two ascents—erotic attraction leads to generation in the beautiful—and to a crucial difference—the generation is of beautiful speeches as opposed to human children. This difference is the mark of the difference between the desire for generation *in the beautiful,* in quest of immortality—the focus of the first ascent—and, more narrowly here, the experience of the erotic attraction *to beauty itself.* Still, it is the similarity that is perhaps most important: in this ascent too, eros for beauty carries with it a creative urge, however it is expressed. We note that this generation of beautiful speeches continues right up the ascent to and includes the penultimate stage, the experience of "magnanimous philosophy" at 210d, which still preserves (as is obviously true phenomenologically) the generation of beautiful speeches. One other difference should be noted from the first ascent. In that ascent, we seek to fulfill our desire for generation *in the beautiful.* Diotima does not say, as she could not say truthfully, that all human children resulting from that generative urge are beautiful. But in this ascent, there seems to be a double presence of beauty. We are *attracted* to the beauty of a beautiful body initially, and that experience of beauty results in the generation of *further beauty,* beautiful *logoi.* Beauty, we are here told, generates beauty.

What is there in our erotic experience of beauty, we must now ask, that drives us beyond the first stage, the love of a single beautiful body? Why do we not simply rest content with that single love? The answer is striking: it is the component of *reason* within erotic experience that makes us "see" that there are other, and eventually higher, beautiful objects to love. Thus the first transition, to the love of the beauty of *all* beautiful bodies, is accomplished as follows: "Then he (the lover who has experienced the beauty of a single body) must *realize (katanoesai)* that the beauty of one particular body and the beauty of other bodies is akin, and that if it is necessary (*dei* is employed again here) to pursue beauty of form, it is *irrational (anoia)* not to believe that the beauty of all bodies is the same" (210b; my emphasis). This is a crucial moment in our understanding of the relation of eros and beauty: it is infused with *reason, thinking.* This ascent is one of eros for beauty, to be sure, but it is at the same time one of reason. Each transitional stage continues this theme, and is accomplished with various verbs of reasoning and thinking: *katanoesai, ennoesanta, kataphronesanta, theasthai.* Far from our erotic experience of beauty being "blind" or irrational, it is infused with reason. This is the crucial difference, as I have indicated previously, between *eros* and *epithumia* (desire), the latter of which we shall see in the *Phaedrus* is explicitly characterized as irrational (*aneu logou*—238b). Eros is inherently *rational;* only as such can philosophy itself be erotic at the core, as we are about to learn.

The ascent now continues to the love of beautiful souls (210c), to the beauty of "laws and institutions" (210c, and note that this is the highest level of the previous ascent), on to the beauty of knowledge (*epistemas*—210c–d), and on again to the penultimate stage, "magnanimous philosophy" (*philosophia aphthono*—210d). It is crucial to notice what is and what is not said about these transitions. The usual interpretation, the one that gives us "Platonism" at least from the Renaissance interpretation onwards—and possibly, as we shall see, the interpretation toward which Socrates himself leans—is that each previous stage in the ascent is *left behind* as one moves to the higher stage. It is this reading that is compatible with the "hatred of the body" and "rejection of the world of appearances" that comes to characterize "Platonism" (not to mention what is now called "Platonic love"). But Plato's Diotima is very careful *not* to say that a previous stage is left behind. The most we could say is that the ascent has the character of a proto-Hegelian dialectical *Aufhebung*. Diotima instead uses the *comparative*: one recognizes that beautiful souls are "more worthy" (*timioteron*) than beautiful bodies; and, in a phrase she employs at four different levels of the ascent, she says that once having achieved a higher stage one considers the previous stage to be "small" (*smikron*—210b8, 210c1, 210c7; *smikrologos*—210d3). But "small" is not "nothing"! If the point of the ascent is to understand, through an insight into Beauty itself, the character of beauty in *all* its manifestations—or what Diotima calls the "wide sea" (210d) of beauty—then we *cannot* leave behind any particular stage, or we would lose our understanding precisely of beauty *in* its various manifestations. If I understand and appreciate beauty in all its manifestations *except* bodily beauty, for example, and am oblivious to bodily beauty and its power, then I simply do not understand beauty. To be sure, that we realize that "lower" stages of beauty are "small" compared to higher ones means that we put the lower stages "in their place" in our lives; we are no longer obsessed, for example, with bodily beauty. But putting these stages in their place means precisely that they *have* a place. We ignore them, or claim to entirely leave them behind, on pain of losing our understanding of beauty in its mortal manifestations.

It is at least possible that in this is the sense in which Socrates himself may have misunderstood the ascent, and Diotima's skepticism about his ability to understand these higher mysteries may be justified. It may be, that is, that Socrates *does* too radically "leave behind" the earlier stages of the ascent, in particular the beauty of human bodies and the human generally, in his almost obsessive focus on the higher stages—knowledge and the forms. That, at least, will be Alcibiades' charge when he delivers his "praise"—which is at least as much a critique—of Socrates shortly:

> You have to realize that *he doesn't care at all* whether someone is beautiful. On the contrary, no one would believe how little regard he has for such matters, or for whether one is wealthy or has anything else the many believe contributes to happiness. I'm telling you, he believes all these sorts of possessions to have no value at all and that *we are worthless as well,* and his entire life is occupied with being ironic and playing games with people. (216d–e; my emphasis)

Alcibiades, of course, is not an objective observer—he is angry at Socrates for refusing his favors and deeply embarrassed by him. But he is also not stupid. If there is a kernel of truth in Alcibiades' charge, it suggests that in Socrates' relentless pursuit of knowledge and the forms, he may fail to love the human sufficiently. Socrates himself thus may be the first to misinterpret Diotima's ascent as a radical transcendence that leaves behind the earlier stages, whereas the real point may be to endeavor to transcend to the higher stages *while preserving the adequate love of the human*. One more question, then, that the *Symposium* leaves for us is this: does Socrates love the human sufficiently? If not, if there is indeed a kernel of truth in Alcibiades' charge, then is this a quiet Platonic criticism of Socrates—that he does not love the human enough, that he is too "otherworldly," too much of a "Platonist"?

So far, the ascent to Beauty itself has occurred discursively in two senses. First, each transition to a higher stage, as we have seen, is accomplished discursively or dianoetically, that is, through a process of *reasoning* that and how the next stage must be higher. Second, each transition has been discursive in its consequence as well: it generates *kaloi logoi*, beautiful speeches by the lover as a result of his or her experience of beauty at each level. To say that the transitions of the ascent are discursive, however, and to say that at each stage *kaloi logoi* are generated, is *not* to give a logos of beauty (as, we must recall, Socrates seemed to be trying to do in the *Hippias Major*). The way up the ascent is something more like the outlines of a phenomenology of erotic experience than itself a logos of beauty. That is to say, something very different is happening in the ascent—indeed in Diotima's entire speech—than the effort at a definitional logos of the sort exhibited in the *Hippias Major*. Whatever we are learning in these passages—and hopefully we are learning much—we are "defining" or giving a focused logos neither of beauty nor of eros.

But now, something different happens as we approach the supposedly "highest" level, the insight into Beauty itself. The difference is signaled by a change in Diotima's language. Whereas its earlier stages were discursive in the sense indicated, the final stage, says Diotima, occurs "suddenly" (*exaiphnes*). This word signifies that the very manner of access to Beauty itself is fundamentally different from the kinds of discursively based insights that we have in the normal course of things, on the way up the ascent. The meaning of its "suddenness" presents an interpretive problem, and the characterization that Diotima gives of this insight will offer us the critical clue. Its suddenness signifies that the final insight is *non-discursive*.[33] We shall consider this further in a moment.

We are now at a high point in the Platonic dialogues. In her description of *auto to kalon*, "Beauty itself," Diotima gives us what is arguably the longest account of a particular "form" in all the dialogues. For it is this insight that the lover of beauty will "suddenly" have. Because it is such a crucial moment, let us quote her description in full:

When someone has been thus far educated in erotic things, contemplating beautiful things correctly and in their proper order, and who then comes to the final stage of erotic things (*pros telos ede ion ton erotikon*), he will suddenly (*exaiphnes*) see something astonishing that is beautiful in its nature. This, Socrates, is the purpose of all the earlier effort. First, it is always (*aei on*); it neither comes into being nor passes away, neither increases nor diminishes. Then next, it is not beautiful in one respect while ugly in another, nor beautiful at one time while ugly at another, nor beautiful with reference to one thing while ugly with reference to something else, nor beautiful here while ugly there, as though it were beautiful to some while ugly to others. Again, the beautiful will not appear to this person to be something like a face or a pair of hands or any other part of the body, nor as some discursive account nor as some demonstrable knowledge (*oude tis logos oude tis episteme*), nor will it appear to exist somewhere in something other than itself, such as in an animal, in the earth, in the sky, or in something else. On the contrary, it exists itself, according to itself, with itself, of one form, always (*auto kath' auto meth' autou monoeides aei on*). All other beautiful things partake of it in such a way that, although they come into being and pass away, it does not, nor does it become any greater or any less, nor is it affected in any way. When someone moves through these various stages from correct pederasty and begins to see this beauty, he has nearly (*schedon*) reached the end. (210c–211e)

what's beyond : the good

What is especially striking about this extended account of insight into a particular "form" is that in it, astonishingly, we are told virtually nothing about what beauty actually is! We are presented instead with a largely "negative way" account: beauty itself is not beautiful in one way, ugly in another; not beautiful to one person, ugly to another, etc. What little we are told positively is in fact an account not of the specific character of beauty itself, but a generic account of any form whatsoever: it is "itself, according to itself, with itself, of one form, always." In sum, in this famous account of the insight into beauty itself, we learn not a single thing discursively about what beauty itself is. We learn only—and this is true again and again in the various accounts of forms throughout the dialogues—a generic account of the nature of formal structure. As it happens, Diotima's very account of this insight tells us why.

For in a crucial phrase of this insight into what beauty itself is *not*, that is, as part of the priestess Diotima's "negative theology," she says that it is *oude tis logos, oude tis episteme,* which I translate as "neither some discursive account nor some demonstrable knowledge." In the *Symposium*, this remarkable claim remains cryptic and unexplained by Diotima (as perhaps befits the pronouncements of a priestess). It is in the *Phaedrus,* to which we shall soon turn, that its significance will be elaborated in greater richness (though even there, that elaboration will not constitute a logos, for the reasons being discussed presently). But at the very least, if Socrates is listening to Diotima, he should be learning from this phrase that the insight into beauty itself, and for that matter into any form, cannot be articulated by any definition (*oude tis logos*) nor even by a more extended discursive demonstration (*oude tis episteme*). This is the real meaning of the failure of the *Hippias Major* to define beauty itself, and indeed, of all the definitional dialogues to define formal structure. Insight into a form is non-discursive, or to put it more positively, it is *noetic* rather than *dianoetic*. Such insight is also not demonstrable knowledge (*episteme*), though *in the light* of such insights we both discourse and have what knowledge we have. The crucial point is this: we are not told what beauty itself is and we never will be told, because the insight into beauty itself (or into any other form) is non-discursive, non-epistemic. To employ again a metaphor congenial to the dialogues, we discourse and know about beauty *in the light of* our non-discursive, that is, noetic, insights. What knowledge we attain is a no doubt complex combination of discursive speech and silent insight, of *dianoia* and *noesis*. But, this passage at least suggest, the *noesis*, the silent insight itself, is neither reducible to nor replaceable by what discourse may lead to it or follow from it. It is this combination whose "phenomenology," a portrayal of the *experience* of beauty and its impact on us, we shall see developed in detail in the *Phaedrus*.

Finally and no less decisively, Diotima concludes her crucial portrayal of an insight into the form of beauty itself, by saying that *after* one has completed the ascent and had the insight into beauty itself, the aspirant has *nearly* (*schedon*) reached the end. Everything hangs on this word *schedon*: "nearly." If Diotima were a "Platonist" she would not, having achieved an insight into the form of beauty, be "nearly" at the end: she would have *achieved* the end. For what else does (what has come to be called) Platonism claim but that the final philosophical achievement, the very goal of philosophy, is insight into the forms? Indeed, Socrates, on the day of his death, before his largely Pythagorean audience, indulges momentarily in just such a Platonistic fantasy, suggesting that the goal of all philosophers is to die and be able, once free of the body, to contemplate the forms forever.[34] And the gods are gods, if we are to believe the mythical teaching of the *Phaedrus*, precisely because they, untroubled as we are by the "black horse" of desire, get to contemplate the forms—there called simply "the beings"—forever, there in that hyper-ouranian place, that place above the heavens.[35] Why, then, does Diotima teach Socrates that having achieved an insight into beauty itself we are only "near" the end of our pursuit? She soon tells us—even if, as is her wont, cryptically, and with as much left unsaid as said.

Again, if Diotima were a Platonist, we might expect her to conclude her speech with something like the claim that there, having achieved an insight into the form, the philosophic quest is complete. Instead, she concludes her speech in such a way as to show just why the insight itself is the penultimate, not the ultimate goal. She concludes as follows:

> What do you think it would be like, she said, if someone should happen to see the beautiful itself (*auto to kalon idein*), pure, clear, unmixed, and not contaminated with human flesh and color and a lot of other mortal silliness, but rather if he were able to look upon the divine, uniform, beautiful itself (*auto to theion kalon dunaito monoeides katidein*)? Do you think, she continued, it would be a worthless life for a

human being to look at that, to study it in the required way, and to be together with it? Aren't you aware, she said, that only there with it, when a person sees the beautiful in the only way it can be seen, will he ever be able to give birth, not to images of virtue, since he would not be reaching out toward an image, but to true virtue (*areten alethe*), because he would be taking hold of what is true. By giving birth to true virtue and nourishing it, he would be able to become a friend of the god (*theophilei genesthai*), and if ever a human being could become immortal, he could. (211e–212a)

Diotima's conclusion challenges us—and challenges Platonism—at several levels. The very claim that seeing and loving beauty itself leads to acts of true virtue might first give us pause. Many of us, aroused by the sight of beauty, could not always claim to be led thereby to acts of virtue. That connection is worth a study in itself, and we will at least begin to see it worked out in the palinode of the *Phaedrus*. There seems to be a crucial difference between our various sightings of instances of beauty, which may but surely also may not lead to acts of virtue, and the non-discursive insight into beauty itself, about which Diotima is confident will surely lead us to such truly virtuous acts. Once more: she does not explain this difference or just how and why acts of true virtue will follow from our insight into beauty itself, but leaves it as a problem. What *happens* in the experience of beauty itself, the culmination of various experiences of mortal beauty, that might lead to acts of virtue? We need, at very least, a phenomenology of this kind of experience that might show us what happens. Diotima the priestess does not give it to us. Socrates the philosopher will do so, to Phaedrus, in the dialogue named for him.

No less importantly for our purposes, we now see that the reason the insight into beauty—and presumably by inference into any other form—is penultimate and not ultimate is because the real *telos* of such insight is *virtuous living*. Perplexing as this at first may seem, the ultimate *telos*, says Diotima, of understanding beauty itself is to live in a certain way, in accordance with human excellence (*arete*).[36] And the decisive point is that *living* in a certain way, though integrally and intimately involved with *logos* and *episteme*, can never be reduced to these. Socrates, and any philosopher, perhaps not without difficulty, must learn this lesson from Diotima. Logos and knowledge are never the end, but always a means—a necessary means to be sure—to an end. The end, always, is a certain way of living. One might say, with the Navajo farewell I have taken as an epigraph for this book, "*Walk* in beauty." They do not say "*Talk* in beauty."

I want to underline how striking the making of this point by Diotima (and Socrates) is, in regard to the question of beauty. For some reason, they—and perhaps Plato—think that it is better or more appropriate or more important to draw out this "existential" implication of the significance of beauty than, say, of justice, or courage, or piety. Somehow, they seem to think, it is the experience of *beauty* that brings home this lesson about virtuous living in the most decisive way. Could this be because it is in the context of beauty that virtue is the most humanly problematic or difficult? At any rate, the movement of thought on this issue seems to be something like this: the question of beauty gets raised, must be raised, as part of an effort to understand the significance of eros. Eros and beauty together point to, indeed are the foundation for, the possibility of philosophy. But philosophy, as we now see emphasized, is a question of *living* in a certain way. That way of living surely involves logos even if it is never reducible to it, and may well include the possibility and the problem of writing: for Plato it did, for Socrates it did not. Everything about this chain of issues in the *Symposium* points to the *Phaedrus* for its culmination.

At the end of Socrates' speech, we are told, Aristophanes is about to respond —which means that Aristophanes *had* a rejoinder to Socrates. (A Platonic provocation if ever there is one. Every serious student of the *Symposium* should write his or her version of Aristophanes' reply to Socrates.) But he is interrupted by the arrival of a crowd of revelers, led by the redoubtable Alcibiades. It is Alcibiades who gives the last recorded speech in the dialogue—and again, it should go without saying that a serious reading of the *Symposium* as a whole must include a careful reading of Alcibiades' speech. Our focus, however, is on the question of beauty, and we will concentrate only on that issue and ones directly bearing upon it as they arise in his speech. We must therefore begin with a consideration of Alcibiades himself, for he is at once an enormously appealing and problematic character.

First of all, he is famously beautiful—the darling, one might say, of all Athens, at least at the time. His beauty matters here. Socrates' reaction—or lack thereof—to his beauty, as Alcibiades will soon report it in his "true confession," must be compared both to Diotima's account of the "lower" level of the ascent and to the much richer account of the experience of a beautiful beloved and the affect on the lover in the *Phaedrus*. Alcibiades enters, as many have noticed, as the very personification of the god Dionysus, and, as Agathon had earlier prophesied, he "judges the wisdom contest" (without having heard the speeches!). He has come, he says, to crown Agathon for his victory in the tragedy contest yesterday. But when he sees Socrates, he puts some of the garlands on *his* head and crowns him as winner "not only recently, as you (Agathon) did, but all the time" (213e). One might say he came to crown poetry, but ultimately crowns philosophy. The judgment of "Dionysus" as to wisdom, then, is something like this: philosophy is the winner, but poetry is a close second and certainly a contender. One might say that the Platonic dialogues themselves are an exhibition of this judgment and its meaning for Plato himself. This may be one inflection of the meaning of Plato's remarks in the Second and Seventh Letters (to which we shall eventually turn) that he has not written his philosophy. His writings are a combination of philosophy deeply inflected by poetry. Or is philosophy itself always already inflected by the poetic?

In addition to his beauty, Alcibiades is an immensely complicated character. On the one hand, he is extremely talented and charismatic. He in principle has a great future in front of him as a political figure and general. But unfortunately, he is both dissolute (as his arrival at the symposium, already drunk, suggests) and is soon to become a scandal: he gets implicated in the infamous profanation of the Eleusian mysteries and mutilation of the Hermes, and eventually becomes a traitor who helps the Spartans defeat the Athenians. By his own subsequent admission, he knows that he should follow Socrates and philosophy, but his desire for public fame prevents him. How, then, are we to interpret his speech? With great care!

The question of beauty is framed existentially by the very encounter of Alcibiades and Socrates. Alcibiades exhibits bodily beauty par excellence. His character, however, is more problematic. Socrates, by contrast, is famously ugly of physique. Yet one of the first images Alcibiades uses to describe Socrates when he begins his speech is that of the Silenus figures, ugly on the outside but with beautiful images of gods within (at 215b, the beginning, then repeated for emphasis at 221e, the end of his speech). By the very use of this image, Alcibiades seems to recognize, even if only intellectually, that inner beauty is somehow "higher" than bodily beauty. At very least, as we shall soon see, he is more than willing to look past Socrates' bodily ugliness to gain what he takes to be the philosopher's inner beauty.

Alcibiades' speech in "praise" of Socrates is as complicated as his own character. He indeed praises Socrates, especially for his courage and to an extent for his *sophrosyne.* But his speech is just as much a severe critique of Socrates. The core of that critique is the passage I have already quoted (216e), where Alcibiades charges Socrates with caring nothing about physical beauty and with contempt for all things human. This charge, as I earlier suggested, must be understood and evaluated in the light of the ascent passage. And we must understand just what it does and does not say. Alcibiades does *not* say that Socrates is unerotic; he is as erotic as can be. But his eros, precisely in the sense developed in the *Symposium*—his incompleteness, recognition thereof and striving for wholeness, coupled with an overflowing overfullness of ability and power—is surely directed primarily on his desire for knowledge, for insight into forms. The question raised by Alcibiades' charge is: is it *primarily* directed there, or *exclusively* so? Stated differently, has Socrates misunderstood the ascent set out by Diotima precisely in the sense subsequently made the standard interpretation of it by Renaissance interpreters: that as one goes up the ascent one *leaves behind* the earlier stages in favor of an exclusive concern with the higher? This is a serious charge, and given the ambiguity of Alcibiades as a fair critic, a difficult one indeed. For it amounts, as I suggested earlier, to the charge that Socrates does not adequately love the human, that his enormous eros is directed more or less exclusively on what he takes to be the divine, the forms. To Alcibiades' charge one might add a further piece of evidence—Socrates' own poignant admission in the *Lysis,* that unlike the two young friends, Lysis and Menexenus, *he has never had a friend* (*Lysis* 212a). If, or perhaps we should say, to the extent

*but before
mention
not
written*

that there is a kernel of truth in this charge of Alcibiades, then it amounts to a certain Platonic criticism of Socrates. In the *Phaedrus,* also at the very end of the dialogue, we shall again see a different but related version of this charge quietly brought by Plato against Socrates: that Socrates never wrote.

At 217a–219d, Alcibiades turns to his qualified praise of Socrates' great *sophrosyne.* It is qualified because Alcibiades was himself the target of this self-control on Socrates' part. Alcibiades here enters upon his "true confessions" tale, his attempt to seduce Socrates and Socrates' refusal to be seduced. Socrates' self-control, then, looks to Alcibiades like a *contempt* for Alcibiades' beauty, and the young man is insulted by this in the very midst of being amazed by Socrates' self-control.[37] A number of things need to be said about this passage.

Alcibiades understands himself in the seduction scene—at least as he portrays himself—as precisely in the situation envisioned by Pausanias in his speech: admiring Socrates' wisdom, and more than cognizant of his own personal beauty, he will grant Socrates sexual favors in return for Socrates' words of wisdom. When the proposition is put to Socrates in this form, he turns Alcibiades down, interestingly and strikingly *not* because the situation is ignoble or even disgraceful, but because the exchange of sexual favors for wisdom is an unfair trade—like the exchange of "gold for bronze" (218e–219a)!

Second, the apparent ease with which Socrates resists Alcibiades' advances (it is worth reminding ourselves that he was one of the leading beauties of Athens—this is no ordinary specimen Socrates is lying down with!) makes Socrates' *sophrosyne* ambiguous in a way closely related to Alcibiades' earlier charge regarding Socrates' lack of interest in human beauty and contempt for humanity. Does his *sophrosyne* arise out of a remarkable control of very strong appetites that he succeeds in overcoming? Is that his *sophrosyne*? Or instead— and this is surely what it looks like in Alcibiades' description—is it in fact *no trouble at all* for him to control himself in the encounter with Alcibiades' beauty because he simply has no strong desire for human beauty? Think back to Diotima's frustration with Socrates when she tried to teach him—an eighteen-year-old with apparently little experience of human eros—about the experience and its meaning! When we turn to the *Phaedrus,* we shall see that a significant portion of Socrates' crucial palinode is devoted to portraying vividly the extremely powerful experience of beauty for a lover (indeed for a "Zeus lover," that is, a philosopher) and the exceedingly difficult time the lover will have (thanks to the force of the "black horse" of desire) resisting the strong desire to consummate the relationship with the beautiful beloved (250e–252b, and again at 254a–256e). To say the least, that hardly seems an accurate description of Socrates himself, at least in his experience with Alcibiades![38] The question, then, becomes one that will be thematic in Aristotle: does a virtue such as *sophrosyne* amount to controlling one's strong desires, or to turning oneself into the kind of person who does not even have such desires? If the latter, is it, strictly, any longer appropriately called *sophrosyne*? In a way, the form of the question being put into play by Alcibiades here is more pointed: is a lack of attraction to human beauty, of the sort exhibited by Socrates, a virtue? Or will such a lack lead to missing out on the kind of powerful if difficult experience of beauty and its consequences portrayed so poignantly in the *Phaedrus*?

We have now completed our study of the very complicated path that the question of beauty takes in the speeches of the *Symposium*. As we turn to the *Phaedrus*, it will be worthwhile briefly to map that path, at least in broad outline, before we see how the question is further developed in the latter dialogue. Beauty first arose as an issue in Phaedrus's speech, but only as a rather general and vague measure of the worthwhile life that will follow from the experience of love or, as Phaedrus subtly developed the point, of having a lover. Pausanias then tied beauty and eros more closely together by drawing the distinction between two modes of eros, a "beautiful" or noble eros and an "ugly" or base one. This was coupled by him with the important point that eros can be either beautiful or shameful, which raised the question of what the criterion for "beautiful" eros might be. Eryximachus then recognizes that the domain of eros extends much more broadly than the personal love affairs that had been the paradigm in previous speeches. He extends the realm of eros, however, not to other psychic dimensions but throughout the physical cosmos. It remains problematic how, given this "materialism," he can make sense of psychic manifestations of beauty. Then, after Aristophanes' noteworthy silence on the question of beauty, it is in Agathon's speech that, for the first time, the specific nature of the connection between eros and beauty becomes explicit: he claims that eros both is beautiful and loves the beautiful. It is this premise with which Socrates begins his speech, first to refute Agathon's claim—to be sure in a complicated and problematic way—and then to begin a complicated development of the connection of eros and beauty: first, that eros loves the beautiful, and then that, strictly, eros loves the good more fundamentally than the beautiful. But beauty reenters the picture when we are told by Diotima that the function of eros is to generate in the beautiful, in quest of immortality. This relation in turn gets complicated still further in the second ascent, where we learn that while there is indeed a genera-tive function to the experience of beauty—this time, "beautiful speeches"—the point of this ascent is less generation than an insight into "Beauty itself," the form of beauty. At least one absolutely crucial point regarding the insight into beauty itself was what I called its non-discursive character, that it is *oude tis logos, oude tis episteme:* "neither some discursive account nor some demonstrative knowledge." But yet again, the point of *this* insight is not simply a knowing of beauty, but living in a certain way—a way that Diotima rather vaguely calls a life of "true virtue." At nearly every step along this path, I had occasion to note the prelimi-nary character of the formulations regarding beauty in the *Symposium*. These formulations usually put a given dimension of beauty into play, or raise them as a question, rather than giving anything resembling an adequate account or even a sufficiently rich portrayal of the phenomena. Again and again, I pointed ahead to the *Phaedrus* for that richer portrayal. It is now time to turn to that dialogue.

THREE

The Question of Beauty in the *Phaedrus*

As my frequent prefigurative remarks have indicated, the *Phaedrus* will develop and enrich the many important issues raised but left more or less undeveloped in the *Hippias Major* and *Symposium* regarding beauty, its connection to eros, and eventually, its connection to philosophy. The way in which the experience of beauty by a lover, in particular the beauty of the beloved, is portrayed—as at once a decisive preparation for philosophy and philosophic friendship, while at the same time putting the possibility of that philosophic experience to the test—is one of the most striking and challenging aspects of the *Phaedrus*, especially for our present, more academic conceptions of philosophy as one discipline among others. These broad themes will necessitate our considering a significant portion of the dialogue, and not just the direct references to beauty, though certainly these will remain our focus. I begin this chapter as I did the last, then, with the acknowledgment that this will not be a comprehensive interpretation of the dialogue, but a highly focused consideration of the complicated connection between beauty, eros, and philosophy as it is developed in the *Phaedrus*.

The setting of the *Phaedrus* is one of the more unusual in the dialogues, for the vast majority of them take place in the city: in the agora, in gymnasia, at private homes, in the law court. The *Phaedrus*, by contrast, takes place in the country. Socrates meets Phaedrus outside the city walls, and Phaedrus explains that he is taking a walk, following doctor's orders, for his health (227a)—though as we soon see, he has more complicated motives as well. Interestingly, we are not told just why Socrates is in the country. That it takes place in the country, as it turns out, has very much to do with the question of beauty, for Socrates shows himself remarkably sensitive to the beauty of the countryside, soon waxing lyrical at the beauty (*kale*) of the location, the trees (including the "Plato"— *platonos*—tree, what we call a plane tree), the fragrances, the cool waters of the spring, the breezes, the grassy slope, and even the song of the cicadas (230b–c). The first instance of beauty in this dialogue, then, is the beauty of nature. This is noteworthy, for we shall see that—just as was intimated in the *Hippias Major* and developed somewhat in the *Symposium*—the core experience of beauty, the "first" and most fundamental, especially for the experience of philosophy, will be the experience of *human* beauty in the person of the beloved. That it is not the only important instance of beauty, however, is signaled by the setting in nature and Socrates' own clear recognition of the beauty of the surroundings. In fact, Socrates will remind Phaedrus—and us—several times in the dialogue of the importance of the beautiful natural setting to what they are discussing.

The surroundings are not just beautiful, however—they are inspiring. The inspiration of the surroundings, the inspiration of nature, introduces us to the theme of inspiration which will express itself in several modes as the dialogue plays out. The inspiration of nature prepares us for the inspiration of the four forms of "divine madness" that Socrates will introduce, the inspirational character of our non-discursive or noetic insights into beauty and the other "beings," and of course, especially the inspiration of eros which will play such an important role in the dialogue.

However, the status of these modes of inspiration is immediately complicated by Socrates' professed ambivalence toward them. No sooner does he comment on the inspirational beauty of the surroundings than he warns Phaedrus: "I am a lover of learning; the countryside and the trees won't teach me anything, but the humans in the city do" (230d). Similarly, at the beginning of his first speech—in response to Lysias's speech of seduction, but in accord with Lysias's negative attitude toward eros—Socrates asks for inspiration from the muses (237a). However, halfway through the speech, he stops to comment on the way in which he is so inspired as to be speaking in dithyrambs (238d), yet speaks of that very inspiration as a "threat to be avoided" (*apotrapoito to epion*) if the gods are willing (238d). (See also 241e, where he expresses a clear dislike of being inspired.) Yet again, after his first speech is concluded, it is his own "familiar" *daimonion* that inspires Socrates (242c) to give the palinode in which he will speak of the benefits of "divine madness" and the inspiration of a beautiful beloved. But then, at its conclusion, Socrates worries that he was "forced to be somewhat poetical" (*enagkasmene poietikos tisin*) by Phaedrus (257a), signaling yet again his obvious discomfort with such inspiration.

This is a very difficult situation to interpret. On the one hand, it may be that the *Phaedrus* is in part a critique of inspiration, dwelling at some length on the senses in which inspiration of some sort is needed and a blessing (the four forms of divine madness, and in this dialogue especially the fourth, eros), while at the same time pointing to its limitations and problems. Alternatively, it could be part of the ongoing (if quiet) Platonic critique of Socrates himself that we have seen in the first two dialogues: in this case, a critique of Socrates' obvious discomfort with the very inspiration on which he depends (as do we all). Perhaps, that is, Socrates is in the end too sober, too insistent on the self-control embodied in his famous *sophrosyne*, to satisfy the philosophic requirements of Plato, his student. We shall have to keep these alternatives in mind as the dialogue plays out. Let us return to the beginning of the dialogue.

Socrates meets Phaedrus walking in the countryside outside the walls of the city. Phaedrus is all agog at a speech he has just heard from Lysias, a sophist and partisan of the democracy, arguing that Phaedrus should give his sexual favors to a *non-lover* (namely, as is made clear, to Lysias himself). We need to think about just why such a speech would appeal to Phaedrus. Much later in this dialogue, we will learn that to be a good rhetorician one must, among other things, know the soul of the person you are persuading. Lysias clearly knows Phaedrus's soul. For as we recall from Phaedrus's speech in the *Symposium*, Phaedrus himself is a non-lover! His understanding of his own status as a beloved, recall, was in contrast to that of the lover, who was *inspired* by eros, clearly implying that the beloved—like Phaedrus—is not so inspired. Phaedrus's general emphasis was on the *usefulness* to a non-inspired beloved of having and using the inspiration of a lover. Lysias, accordingly, emphasizes throughout his speech the usefulness of giving in sexually to a non-lover. Not surprisingly, therefore, Phaedrus regards the speech as "clever" (*deinotatos*—228a). (Later, when Socrates takes back his own first speech and prepares for his palinode, he will play on the ambiguity of the term, describing his first speech as a "terrible, terrible speech": *deinon, deinon logon* [242d].) On the other hand, Phaedrus seems to forget that his own strategy was to use the inspiration of the lover to his own benefit, which, if he accepts Lysias's seduction, he presumably won't be able to do. Or is this precisely what he finds so "clever" about it?

To Phaedrus's enthusiastic summary of the speech Socrates responds sarcastically "How noble!" (227d), and immediately mocks the thesis of the speech that he has not yet heard. Socrates then shows that he too knows Phaedrus well. He knows that he wants to memorize Lysias's speech, but when Phaedrus wants to practice his memorizing on Socrates, Socrates makes him read it instead. To Phaedrus's suggestion that he begin rehearsing the speech, Socrates replies: "After you first show, dear friend, what you're holding in your left hand under your cloak! I suspect you have the speech itself. If that's so, believe this of me, that though I am of course your friend, if Lysias himself is here, I have no intention of making myself available for you to practice on. Come on, show it" (228e).

We shall have to remember this scene when we turn to Socrates' famous "critique of writing" toward the end of the dialogue. For this scene is in clear tension with his later claims in at least two ways. First, we will be told that writing detracts from our ability to memorize (275a ff.). But here Phaedrus is using the written speech *as an aid* to memorization.[1] Second, in Socrates' later critique of writing he will indicate a clear preference for oral speech on a variety of grounds (275c ff.). But here, presented with the actual choice between an oral presentation that depends on memory and a written speech that will be read, Socrates *prefers the written speech,* and for very good reasons. It will, in fact, be more dependable—given Phaedrus's rather weak capacity for memorizing. Moreover, once the speech is read, Socrates will have not the slightest hesitation in criticizing it, even though, as he will later say, its "father" is not present. Indeed, one might note, third, that here, in contrast to his later critique, Socrates takes the presence of the written speech as the functional equivalent of the presence of *Lysias himself:* "if Lysias himself is here" (*parontos de kai Lysiou*). The existential drama of the beginning of the dialogue will thus call into question the spoken words of Socrates at the end.

A few more items in the dramatic background need our attention before we turn to the reading of Lysias's speech by Phaedrus. The first is Socrates' characterization of himself at 228b, teasingly reminding Phaedrus that he knows he has the speech under his cloak and wants to rehearse it, as having a "sickness for *logoi*" (*to nosounti peri logon*). This may be seen as a preparation for the introduction of the notion of "divine madness." In a moment, Socrates will characterize himself, more moderately, as a "lover of speeches" (228c), and much later in the dialogue, as a "lover of divisions and collections" (266b). These passages help make sense of an otherwise perplexing problem with this dialogue: why should Socrates spend so much time with a dilettante like Phaedrus? Why should he try so persistently to seduce Phaedrus to philosophy, which he manifestly does? (We will note later that Socrates' prayer at the end of his palinode is that Phaedrus turn to philosophy [257b].) For in many ways, Phaedrus is the strangest of those whom Socrates tries to invite into philosophic living. And dramatically at least, we can suppose that Phaedrus was one of those whom Socrates made a sustained effort to offer that invitation. As we have seen, he is present in the *Symposium,* even if Socrates does not have the opportunity to engage him in dialogue. Here in the *Phaedrus,* Socrates has him alone: indeed, Plato portrays this as the longest, most sustained conversation Socrates has with a single person, alone. Yet Phaedrus hardly seems like one with the qualities necessary for philosophy. He is, as we see in the *Symposium* and here, a devotee of the sophists, and a second-rate one at that. His speech in the *Symposium* is surely the weakest of all the speeches, despite the fact that he is called the "father" of the speeches by Eryximachus. He is, moreover, morally suspect: we know that he was one of those implicated in the notorious profanation of the Eleusian mysteries and the mutilation of the Hermes. And in the *Phaedrus* itself

Phaedrus expresses great enthusiasm at a speech by Lysias—which we shall examine in a moment—that expresses the morally repugnant position that it is better to grant sexual favors to a non-lover than to a lover.

Moreover, as we have already briefly noted, the dialogue opens with a reference to the problematic character of Phaedrus's memory. As Socrates supposes and Phaedrus confirms (228a ff.), Phaedrus made Lysias repeat his speech of seduction several times so that he could memorize it, but, unable to, he requested the written text to take with him so that he could continue to try to memorize it. And Socrates, clearly distrustful of Phaedrus' weak memory, insists that he take out the written text that he has under his cloak and read it, rather than exercise his faulty memory. As we have noted, Socrates, much later in the dialogue and speaking in the name of Thamus, will name as one of the defects of writing—indeed as its first defect—that it will not aid memory, as Theuth had supposed, but inhibit it (275a). Yet here, at the opening of the dialogue, Socrates prefers hearing the written text to depending on Phaedrus's faulty memory. Nor does he seem troubled here, as he will be in his critique, by the absence of the author: undetained by the unavailability of Lysias, Socrates does not hesitate to engage with Phaedrus in a critique of the written text, authorial absence notwithstanding.

What, then, is Socrates' attraction to Phaedrus? Why does he engage with him in this sustained conversation and pray at the end of his palinode, despite all the negative indications, that Phaedrus turn to philosophy? Phaedrus manifestly lacks the intelligence and nobility of a Theaetetus, or even a Lysis or Menexenus. What he does have, and what surely attracts Socrates to him, is a love of speeches. This seems, if anything, to be Phaedrus's defining characteristic. It is he who generates, according to Eryximachus, the speeches of the *Symposium* (177a), and Eryximachus calls him the "father" of those speeches (177d). The *Phaedrus* opens with his wild enthusiasm for Lysias's speech, and Socrates, upon the occasion of his second speech (the palinode) says that Phaedrus has probably caused more speeches to be given than anyone, with the possible exception of Simmias (242b). Phaedrus is thus a "fellow reveler" of Socrates who is himself "sick about speeches." The attraction of Phaedrus for Socrates, then, is his inordinate love of logos. Despite his problematic character, Phaedrus, at least as Plato portrays him, shares with Socrates at least this quality—a deep and passionate love of logos—that might make him philosophical. Socrates sees in Phaedrus, then, an inferior version of himself.

The problem is, Phaedrus's love of logos is indiscriminate, as the appeal of Lysias's speech demonstrates clearly. Socrates' particular predicament in this dialogue, then, will be not so much to encourage a love of logos as to moderate and control it. He will do so through what amounts to a sustained critique (again in the Kantian sense) of logos throughout the dialogue. This critique will take several forms. It begins with a critique of Lysias's speech, at first in terms of form, and then of content; it moves to a revelation (in the palinode) of a double limiting of discursive speech, first through the non-discursive experience of beauty, and then through the non-discursive noetic insight into beauty itself that this experience generates; it will move from there to a critique of rhetoric, and will conclude with the critique of writing that ends the dialogue.[2]

We can turn now to a brief consideration of Lysias's speech that so enchants Phaedrus. The first thing that must strike us is that eros is denigrated throughout the speech. It is identified—and Socrates will reiterate this and make it explicit in his own first speech—with irrational desire (231d, 232a, 233b). Lovers, says Lysias, will be calculating and fickle, are sick, irrational, blabbermouths, jealous, inconstant, and selfish. It is dubious, of course, that these negative generalizations could be supported as always so, but Lysias merely asserts them. The non-lover, by contrast, appeals throughout to the beloved's self-interest (231a, 233c, 234). The general tenor of the speech is that it will be more in the beloved's self-interest to give his favors to the non-lover; Lysias shows that he knows very well what will appeal to Phaedrus. One might say that Lysias presents the position of "cynical reason" regarding love. At the very end of his speech, however, Lysias trips himself up: he closes by trying to cut off the implication that the beloved should give in to *all* non-lovers, thus betraying that this "non-lover" is as jealous as the lover is reputed to be (234c)! This prepares the way for the transformation, in Socrates' speech, of the non-lover into the "concealed lover."

Yet Lysias's speech is not without philosophic interest and merit. It sees the need, for instance, to join *reason* with our erotic experience. It sees the potential dangers of unbridled passion. It makes a legitimate appeal to the beloved's self-interest. All these themes will be preserved not just in Socrates' first speech, which he will give with his head covered in shame, but in his palinode as well. It should be noted, however, that next to nothing is said in the speech of the issue of beauty.

At the end of this speech that Phaedrus finds so enchanting, Socrates dismisses it on grounds both of its content and its rhetoric. It just said the same thing again and again, he says (235a). Indeed, Socrates says, he could do better, and, after more playful teasing with Phaedrus (235c–237a), he agrees to give a better speech in the same spirit as Lysias's—one that he attributes to "the beautiful Sappho or the wise Anacreon" (235c). Nevertheless, he warns, he will give this speech with his head covered in shame and as fast as he can, signaling clearly his dissatisfaction with what he is about to say (237a).

Almost immediately, however, Socrates transforms Lysias's speech in important ways. It is, for one thing, much more "intellectual," and begins with the importance of getting clear on our terms before doing anything (237c).[3] This gives Socrates the opportunity to "define" eros, which he does at first as "some sort of desire" (*epithumia tis he eros*—237d), then later and crucially as "irrational desire," or more literally, "desire without logos" (*epithumia aneu logou*—238c). This will be a severe problem with the first speeches: they conflate love and desire, *eros* and *epithumia,* and this is something Socrates will have to correct in his palinode. We have already seen the way paved for this correction in the ascent passage of the *Symposium,* where, recall, the ascent was accomplished thanks to the presence of reason in eros.

At 238c, having "defined" eros as irrational desire, Socrates interrupts his speech to comment on how poetically inspired he is; he is speaking, he says, in dithyrambs. We have already briefly noted this passage. Socrates here clearly is discomfited by the very poetic inspiration that in a moment, at the beginning of the palinode, he will praise as "divine madness," the best thing that can happen to a human being. Socrates personally is more ambivalent about the inspiration of divine madness—and particularly in its form as poetic inspiration—than his words of praise suggest. Either we will have to moderate our own judgment regarding the forms of divine madness, or we will have to consider whether this is an important difference between Socrates and the dialogue's author. Perhaps, as suggested earlier, we are to see that Socrates is more "sober" than Plato—or than Plato believes a philosopher should be. All this will culminate in the critique of writing at the end of the dialogue.

The rest of Socrates' first speech, in accord with the negative definition of eros, assumes that love is irrational and bad. Lovers will want to keep the beloved inferior and of weak intellect (239a), will be jealous (239b), will keep them from "divine philosophy" (239b), and, implausibly, will even want to keep the beloved's body weak (239c–d). In sum, love is totally denigrated (241c). A particularly important passage in this catalogue of love's defects occurs at 241a, when Socrates describes what happens when a former lover falls out of love: *nous kai sophrosyne,* "intelligence and self-control" replace *eros kai mania,* "love and madness." A number of important issues are adumbrated here. On the one hand, eros is associated with madness, but only in the negative sense. This will have to be corrected by the introduction of the notion of divine madness in the palinode. But because of this association of eros and madness in the negative sense, eros is contrasted to *nous* and *sophrosyne.* Once we see that the madness of eros is divine madness, these will no longer be incompatible. Still, this first speech does recognize the need for the presence of reason and self-control in eros, even if it denies that presence. Socrates, in his palinode, will somehow have to transform our understanding of eros so that it is compatible with *nous kai sophrosyne,* and that is what he will do in a very complex and surprising way, since the compatibility will be exhibited in the context of the experience of the beauty of the beloved.

One might say, then, that despite their vulgar teaching, the first two speeches are not entirely wrong: love, after all, *can* be irrational and destructive. It hardly follows that one should gratify non-lovers. The issue for Socrates now, as in the *Symposium,* will be to understand both the promise and danger of love, and to think about how to stand in proper relationship to it. This, as we shall soon see, will have everything to do with the way we respond to beauty, to the experience of a beautiful beloved.

Socrates ends his first speech with his critique of eros (241d), much to Phaedrus's dismay, since he expected Socrates to now turn to the desirable traits of the non-lover. Socrates indicates his distaste for the entire standpoint by simply saying that one can attribute to the non-lover the opposite of what was said of the lover (241e)! At the same time, he once again indicates his dismay at the way he is speaking in poetically inspired terms. He is about to leave the spot and go home when his customary *daimonion* stops him. He has committed a "sin against eros" (242c); it was a "terrible, terrible speech" (*deinon, deinon logon*) he just gave. He knows, he says, that eros is in fact "a god or something divine." So he must atone for his sin with yet another speech, a palinode, which he yet again attributes to someone else—this time to Stesichorus. This palinode, to which we can now turn, is surely one of the more memorable speeches in philosophical literature.

We need to keep in mind the two explicitly stated intentions regarding Socrates' second speech. First, it is a palinode, meant to correct the "sin against eros" of Lysias's speech and Socrates' first speech. We shall have to watch with care, then, the very different account of eros given here, particularly in its connection to beauty, which, as we saw, was barely mentioned in the first two speeches. Second, the palinode is especially directed to Phaedrus—as Socrates acknowledges in his prayer at the end of the speech—in the hope that Phaedrus will be turned away from his indiscriminate infatuation with sophistic rhetoric and toward philosophy. We shall have to evaluate the success of this intention as well, but of course, only at the end of the palinode.

The first issue Socrates raises in the palinode is that of "divine madness" (244a–245b). We have seen that both early speeches treated eros as a form of madness, but in the entirely negative sense of the term. Socrates' interesting recantation on this particular issue will not be, as one might expect, to deny that eros is madness, but instead to distinguish between sorts of madness: a "divine" madness which is a great blessing to its sufferer, and a "human" madness which is the worst thing that can happen. Socrates introduces four forms of divine madness, indicating explicitly, however, that there are other forms of divine madness as well. His list is exemplary, but not exhaustive (245b). The four exemplary types of divine madness that Socrates mentions are: prophetic, "religious" (purifications, rituals, mystical experience), poetic, and erotic. So the early speeches were right that eros is madness; they were mistaken in not appreciating, as Socrates will now try to exhibit (*apodeixis*—245c), that eros is a form of *divine* madness.

It must not be forgotten, however, that divine madness is *madness*. As such, it presumably refers to an experience over which we do not have technical control. We cannot avoid it with *sophrosyne,* nor can we call it forth at will.

Instead, something "comes over us," as if from an outside force of some sort—we ourselves are not its source. When this "possession" by some force outside us has negative results, we call it simply *madness*. What do we call it when it has positive results? Typically, something like *inspiration*. (The Greek term for this is instructive: *enthusiasmos*—literally, "the god is in us.") Now, most of us easily accept this notion when it comes to poetic or artistic inspiration. We are not so given to this language when it comes to philosophy, although we certainly speak more generally of the "inspiration" of love. Especially because the focus of the erotic experience that Socrates will describe in the palinode will be what he calls "Zeus" friendships (250b)—that is, philosophic friendships—we should note the implication that philosophy, as a mode of eros, involves a similar sort of "inspiration" to that of poetry and art. To the extent that this is so, it prepares us for the recognition that philosophy cannot be simply a "logical" activity but is one, like the arts, that involves inspiration. This is the striking claim that will be set out in the palinode, and we shall see that Plato sustains it in the Second and the Seventh Letters, to which we shall turn after addressing the palinode. That philosophy is somehow inspired reminds us of Socrates' tendency to *resist* inspiration; we saw this in his first speech as well as in his introduction to the palinode. We should note as well how "poetic" the palinode will be, with its image of the charioteer and two horses, journeys to the hyper-ouranian place, etc.

If eros, and so philosophy, is a form of divine madness, is it *always* divine? Or is it sometimes divine, and sometimes human madness? A little later in the palinode (248c ff.), Socrates will present a list of the types of lives that devolve based on how much of "the beings" souls have seen. There, "someone devoted to the Muses," that is, *inspired* art, is placed in the highest position along with philosophers, lovers of beauty, and lovers (248d), while "imitative poets" are placed way down in sixth place (out of nine).[4] This suggests clearly the distinction between inspired poetry or art and "merely" imitative poetry. (We should note that in the notorious "criticisms" of poetry and art in the dialogues, it is nearly always their imitative and not their inspired character that is criticized, a distinction not sufficiently observed in most discussions of Plato's supposed "distaste" for poetry.) Might something like this same distinction be true of eros and so of that mode of eros which is philosophy—that there is *inspired* (divine) eros and *sick* eros as well? If so—and doesn't it seem to be so?—determining the difference will be a decisive but no easy task.

Whether eros is divine or human madness, it is not entirely within our control. This means that eros—and so its manifestation as philosophy—will exhibit a certain resistance to our efforts at *sophrosyne*, at that self-control which seems so important to Socrates. We ask again: is Socrates' discomfiture at being inspired a certain limitation on his character as a philosopher that Plato is quietly observing? Is Socrates just a bit too *sober* for Plato's understanding of philosophical life? One is reminded here of Nietzsche's Zarathustra: "There is always some madness in love; but there is always some reason in madness."[5]

Alternatively, and broaching the possibility of paradox, might *sophrosyne itself*—particularly insofar as, in the *Charmides,* it is revealed as that self-knowledge which is philosophical living[6]—be itself a mode of inspiration? That is, must we somehow be inspired in order to be self-controlled, inspired *to be* self-controlled? Or at least philosophically so? One is reminded here of Socrates' own self-questioning earlier in the *Phaedrus:* "Am I a beast more complex and agitated than Typhon, or a gentler and simpler animal, possessing by nature a divine and un-Typhonic lot?" (230a).

In sum, the introduction of the issue of divine madness presents us with a number of difficult questions. If the "secular" version of divine madness is easy enough to grasp in principle—it refers to the phenomenon of inspiration—how do we determine in specific instances of madness whether it is divine or human? To what extent, and how, is philosophy itself, as manifestly a mode of eros, itself a form of inspiration? And is it always so, or only in some of its instances? If, as it certainly appears, it is the latter, how do we determine whether those instances are divine or human? It cannot be said that Socrates answers these questions in the palinode. But he certainly shows us that they are at stake in understanding the philosophical living that he will now try to persuade Phaedrus to adopt.

Socrates turns next to his so-called "proof" of the immortality of the soul (245c ff.). It should be noted that the word Socrates uses throughout is *apodeixis,* not the stronger *tekmerion. Apodeixis* has the looser sense of "exhibition," rather than the stronger sense of "proof" or "demonstration" embodied in *tekmerion.* Indeed, Socrates prefaces his "exhibition" with the following instructive warning: "Our exhibition will be persuasive (or 'trustworthy'—*piste*) to the wise, but not to the clever (*deinois*—keep in mind the ambiguity of this word)" (245c). Socrates here virtually announces that the argument for immortality will not be logically rigorous, but that such is not the real issue. The "clever" will only look at its logical validity. The "wise" will look deeper. Especially given the mythical character of what is to follow, and keeping in mind the Greek (and Platonic) sense of myth as a truth couched in fiction,[7] we could say that the wise will look for the truth within the fiction of the myths to follow. The wise, that is, will find what is worthy of *trust* in the exhibition, and not obsess on the logical validity or invalidity of the "proof."

Socrates introduces the exhibition as follows: "We shall determine the truth about the nature of the soul, both human and divine" (245c). The claim that what follows will be about the nature of the soul will become striking when we have gone through the development of what ostensibly looks like an image of the soul (the charioteer and two horses, etc.). For we will then be told by Socrates that "the whole speech so far has been about the fourth kind of madness" (249d)—i.e., about *eros*—rather than the soul. Let us leave this as a provocation for the moment, but let us not forget it.

The exhibition begins, "All soul is immortal": *psyche pasa athanatos* (245c). There is an apparently intentional ambiguity in this opening sentence, which has at least three possible senses. It could mean, first, something like "each soul" is immortal, thus arguing for the immortality of the individual soul in the orthodox sense. This possible interpretation is imposed on the reader by those who translate the sentence as "Every soul is immortal."[8] Or, it could mean something like "soul taken as a whole" is immortal.[9] Still again, it could refer to some sort of "world soul," as in the *Timaeus*.[10] Fortunately, we do not have to resolve this issue here: the matter of utmost importance for us will be Socrates' emphasis, throughout his exhibition, on self-motion. This, we are told in an arresting statement at 245e, is the *ousian te kai logon,* the "being and discursive account" of the soul. What is so striking here is the strength of the claim. Socrates is not just saying that the soul has, as one of its *attributes,* even an important one, that of self-motion. He is saying that the very *being and logos* of the soul is self-motion. What soul *is,* is self-motion. Among other things, this is tantamount to a denial that the soul is some sort of *substance* which has as one of its *attributes* self-motion. Again, the soul *just is* self-motion.

If self-motion is not just an attribute but the very being of the soul, then its *logos* will also be unusual. First, everything will now depend on what sort of motion the self-motion of the soul really is—and Socrates' brief "exhibition" does not say what it is, but leaves it abstract. Only later will we learn what the specific self-motion of the soul is. But in any case, whatever its specific motion is, if the being of the soul is self-*motion,* then its logos, it seems, will also have to *move* along with the moving being of the soul. That is, both the being and the logos of the soul will be in motion. "The soul has a logos, which increases itself," said Heraclitus, who seemed to presage fully what Socrates is driving at here.[11] If the very being of the soul and its logos are self-motion, then whatever that motion turns out to be, as moving—that is, as constantly changing—can there possibly be an *idea* of the soul in the formal "Platonic" sense? Socrates is about to entertain briefly and problematically that idea, but nothing in this or other dialogues suggests that it will be possible.

Almost immediately, at 246a, Socrates introduces this very notion: "As for the immortality of the soul, that is enough, but as for its *idea,* we must say the following." The problem is this: given the nature of the soul that is here claimed as self-motion, given the intimacy of soul and eros that we have already seen in the *Symposium* (eros, which has no "idea" but is "in the middle"), given as well the strange nature of Socratic *self*-knowledge as "knowing what I know and what I do not know," there should not *be* an "idea" of the soul in the technical, Platonic sense. And indeed, this is the only place in all the dialogues where such a possibility is mentioned.

The very next sentence Socrates utters helps clarify our problem. "To specify what sort of thing it (the soul) is would by all means be a task for a god and a lengthy exhibition, but to say what it seems like (*eoiken*) would be briefer and something a human being could do" (246a). Only a god could tell what the soul really is. How it *seems* is a proper matter for human discourse. This surely means, at very least, that there can be no "proof" of the soul's nature. What it *seems* like will now be articulated by Socrates in his remarkable image of the charioteer and two horses. In this case, then, the "idea" (literally the "look") of the soul must refer not at all to a "Platonic idea of the soul," but precisely to the charioteer and horses image that Socrates is about to develop. The "idea" of the soul, then, will be its "look"—how it seems to us. We can turn now to the remarkable image of the soul as a charioteer and horses.

We shall concentrate, yet again, only on those aspects of the charioteer/horses image that prepare us for the way beauty is addressed in the palinode, where it becomes thematic. The image is introduced to us at 246a, and is sustained throughout the rest of the palinode. The image begins with the assertion of a certain kinship between the gods and us. We all have souls that are comprised of a winged charioteer and two winged horses. Here, however, the similarity ends. For the gods apparently are, as without bodies, *nothing but* these charioteer/horses souls; whereas, as we are about to learn, we humans are embodied (246c). The second crucial difference is the makeup of the team of horses. Both the horses of the god-souls are "of good stock" (246a), whereas we humans have a white horse of good stock, but also a black horse which proves to be troublesome in the highest. It is instructive that our white horse is described as *kalos te kai agathos,* usually translated "noble and good," and the black horse as "the opposite" (246b). Our souls, then, are comprised in part of a mixture of the beautiful and the ugly. This also means that our souls are thus "triadic," and the function of each member of the triad is fairly clear. The black horse represents desire (*epithumia*), the white horse something like spiritedness (*thumos,* though it is never quite named as such), and the charioteer is reason (*nous*), and serves the double function of controlling the two horses as well as "seeing" the beings.[12] This is the beginning of the correction of the claim in the *Phaedrus*'s first two speeches that eros is merely desire, that is, that eros would be simply the black horse. *Epithumia,* the black horse, is *one constituent* of the soul, and so, as we shall see, of eros.

Next, we are told how and why we are mortal (246b–d). The souls that are "perfect" and have wings circle the cosmos and participate in the governance of the whole. However, some souls lose their wings and thus sink down, settling in a body. (There is a certain interesting implication here that the body therefore "supports" the soul, in which case it can hardly be all bad, as the soon to be introduced "oyster in its shell" analogy also will suggest.) This united whole (*xumpan*) is called a living being (*zoon*) and mortal (*thneton*—246c). The next sentence is particularly instructive: "It is not immortal by any coherent logos" (*Athanaton de oud' ex henos logou lelogismenou*); and we construct our idea of an immortal being after an image of our own embodied nature, though we cannot, says Socrates, adequately conceive (*hikanos noesantes*—246d) of a god.[13] Note that the image of the gods nevertheless constructed here is that they are "pure minds" with no bodies—again, an interesting prefiguration of Aristotle's

"Unmoved Mover" as "thought thinking thought." Presumably (but not certainly) the reason we lose our wings, fall to earth, and become embodied has something to do with our black horse of desire. If so, there is raised here implicitly the question of the connection of desire and the body—to say the least, an enduring philosophic question.

Next, we are presented with the interesting account of the arrangement of this heavenly train (247a ff.). The eleven gods circle the heavens and easily contemplate "the beings," and all other souls follow the lead of one or another of the gods.[14] The image thus suggests that we humans have different character types according to the god that we follow. Philosophers, for example, are followers of Zeus, warriors of Ares, etc. (252d). The image suggests that the various human character types are many, but not infinite, and there is a way of making at least some sense of the source and nature of those character types. This will become crucial for an understanding of our experience of beauty, for as we shall see (252d ff.), what god you follow will determine both the kind of person you find beautiful as well as the way you love that person. So it will indeed be the case that "beauty is in the eye of the beholder," but this will not be pure relativism; rather, each person's judgments of beauty, as well as the way they respond to the beautiful, will be a function of the "god" that he or she follows.

The gods, we are told, travel easily to this "hyper-ouranian" place, which turns out to be the realm of true being. (Plato's language is hyperbolic here: it is the place of "the being that beingly is": *ousia ontos ousa* [247c].) Of the experience of the gods as they circle the beings, we are told a number of important things. First, in an obvious departure from popular Greek theology, *all* the gods are apparently wise—they all circle the heavens and nourish themselves on being. They do so, second, only with *nous,* which alone can behold being. Indeed, third, all "true knowledge" is of being. Thus, the thought (*dianoia—* 247d) of the gods is nourished by *nous kai episteme,* perhaps something like "thought and knowledge." This must refer to the charioteer of the gods' souls, since we are told that after circling the heavens and contemplating the beings, the horses of the god-souls are nourished by ambrosia and nectar (248a).

This passage is extremely instructive, especially by contrast to the human experience that will be described in a moment. For it makes ultimate intellectuals of the gods! They are portrayed by Socrates as basically *nothing* but contemplators of being. Indeed, the presumed differences among the gods are virtually washed away by this image: they all seem to do the very same thing, all the time. No less important, the gods apparently do not speak. They apparently do not speak on the way to the heavens, they do not speak while contemplating the beings, and no indication is given that, after returning, they share their appreciation of the beings with each other.[15] There is a good reason for this: since the gods' noetic visions of the beings are complete and unadulterated (they have no black horse, remember, to interfere with their visions), they have no *need* of logos. We note again the kinship to Aristotle's god, who is pure *nous.* Logos is required only by those whose noetic insights are not complete or perfect. The implication is clear: only humans speak, not the gods. Only humans have—that is, *need*—logos. Put differently, logos is a peculiarly *human* phenomenon, which is to say, it is somehow a function of our mortality, the incompleteness of our noetic visions—or, one might say in anticipation, of our eros.

We are presented with the contrasting experience of human souls at 248a–b. It is a vivid image of the struggle, trampling and jostling, and suffering we undergo to fight our way up to the circle of the beings, such that—unlike the gods, who can contemplate the beings presumably at leisure and perfectly—we can at best get only occasional and utterly partial *glimpses* of the beings. And, importantly, it is not just the inferior horse that keeps us from attaining to full noetic visions of the gods, though that is surely part of the problem. It is also that we humans have *bad charioteers: kakia henioxon* (248b). This is a crucial image of the *finitude* and incompleteness of all human knowledge. Our *dianoia*, our discursive, *logical* (in the literal sense) efforts toward knowledge lead us to occasional noetic visions which are *partial*. As will become clear, the situation is even more complex. Our intellectual experience, as opposed to that of the gods, is in fact not of one but of two noetic moments, joined by logos. We first have a noetic, that is, non-discursive, experience that *begins* the effort to see the beings. In ordinary terms, something has to "happen" to us to make us *want to know* something—want to begin the discursive struggle to knowledge. As we shall see presently, this originating non-discursive experience has everything to do with the paradigmatic experience of beauty. That originating insight or intuition in turn awakens our *dianoia,* our discursive struggle via speech (*logos*) to understand. Occasionally, if we are lucky, that discursive effort leads us to a *culminating* noetic, non-discursive experience—an occasional "vision," always partial, of this being or that. Human knowledge is thus finite, partial, incomplete from beginning to end. The originating noetic, non-discursive experience that gets us started is finite. The discursive logos that moves us forward is also finite (this, one might say, is the great lesson of the *Hippias Major* and the other "definitional" dialogues), and what culminating noetic insights we might from time to time attain are (thanks to our "bad charioteers") also inevitably finite.

Moreover, we begin to see here the decisive but double-edged role of logos, of discursive reasoning. Logos is, in effect, "in the middle" between our originating and our culminating intuitions, and it—always finitely—joins the two together into a whole. Logos, that is, plays precisely the role here played in Diotima's speech by daimonic eros: in the middle between the mortal and the divine, binding the two together into a whole (*Symposium* 202e). There, we were told that "there are many of these daimons of all sorts, and one of them is eros" (203a). Perhaps another of these crucial daimons, at once the source of our finitude and our transcendence, is *logos*. Discursive speech, that is, both makes possible our transcendence (our visions of the beings), while at the same time it is that very speech that keeps such transcendence from being complete.[16]

Socrates' next step in the palinode is to present one of the several versions of reincarnation myth he presents in the dialogues (248c–249d). Several points about this myth within a myth are important for our purposes. First, Socrates relates that the lives we live—or rather, as we learn at 249b, the lives we choose—are a function of the amount of being we have seen, the extent to which we have glimpsed being. When we lose our wings and fall into embodiment, we choose a life accordingly. As we have seen, Socrates mentions nine categories, some of the elements of which are hardly surprising: philosophy is mentioned in the first category, for example, sophistry in the eighth and tyranny in the ninth. So far, so Platonic. But things are immediately complicated in the very first, the highest category, where not only philosophy is mentioned. Rather, those who have seen the most of being will become "a philosopher, or lover of beauty, or of one of the Muses and of love": *philosophou e philokalou e mousikou tinos kai erotikou* (248d). That philosophers are in the highest category is typical of Socrates' reincarnation myths and not surprising. More interesting is the point we already have noted, that "lovers of the Muses"—i.e., all those devoted to the arts—are included in the highest category. So much for Plato's "hatred of art," one might say. Yet as we have noted, that "poets and other imitative artists" are located at the *sixth* level (out of nine), suggests that Socrates has in mind a distinction between "mere" imitative artists, who are denigrated to a low level, and *inspired* artists—i.e., those who experience a form of divine madness—who are placed at the very highest level.

Most interesting of all, however, and perhaps most striking, is the other group placed in the highest level: "lovers of beauty." This is an important preparation for what is to come. Surely Plato wants us to be struck by this inclusion: those who love beauty are among those living the very best lives, those who, prior to embodiment, have seen the most of being. As it is presented in this list, it is unexplained and remains a mystery why it is so. But as the palinode builds to its conclusion, we shall see that there is very good reason for placing lovers of beauty at the highest level. They have seen something that few have seen.

One other thing needs to be noted about the list of nine categories of life: prophets and mystery priests are ranked in the fifth class, which is hardly a distinguished level. This is at first puzzling since these represent, we recall, two of the four types of divine madness mentioned at the beginning of the palinode. Perhaps a clue to this puzzle is the just-mentioned problem regarding poetry and poetic divine madness. Perhaps in a similar fashion, Socrates is suggesting a distinction between *inspired* prophets and mystics, and those who are not inspired—of whom there were many and notorious examples in Greek culture. But if this is true of poetic, prophetic, and mystical divine madness—namely, that not all who go under those names are truly inspired—might it not also be true of the fourth form of divine madness? That is, might there also be *uninspired lovers*, those, one might say, who give love a bad name? And so, uninspired philosophers? We should watch for this as the palinode continues.

At 249a–c, elaborating on the reincarnation myth in terms of the cycles of types of existence, Socrates makes a claim of the greatest importance for our understanding of beauty. Not all souls, he says, enter into the life of a human being when, in the cycle, it comes their time to choose their next life. Only those who have "seen the truth" (*idousa ten aletheian*) can enter into a human form. Socrates explains why, and the passage is worth quoting:

> It is necessary for a human being to acquire understanding of what is said according to forms (*kat' eidos legomenon*), gathering together many perceptions into one through reasoning (*logismo*). This is a recollection (*anamnesis*) of those things which our soul once beheld when it traveled with a god, and lifting its vision above that which we now are, rose up into what really is (*to on ontos*). For this reason it is just that only the thinking of a philosopher (*he tou philosophou dianoia*) will make the wings grow, because, through memory (*mneme*), he is always, as much as he is able, together with those things whose proximity make a god divine. When a man uses correctly these reminders (*hupomnemasin orthos chromenos*), he is always initiated perfectly into perfect mysteries, and he alone becomes really perfect (*teleous aei teletas teloumenos, teleos ontos monos gignetai*). (249c)

Let us remark on several of the points made in this passage. First, humans must understand what is said (*legomenon*) according to forms (*kat' eidos*). Two important issues are signaled here. We understand "according to forms," and this is accomplished via a certain "gathering" of many perceptions into a one. To say the least, this points to a complicated situation indeed. I emphasize here only that it is we humans who do the gathering of many into one, that we are the gatherers here. But second, what we come to understand through this gathering is *what is said*. And we do so *by reasoning* (*logismo*). Logos is all over the place in this passage. The gathering of many into one, according to forms, is accomplished via *logos*. We are reminded again of the role of eros, according to Diotima, which, in the middle between the mortal and the divine, "binds the two together into a whole" (*Symposium* 203a). Logos, once again, is one of these daimonic gatherers or binders, similar to eros, that enable us to construct a coherent world. Second, however, this experience of gathering many perceptions into one, Socrates now says, is enabled by a *recollection* of our former insight into the beings when we followed a god. It looks very much like the human experience to which the myth of recollection refers is something like our occasional non-discursive *insights* or intuitions (always accompanied by but not reducible to logos) into formal structure that enable us to understand.

Finally, Socrates concludes in a hyperbolic repetition of variants of the Greek word for "perfection" or "completeness" that it is these reminders (*hupomnemasin*)—these occasional experiences of insight into formal unity, we may say—that make us as perfect as can be. We presently will have occasion to remind ourselves of the use of this word. Here, let us note, "reminders" are *good*. They are a crucial element in our gaining what knowledge we, as humans, may attain. We shall need very much to recall this when we turn to Socrates' critique of writing, which in part will be predicated on the *denigration* of precisely this phenomenon of "reminding." But this must await our address of that passage in a later chapter.

And now, at 249d, after some four utterly rich pages of his account of the soul in terms of the charioteer image, and just before he turns to the experience of beauty and its effect on the soul, Socrates says something truly remarkable: "The whole speech so far has been about the fourth form of madness": *Estin de oun deuro ho pas hekon logos peri tes tetartes manias*. All this talk about immortality of soul, about the image of the charioteer and its horses, about our struggle to see the beings, *before* the explicit discussion (soon to follow) of the experience of eros for beauty—all this has been about eros? It *seemed* to be about the soul! What could it mean for Socrates now to say that it has *all* (*pas*) been about eros? How can an apparent account of the soul in fact be an account of eros?

There is at least one way in which this strange sentence could make sense. It would if the specific "self-motion" that constitutes the being and logos of the soul is in fact the motion of eros—for eros surely is a motion. Very much more, of course, needs to be said about the specific character of eros's motion. In the *Symposium* we have seen it characterized largely in terms of the impetus or drive for completeness: eros is that which leads us to strive for wholeness out of our experience of incompleteness. Here in the palinode, we note that the source of the soul's motion is located in part in the two horses; in part in the charioteer himself, who controls whether the horses charge forward and also, as reason, decides on the direction of travel; but ultimately it is in the *wings* shared by both the charioteer and its team of horses. If eros is the "being and logos" of the soul, its specific self-motion, then what appears to be an account of the soul could in fact be an account of eros. Is there any further evidence within the speech that would warrant making this striking identification?

Right from the beginning of the charioteer image, we are told that both the charioteer and the two horses are winged (*hupopterou*—246a). The wings of the god-charioteers and their horses are strong, indeed "perfect" (*telea*—246b). Our wings, however, are often injured and ruined, due to the battle and struggles necessary for us to work our way up to a glimpse of the hyper-ouranian place (248b). If the charioteer and horses are an image of the soul, then it is ultimately the wings of the soul—whether of the gods or humans—that enable it to move. The soul's movement—its self-movement, which is its being and logos—is a function of its wings.

As Socrates, after the completion of the charioteer image, turns to the actual experience of eros for beauty, he gives Phaedrus an apparently playful etymology of eros. At 252b, he says:

> Well, you beautiful boy for whom my speech is given, human beings call this experience eros, but when you hear what the gods call it, because of your youth, you will probably laugh. I believe some Homericists quote two verses to eros from the secret epics, of which the second is quite hubristic and not very metrical. They sing as follows: "Mortals do indeed call the winged one Eros, but immortals call him *pterota* (feathered), because he necessarily develops wings."

This "winged one," the soul, *is* eros. The source of the soul's self-motion, and so indeed its very being and logos, is eros. Once again we must emphasize the implication here: eros, love, is not just one of the things that occasionally happens to the soul among other experiences. As the very self-motion of the soul, eros is the being and logos of the soul.[17]

We may return to the movement of the palinode from Socrates' remark at 249d that the whole speech so far has been about the fourth kind of madness. Socrates now begins the movement toward an explanation of the special appeal of beauty for human being by emphasizing the power of our original experience, before embodiment, of following in the train of our particular god and glimpsing the beings. He emphasizes the difficulty and partiality of our efforts— as we are now, embodied—to recall or recollect those "original" experiences of the beings:

> For as has been said, every soul of a human being by virtue of its nature has seen the things that are, otherwise it could not have entered into this kind of living being; but it is not easy for every soul to recollect those things on the basis of the things of this world. Some barely saw the things there at the time, and others who fell to earth had the misfortune of being corrupted by some of their associations and have forgotten the sacred forms they saw before. Few are left who have a sufficient memory of them, and they, when they see some likeness of these things, are astounded and delirious, although they do not understand the experience because their perception is so unclear. Thus there is not sufficient light (*pheggos*) in this world's likenesses of justice, *sophrosyne*, and all the other things souls hold worthy. (250a–b)

Socrates goes on to paint a contrasting picture of our "original position" when we saw the beings in their clarity and brilliance, before we fell into bodies and were "imprisoned in it like an oyster in its shell" (250c).[18] The passage quoted is a strong indication of the finitude of all human knowledge. Even the best of our claims to knowledge, the passage suggests, are in the end functions of our always compromised recollections of the beings.

There is, however, one particular experience we have that gives us an especially vivid recollection of the being in question. That experience and that being, says Socrates, is beauty. "Concerning beauty, as we said, it shone brightly along with those things, and, since coming here, we have grasped it shining most distinctly through the most distinct of our senses. For sight is the keenest of the sensations coming through the body" (250d). This is a crucial passage for our concerns. Socrates is trying to make sense of an important human phenomenon: for most of us at least, the experience we have of beauty is not quite like the experiences we have in our embodied states of the other "beings"—of justice, *sophrosyne*, or wisdom. Moved though we may be by such experiences, they lack the utter power over us and the effect on us that the experience of beauty gives us, and which Socrates is about to describe in dramatic detail. One could hardly match the portrayal of this experience that Socrates is about to give. What he is trying to do, clearly, is to give us a sense of the extraordinary effect on us, indeed, the overwhelming power of our experience of beauty.

When we see beauty in this world ("here"—*to tede*), we are reminded of true beauty and our wings begin to grow. We should note the change in the epistemological relation here, from that of the *Symposium*. It is not, as with Diotima, that once we see beauty itself we realize that it is the source of all these other manifestations of beauty and so understand them. It is rather the converse relation: seeing—and hence recognizing—beauty "here" *reminds* us of beauty itself. The two directions may of course be compatible. In both cases, however, our "understanding" of beauty, such as it is, seems to be a function of our *non-discursive* recognition of it: either the explicitly non-discursive insight into "beauty itself" in Diotima's account (recall, *oude tis logos, oude tis episteme*); or the present non-discursive "recollection" of true beauty (the "being"), which is itself the result of our non-discursive *recognition* or experience of beauty "here." In this account, as before, there are two non-discursive experiences in play—one that originates and one that culminates our (always finite) understanding of beauty. First is the non-discursive but extraordinarily powerful *experience* of beauty "here" which, in turn, will "remind" us of our *previous* non-discursive experience of beauty itself when we were with our god. One crucial consequence of this situation needs to be reiterated, for it supports and sustains what we have discovered in the two earlier dialogues: what beauty is cannot be reduced to any sort of "definition," even an elaborate one. Indeed, it cannot even be reduced to a logos. It is inseparable from non-discursive insight. Once again, this is why the attempt at the definition of *to kalon* in the *Hippias Major* simply had to fail.

Socrates underlines the special character of the experience of beauty by imagining what it would be like if we could experience the other beings with the same power that we experience beauty. It would give rise, he hilariously conjectures, to "terrible erotic urges."

> Wisdom (Socrates somewhat curiously switches here from *sophia* to *phronesis*) is not visible to it (i.e., sight), because the sort of clear image of itself that would be required for sight would provoke terrible erotic urges (*deinous gar an pareichen erotas*), as would be the case with the other objects of love. It is beauty alone which has this destiny, and thus is the clearest and loveliest (*ekphanestaton einai kai erasmiotaton*). (250d–e)

We note the enormous power that Plato here grants to the experience of beauty. Thanks to its shining power, he suggests, the beauty we humans experience—which is paradigmatically that of another beautiful person—is one of our most powerful experiences. It is worth thinking back in this regard to the *Hippias Major* where, we recall, "power" (*dunamis*) was presented by Socrates as a putative definition of beauty itself (296a ff.). That "power" there fails as a comprehensive definition of beauty, we now see, hardly denies that the sheer power of beauty as we experience it is a central feature of any more adequate understanding of beauty. The literal visibility of beauty, and thus its sheer power over us, makes this experience and our ensuing recollection of its "being" something of a paradigm for our other experiences of "the beings."

There is one other way in which the experience of beauty functions as a paradigm for humans. As the most visible of the beings, Socrates says, beauty *shines*—shines more brilliantly than the other beings—and so its manifestations "here" also shine more brilliantly than other phenomena. Beauty thus shines forth and in so doing shows us what it means for things to shine forth, to thus reveal themselves, to come to unhiddenness—what the Greeks named *aletheia*, truth. Especially for the Greek experience of truth, then, that which paradigmatically shines forth, beauty, is also a paradigm for the shining-forth of things, for their truth. Unlike a later age which tended to separate the question of beauty from that of truth, beauty in the *Phaedrus*, in its excessive shining, functions as a paradigm for truth.[19] No wonder, then, that it is so often such a crucial element in the dialogues.

Socrates now enters into a vivid portrayal of that altogether erotic experience of beauty (251a–252b). The description constantly plays on the edge between a strong description of the experience of beauty and a straightforwardly sexual experience. We are told that in response to the experience of the beautiful beloved, the previously hardened follicles of our damaged wings are softened, that a "nourishing moisture flows over them," that "the shafts of the feathers begin to swell and grow," that the entire soul "throbs with excitement," and that when the soul looks at the beloved's beauty "a flood of particles flows from him" (251b–c). One can only imagine Plato chuckling to himself as he wrote this passage, combining as it does an almost perfect blend of images of male and female sexual arousal (swelling and growing, moistening and softening). The no doubt intentional ambiguity of this image of sexual experience and the experience of beauty underlines an important point that we have noted in both early dialogues. The paradigm experience of beauty is the beauty of a human being whom we love; that means that the paradigm experience is the explicitly *erotic* experience of beauty. Just as the first example of beauty that occurred to Hippias was that of "a beautiful girl"; just as Diotima taught Socrates that "it is *necessary*" to begin with the love of a beautiful human body; so Socrates here simply assumes that the most vivid and powerful experience of beauty we have (which to be sure may open the way for other experiences of beauty and indeed for experiences of the other "beings") will be the erotic experience of a beautiful beloved—an experience that he describes in almost lurid detail.

Nevertheless, his description is not without careful qualification. At 252a, Socrates acknowledges that the lover will not leave the beloved willingly, and values nothing more highly than the beloved's beauty. The lover's soul "forgets mother, brother, and all associates, and if property is lost through neglect, thinks nothing of it. It now despises decency and taste, which it used to take great pride in, and is ready to be a slave and sleep wherever it is allowed to, as near as possible to the object of its longing." One is reminded by this passage of the depths of vulgarity into which Pausanias's speech finally fell in the *Symposium*. It certainly does *not* remind us of Diotima's confident claim at the end of her speech that seeing beauty itself will lead to "true virtue." There is a subtle but important difference in the two situations: in Diotima's speech, it is *after* the insight into beauty itself that she says we will live lives of true virtue; here in the *Phaedrus,* it is simply the *experience* of the beloved's beauty that leads us to behave otherwise. Perhaps we need to be "reminded" of beauty itself before what might otherwise be deplorable behavior is transformed into virtuous living. That is just what we are about to see described in the battle between the black horse of desire and the charioteer and white horse of the "Zeus lover," the philosophic lover. In the *Symposium* it was recognized by almost all of the speakers that eros had a dangerous side, that its "double-edged-sword" character meant that it could destroy us as well as bless us, and yet that the insight into beauty itself could also culminate in "virtuous living"; similarly here, we see that the erotic experience of the beautiful beloved can indeed be "divine madness" that will lead us to philosophic living—as Socrates will presently describe—yet it can also reduce us to vulgarity. But this raises a crucial set of questions: how can we work through the connection of the inspirational dimension of the eros for beauty with its capacity to generate vulgarity and baseness? Can the latter be avoided, or is it an inevitable consequence of the erotic inspiration of beauty? How, then, can we reconcile this danger of the eros for beauty—and must we not admit that it is a real and present danger?—with the claim that seeing beauty will give rise to virtuous living, as we saw in the *Symposium* and as Socrates is about to develop at length here?

After the playful etymology of eros which we have already addressed (252b), Socrates elaborates on the differing experiences of and reactions to beauty according to the different gods that we follow. Socrates first describes Zeus followers and Ares followers, and how the followers of these gods will react to their experiences of the beloved in different ways. In this case, the Zeus lovers react in a "more dignified" (*embrithesteron*) way, and Ares lovers more violently (252c). Moreover, he continues, each of us will also *choose* our beloveds—find one or another beautiful—according to our god. Again Zeus lovers are the lead example: "The followers of Zeus want the person they love to be a Zeus-like soul. So they search for one who has the nature of a philosopher and a leader" (252e). (It is similar, Socrates adds, with followers of Hera, Apollo, and the other gods.) Much is being accounted for in these two sets of examples. In the first case, we *react* to the experience of beauty according to the god we follow. This refers to the many different reactions among humans to the experience and love of beauty. But also, as the second set of examples shows, we even *choose* our love object—that is, find different people beautiful—according to the god we follow. This accounts, then, for the many different *objects* of love. This is the way Socrates makes sense of the phenomenon that *to a certain extent,* "beauty is in the eye of the beholder." Beauty is, in a way, relative—yes, but relative to the *god* we follow. One might say, in paraphrase of Aristotle, that beauty is experienced in many ways. Many ways—but presumably not an infinite number. There are indeed a number of different ways in which beauty might be experienced. It is in a sense, then, relative. But it is a limited and one might say, a grounded or determined relativism: determined by the nature of the god we follow. There is no "radical" relativism here. Nor is it a version of the Protagorean "man is the measure of all things," for man is not the measure: the god we follow is.

What would be the demythologized or secular version of this? I take it that Socrates is saying something like this: there is a variety, a significant but not unlimited variety of (more or less) legitimate ways in which one experiences beauty, and a similarly limited variety of objects (in this case humans) that one finds beautiful. Even within this limited range, however, there is a certain hierarchy whose measure is not beauty itself, but the quality and variety of lives (philosophers, warriors, etc.) that lead to different choices and experiences and that follow from these choices and experiences. As Socrates will now develop at some length, the highest life in the hierarchy is that of Zeus lovers, who—as he has just reminded us—become philosophers, love young philosophic souls, and find philosophic types to be beautiful. The difficulty now becomes: since the erotic experience of beauty for the Zeus lover (again, the philosopher) is nevertheless *erotic,* it will still embody the danger of erotic experience that has been discussed—the danger, that is, of falling into vulgarity. How, then, is a philosophic type, who falls in love with a beautiful beloved, to conduct their love affair so that it becomes a *philosophic friendship*? Not without a great struggle, as the ensuing—and quite long (253d–256e)—account of the experience of a Zeus lover will attest.

Socrates' description of the experience of a Zeus lover of falling in love with a beautiful beloved begins with a return to and significant elaboration of the charioteer/horses image (253d ff.). We are treated to a sometimes lurid description of the struggle of the philosophic soul to resist the demands of the black horse—that is, of desire (*epithumia*)—to consummate the relationship sexually, indeed to rein in those desires so that a philosophic friendship may develop. Let me comment on several specific points regarding this long passage, then reflect on its significance as a whole.

First, it is important to recognize that this is a description specifically of the struggle of a *Zeus lover* to resist the desire for sexual consummation and to achieve a genuinely philosophic friendship. This means, in the first instance, that Zeus lovers too have the black horse of desire. Presumably this includes Socrates. Earlier we had occasion to wonder whether Socrates had these strong desires at all or whether—as Alcibiades attested—Socrates was simply *playing at* erotic arousal at the young man's beauty. According to the present account, even a philosophic lover will be subject to these desires in a very real way, and have to overcome great erotic temptations to preserve philosophic friendships. If this is not true of Socrates, then he is simply defective erotically. Moreover, it is important to remember that this is not a general description of *all* erotic experience of beauty, but only that of philosophic lovers. This becomes crucial in passages such as 256a–e, where Socrates describes the difference between the successful philosophic friendship, which avoids sexual consummation, and the defective— but still somewhat worthy—experience of those who cannot resist the demands of the black horse of desire. If, as the passage is too often read, this is taken to be an account of *all* erotic experience, then it would mean that Plato is having Socrates here issue a general condemnation of sexual consummation in love affairs, which would be strange indeed. But the passage is much more limited than that—limited, again, to a description of the efforts of a Zeus lover to resist the temptations of sexual desire in favor of philosophic friendship. One could hardly imagine, for example, that a follower in the train of Aphrodite would or could resist such temptations. Rather, the teaching here is the more limited one that, first, even Zeus lovers have their black horse of desire and *will be sorely tempted* by sexual desire; but also that, if one wants to have a philosophic friendship, it is probably best to resist this temptation. As the poignant description of a pair of Zeus lovers who do not quite succeed in resisting this temptation shows (256c–d), if one does enter into a philosophic relationship—a Zeus-love—and that relationship becomes sexual as well, its purely philosophic character is likely to be compromised. And is this not true?

Second, it is noteworthy that even in the midst of the description of a no less passionate affair (254b–c), we are reminded that the sight of the beautiful beloved serves to remind the lover of his "prior" experience of beauty itself when it stood with *sophrosyne* on a sacred pedestal. This is in a way a striking claim. Even in the very midst of the intensity of erotic passion, Socrates seems to be saying, there is some *intellectual* apprehension in play. Deeply immersed in our passion, we nevertheless *see* something—and what we see, what we recognize, is that the beauty of the beloved is a reminder of true beauty. Indeed, it is this very recognition that so inspires us. But this co-presence of sexual desire and intellectual insight reminds us of the double role or double challenge of the charioteer, our reason: on the one hand to *control* the black horse of sexual desire, and on the other hand to adequately *see* what is really at stake. Only if, once "reminded" of the true beauty it has seen, the charioteer succeeds in controlling the desires of the black horse, will the experience be transformed from the potentially vulgar one that every erotic experience risks to the virtuous living promised by Diotima and limned here in the tale of the successful charioteer.

Does this amount to the claim that, for Plato, the lover really just uses the beloved for his own intellectual ends? That for Plato love is in the end selfish and indeed exploitative of the beloved—a charge often enough leveled against him? Such a reading is, I think, unnecessary and even bizarre. In this entire passage there is not the slightest suggestion that, since the beauty of the beloved reminds the lover of beauty itself, this somehow *diminishes* or makes less genuine the lover's love of the beloved. Quite the contrary: it leads the lover to treat the beloved as well as possible, indeed, to do everything possible to lead the beloved into philosophy. Moreover—against yet another charge often leveled at Plato—the poignant description of the experience of the *beloved* as he too falls in love, testifies that this love is reciprocal. The two benefit *each other*.

Finally, toward the conclusion of the palinode, describing what will happen if the Zeus follower and the beloved are successful in resisting sexual temptation and achieving a philosophic friendship, Socrates says:

> If now the better elements of the mind (*dianoia*) prevail, which lead to a well-ordered life and to philosophy,[20] they live a life of blessedness and harmony here, self-controlled and orderly, holding in subjection that which causes evil in the soul, and freeing that which causes virtue. When they have accomplished this they are light and winged, for they have won one of the three truly Olympian contests. Neither human *sophrosyne* nor divine madness can confer upon a human being a greater good than this. (256b)

We now see that what has been developed in the palinode is an elaboration of the claim made but not defended by Diotima in the *Symposium*, that the experience of beauty itself could lead not merely to "knowledge of what beauty is" but to "true virtue." It can be accomplished, to be sure, but only with a struggle, the struggle to control the very human desires of the black horse, and the "true virtue" to which it will then lead is that of philosophic living. And this philosophic living, the story tells us, is inseparable from—one might even say impossible without—philosophic friendship. Moreover, and this is in a way the most stunning claim of the palinode, this philosophic living and this philosophic friendship are generated by, and so impossible without, the erotic experience of *beauty*. The experience of beauty then, at least for certain types of human beings, generates philosophy.

What, then, can be said about the treatment of beauty in this palinode? I am struck most of all by the decisive role of the non-discursive elements in the experience of beauty. It is almost as if the speech is a certain kind of loose proto-phenomenological account, the point of which is to bring us to "see," that is, to have the appropriate intuitional experience of beauty and its significance. We are thus as far as possible from the apparently naïve optimism of the *Hippias Major* (and for that matter the other "definitional" dialogues) that to understand something like beauty is a matter of discourse alone, that if only we can get an adequate *definition* of beauty we will have what we want, we will "know" beauty itself. Both the *Symposium* and the *Phaedrus* suggest, almost, that a category mistake is being made here. Beauty (as perhaps, or in all probability, the other "beings" as well) is simply not the sort of thing that is susceptible of complete discursive articulation. To *know* the "beings" is something very different from being able to *say* definitively what they are. Moreover, as we suggested earlier, this non-discursive moment bounds any discourse, any logos, on both sides. Our experience of beauty, first, is *originally* non-discursive: we *see* something beautiful, and if these two dialogues are right, this first beautiful object is usually or rather necessarily a beautiful person. This non-discursive experience, as both dialogues suggest, leads us to generate "beautiful *logoi*"—that is, it leads us to speak *in the light* of our non-discursive experience. And *this* discourse may lead us toward a certain culminating experience which is *also* non-discursive: the insight, as the *Symposium* has it, into "Beauty itself," or as the *Phaedrus* puts it, the recollection of our "earlier" non-discursive experience of beauty itself. But this in turn suggests, or reminds us, that Plato is not turning the experience of beauty into some sort of mystical experience, unless you think that every time you experience beauty you have a mystical experience. In the accounts of both dialogues (themselves discursive, let us not forget, in however complicated ways), logos is all over the place: the *kaloi logoi* of the *Symposium*'s ascent passage; the "understanding of what is said according to forms, drawn together by reasoning, into a unity out of a multiplicity of perceptions" at *Phaedrus* 249c; the logistic "love of divisions and collections," as it will presently be succinctly reformulated by Socrates (266b); and of course, the written (and dramatically spoken) discourse of the dialogues themselves. What, then, is the relationship between our speech, our discursive logos, and the non-discursive experiences that bound them? From the standpoint of a certain Hegelianism,[21] this speech would amount to a full and adequate articulation of our intuitive experiences, and so, finally, to a *replacement* of intuition by discursive speech. I do not think the dialogues are so optimistic. One might say, the Socrates of the "definitional" dialogues is pretending to be such an Hegelian—to reduce our knowledge of things to discourse. But the Socrates of the *Symposium* and *Phaedrus* is not so confident. The discursive speech that always occurs along with our non-discursive experiences will never *replace* that experience, but it nevertheless will occur—and I am forced to use a metaphor here—*in the light of* that non-discursive experience. Think of the famous "sun analogy" of the Good in the *Republic:* the gift of the sun is not to enable us to see the sun itself.[22] No, the gift of the sun is to enable us to see the things of our experience, of our world, literally this time *in the light* of the sun which itself is not directly "visible" on pain of blindness. Similarly here: our speech about beauty, or presumably about any of the "beings," will be enabled by, and so occur in the light of, our non-discursive experiences of beauty. It will not be a direct or comprehensive articulation of that experience, any more than we directly "see" the sun. But it is nevertheless the knowledge, the *human* (and therefore finite) knowledge that we have. Indeed, finitude seems almost the defining characteristic of our experience of knowing. Our logos, our discursive speech, is always finite, and it is bounded on both sides by non-discursive experiences that are each also, for varying reasons that we have seen, finite as well. We might say, then, that human thinking, mortal thinking, is the joining—or rather an attempted joining—of our interminable yet always partial fluctuation between a finite originating and a finite culminating *noesis* by a finite logos. In the words of Alcmaeon, "Humans die for this reason, that they cannot join together the beginning and the end." But again, this finite logos and finite *noesis* are what we have. They are virtually our only path to transcendence—a transcendence, it must be emphasized once more, not to god-like vision of pure form but to a higher *living*—a living in the light of human excellence, human virtue.

Socrates concludes his palinode with a prayer that is altogether consistent with his culminating section on the efforts of a Zeus lover and beloved to live a philosophical life. He prays that the "erotic *techne*" that he has been given by the god will be preserved; that he will be esteemed even more in future by those who are beautiful; and crucially, that Phaedrus will "cease being ambivalent, as he is now, but will dedicate his life entirely toward eros with philosophical discourses (*erota meta philosophon logon*)" (257b). As we shall see presently, this last petition, at least, will not be answered.

For a long time now, at least through the *Symposium* and *Phaedrus* and implicitly in the *Hippias Major* as well, a theme especially important for our topic has been quietly developed by Plato—one might say that he has been quietly putting it into play without making it a focal issue. The theme is played out as much in the drama of these dialogues as in their explicit "arguments," such as they are. This theme is the intimacy between the experience of beauty and the possibility of philosophy, or as I prefer, following the dialogues, of philosophical living. The theme has been insinuated right to the verge of explicitness: in the *Symposium,* when Diotima teaches that the "ascent" that might lead to philosophy is the ascent of a love of beauty that "must" begin with the love of a beautiful body, and whose culminating insight into "beauty itself" will result in "true virtue"; or in the *Phaedrus,* when the experience of falling in love with a beautiful beloved, if done in a certain way (the way of "Zeus") will lead to a philosophical life. To be sure, we are never told, nor is it even intimated, that the experience of beauty is the *only* way to originate philosophy—and I doubt very much that such a view could be sustained through all or most of the dialogues—but it surely seems to function as a paradigm. Nor, alas, does *every* erotic experience of beauty lead to philosophy. Nevertheless, I think it would be fair to say that the dialogues we are addressing quietly teach us that the erotic experience of beauty, *if experienced in a certain way,* is the paradigmatic experience that might originate philosophic living.

We have seen, however, that the experience of beauty is, this time in the literal sense, de-fined—bounded at its beginning and its end—by certain non-discursive elements. Non-discursive elements that, to be sure, give rise to what Diotima calls *kaloi logoi,* "beautiful discourses." The question then arises, is the same thing true of philosophy itself? Might philosophy arise out of such an experience of beauty? Is philosophy too bounded at its beginning and its end by certain non-discursive experiences that cannot be reduced to discursive speech even if they give rise to that speech? Philosophy, for the Greeks as much as for us, is nothing if not logos. To be sure. But is it *only logos*? Is philosophy *reducible to logos*? To put the question another way, is the irreducibly non-discursive or noetic element in the experience of beauty carried over to the possibility of philosophy?

The dialogues themselves seem to intimate—but only intimate—that the answer is affirmative. It is intimated, for example, in the many instances in the dialogues where Socrates affirms what too often has become a trivial cliché, that "philosophy is a way of life." Perhaps the most famous example is the *Apology*, which is a defense, after all, of Socrates' *life* as a philosopher—not a defense of this or that philosophical *position* that he thinks he can discursively articulate and prove. The most famous maxim of that dialogue, it should be noted, is not "the unexamined thesis is not worth defending," but "the unexamined *life* is not worth *living*." And life, I think we can all agree, is not reducible to discourse, though discourse is surely a decisive element—Aristotle will teach us it is the defining element—in human living.

Strangely enough, it is not in the dialogues, then, that the non-discursive element in philosophic living is made explicit and thematized as such, but in certain other of Plato's texts—his Letters, in particular his Second and Seventh Letters. This non-discursive element of philosophic living is elicited, appropriately enough, within a discussion of the problematic character of *philosophic writing*. In order to pursue the question of the non-discursive element in philosophy, then, we shall turn in the next chapter to the Letters and take up the issue within its own explicit context, that of the question of philosophic writing. That, in turn, will return us in the last chapter to Plato's most well-known critique of philosophic writing, and so to the conclusion of the *Phaedrus*.

FOUR

The Second and Seventh Letters

I addressed in the introduction what many regard as the most vexing question regarding the Letters, the question of their authenticity. The gist of my position is that the issue, quite especially for us in this time of the "decentering" of authorial authority, is less whether the Letters were really written by the one man, Plato, than whether they shed light on the issue at hand—in this case, the question of the non-discursive element in philosophic living and with it the question of the efficacy of philosophic writing. The powerful consistency of what will be said in the Letters with the views I have elicited from the dialogues might well be taken as circumstantial evidence for their authenticity, and informally I would argue for that position. But that is not the point of the present study.

If it is true of the Platonic dialogues that the statements of this or that participant must be interpreted in the light of their context—of the characters who are speaking together, of the existential situation in which and out of which they are speaking—surely that is at least as true of the Letters. For an initial drama of the Letters—and we should at least consider whether this drama might not have been intended by Plato—is that we, the readers, are not the ones for whom they were apparently intended. We are interlopers, perhaps thieves, stealing the letters from their rightful recipients. Indeed, in the case of the Second Letter, to which we shall turn first, the putative recipient is told to read the letter several times and then burn it (314c)! Even if the intended recipient, the Syracusan tyrant, Dionysus, was in fact sent the letter (or did Plato intend it for a different audience?), and even if he received it, he did not obey its commands. So we, today, can read it. One way or the other, then, we are in the situation of at least reading over the shoulder of its intended recipient.[1]

The Second Letter is written to Dionysus, the Seventh to friends of Dion. The general context is sufficiently well known. Plato, at the urging of his Syracusan friend Dion, makes several trips to Sicily in what proves to be the vain hope of educating a still youthful tyrant to be a just ruler. The tyrant, Dionysus, does not respond as Plato hopes. Most alarmingly, perhaps, Dionysus has apparently written and spoken of knowing Plato's "teaching"—indeed, to claim it for himself and to spread it abroad. Plato writes both letters, then, the Second to Dionysus himself, the Seventh to Dion's friends, trying to clear up the misunderstandings apparently perpetuated by Dionysus. The psychological, emotional, and political complexity of this situation reminds us of an important lesson gleaned from the same sorts of complexity as they are portrayed in the dialogues: if there is Platonic irony—if, to put it in its broadest formulation, things are not always as they seem and what is said is not necessarily simply what is to be believed—if that is true of the dialogues, then surely it is at least as true of the Letters. And if, in addition, the Letters were originally intended for a broader audience than the named recipients, then interpretive caution is even more appropriate. Still, the drama of the Second Letter, its dramatic situation, is that it is a somewhat scolding letter to Dionysus. Let us turn to it with a particular eye to what it might suggest about Platonic philosophy, Platonic writing, and their relation to Socrates.

The Second Letter seems in many ways more odd than the Seventh. In the opening passages, Plato seems deeply concerned with the danger to his reputation that might accrue from his by then well-known association with the young tyrant, a relationship of philosophy and political power, he notes, that is repeated again and again in history and in literature. He emphasizes, for example, the importance of Dionysus taking the lead in the conduct of their relationship, lest it appear that Plato is playing the sycophant. At the same time, he encourages the young tyrant in his apparent procedure of talking with other philosophers; Plato seems satisfied with the prospect of Dionysus considering other philosophic teachings, comparing them with Plato's and making his decision.

But then things turn more strange, and it is in the subsequent passages that the impression is given that Plato has a particular teaching, a teaching that he for some reason wants to keep secret. So concerned is he with the importance of secrecy that he now, in apparent response to some questions that Dionysus has, speaks in riddles. Plato writes as follows:

> For according to his (Archedemus's) report, you say that you have not had a sufficient demonstration of the nature of the first (*tou protou*). I must speak of this matter to you in enigmas (*di ainigmon*) in order that if anything should happen to these tablets "in the recesses of the sea or land," whoever reads them may not

understand our meaning. It is like this: related to the king of all are all things, and they are for his sake, and he is the cause of all beautiful things (*hapanton ton kalon*). And related to the second are the second things, and related to the third the third. About these, then, the human soul strives to learn, looking to the things that are akin to itself, though none of them is adequate. But as to the king and the objects I have mentioned, they are not of this sort. The soul then asks, "but of what sort are they?" This is the question, O son of Dionysus and Doris, that causes all the trouble, or rather, this it is that creates such travail in the soul, from which, unless he delivers himself from it, he will never really attain the truth. (312d–313a)

One is tempted, of course, to turn immediately to the question of the meaning of the enigma. Is "the first" the Good, "the second" the Ideas, "the third" phenomena? Or some other possible triad derived from somewhere in the dialogues? And what is the connection of these three to the *fivefold* that plays so prominent a part in the philosophic discussion of the Seventh Letter to which we shall presently turn? But for our purposes, I want to turn to what I take to be a prior question: the set of assumptions underlying the very presenting of this enigma. For it might seem to suggest, first, that there *is* a certain teaching that is at stake here, about which Dionysus has questions. Let us suppose, plausibly but not certainly, that the "teaching" in question is one that Plato has been presenting to Dionysus. But "Plato" presents many, many teachings in the dialogues, and not all of them, certainly, are ones that he would espouse. Is the teaching in question here, then, a teaching that is Plato's own? If it is (and I think that is a real question, given the recipient), then a second question arises: why would Plato have a teaching that he feels the need to keep secret—a secret teaching, as the esotericists say? To anticipate briefly, this is a very different situation from the one to be presented in the Seventh Letter, where the highest truths of philosophy also cannot be put into words—not in the sense that they *can* be put into words but are not for the many to hear, but in the sense that they *cannot* be put into words at all. Here in the Second Letter, one possible implication is that the teaching in question can indeed be put into words, but is not for everyone's ears: a teaching to be remembered, but not to be written down (at least not explicitly) lest it be available to the wrong people; a teaching, it should be noted, that Dionysus has forgotten.

Why must it be described in enigmas? Is it a politically explosive teaching? One that might get Plato into political or religious difficulty? That is not the explanation that Plato subsequently gives. Instead, he suggests, the reason for the caution has to do with the easily misunderstood simplicity of the teaching.

> Beware, however, lest these be disclosed to the uneducated. Nothing, I believe, could be more laughable to the many than these sayings, or on the other hand more wonderful and inspiring to those of good natures. For it is through being repeated and listened to frequently for many years that these sayings are refined at length, like gold, with prolonged labor. But listen to the most remarkable result of all. Quite a number of men there are who have listened to these, men capable of learning and

capable also of holding them in mind and judging them by all sorts of tests, who have been hearers of mine for no less than thirty years and are now quite old; these men now declare that the opinions (*doxanta*) that they once held to be most incredible appear to them now the most credible, and what they held the most credible now appears the opposite. (314a–b)

One is reminded here of Heidegger's phrase from *Aus der Erfahrung des Denkens:* "the splendor of the simple."[2] It is not, presumably, that the teaching in question is political dynamite, nor that it is religiously suspect, nor even that in any normal sense it is "elitist." Rather, the "sayings" (*legomena*) are so deceptively simple that they will appear laughable to those unwilling to spend years meditating on their depth. We begin to move closer to the spirit of the Seventh Letter, to the notion that the highest insights of philosophy "cannot be put into words like other subjects." Here the suggestion is that when they are put into words, they will inevitably appear more simple, indeed, more "laughable" (*katagelastotera*) than they are. It is not, then, a potentially volatile "secret teaching" that Plato is concerned not to divulge. To the contrary, it is something that ordinary hearers, thoughtless hearers, perhaps in the end hearers such as Dionysus, will think that they understand all too well—something simplistic, something that one can easily pass by. Perhaps it would be something like Heraclitus' *hen panta* or Parmenides' *estin.*

This prepares us to turn to what, for our purposes, is the decisive passage of the Second Letter: the passage where Plato makes the stunning and puzzling remark concerning his own writing.

> The greatest safeguard is not to write but to learn by heart; for it is not possible that what is written down should not be disclosed. For this reason I myself have never written anything concerning these things, and there is not and will not be any written work of Plato's. Those that are now called so are of a Socrates become beautiful and young (*ta de nun legomena Sokratous esti kalou kai neou gegonotos*). Farewell and believe; and now read this letter once and many times, and burn it. (314c)

The initial shock of this claim, that Plato has never written his philosophy, has been sufficient proof to many that the letter is inauthentic. Thirty-some dialogues, and Plato has not written his philosophy? Did he indeed have a "secret teaching," his real "philosophy," that he excluded from his writings and divulged only orally to select members of his Academy—and perhaps, but just perhaps, to Dionysus? But why then would a serious person spend what must have been a good part of his life writing this enormous body of work, if none of it contains his true teaching?

But if, as I suggested earlier, the issue is not that of a secret teaching but rather of one—as the Seventh Letter will soon suggest—that "cannot be put into words like other subjects," then this still stunning remark begins to make more sense. Then it is not that Plato *withheld* his true teaching from the dialogues, but rather that *no* writing can adequately express the deepest truths of philosophy. We still do not know what this claim would mean in depth, and we must presently turn to the Seventh Letter to reflect on it more deeply. But we now know that it at least means something like this: Plato has not written "on these things" (*peri touton*), because any attempt to do so would only appear laughably simplistic.

But Plato here does not leave it at this simple denial. In a striking way, he *does* tell us what he has written about: the writings that are called his—and this can only be the dialogues—are those of a Socrates "become beautiful and young." So Plato, by his own apparent admission, has written a "Socratic memorabilia" of sorts. But if so it is a strange memorabilia indeed, for it makes no pretense, as memorabilia usually do, of historical accuracy. Plato's is a "memory" of a Socrates transformed, become (*gegonotos*) other than he is—and become so not, in the way of all memory, in a manner beyond the intention of a finite memory (given the softenings and exaggerations of nostalgia) but *transformed* by Plato according, presumably, to a set of intentions of his own. This raises two questions immediately: first, in what way is Socrates transformed in Plato's "memorabilia"? And second, for what purpose the transformation? Only the first is answered in the Letter with any explicitness, and that, as we shall see, ambiguously. Let us turn to this question.

In my quotation from the Second Letter, I employed a fairly standard translation: Socrates, in what are called Plato's writing, has become "beautiful" (*kalou*) and "young" (*neou*). If we stay with this translation for the moment, there is considerable irony. For in only one Platonic dialogue is Socrates explicitly portrayed as "young": in the *Parmenides,* Socrates is portrayed as quite a young man talking to a very old Parmenides. Though young, Socrates is not too young to have a remarkable set of philosophic notions which he calls first "forms" (*eide*), and later in the dialogue, "ideas" (*ideai*), and which the aged Parmenides proceeds to criticize. However, even this portrayal is complicated. For in the *Parmenides,* Socrates is not portrayed *directly* as young, portrayed, that is, by Plato the writer as in the immediacy of his youth. Instead, the dialogue is one of a number of Platonic dialogues that are "second hand": told much later than the event portrayed, by one who is in a position to know. In the case of the *Parmenides,* the interlocutor is hardly dependable. It is a man named Antiphon, who was present at the meeting when he was young and apparently cared enough and took the time to learn to recite the account from memory (*Parmenides* 126c). (And the *Parmenides* is a complicated account indeed!) We marvel at the capacity of the young Antiphon, who could memorize one of the most conceptually complicated exchanges in all literature. But any confidence we might initially summon up is immediately shattered by what we learn next about this Antiphon: now, as an adult, Antiphon "devotes most of his time to horses" (126c). How dependable, then, is the memory of a man such as this to be? Why else would Plato write such a description of the narrator into a dialogue, than to agitate our confidence in his memory? So this memory of a Socrates made young is in fact a double memory: the memory of Plato, admittedly a transformed one, mediated by the fictional memory of a man whose chief passion in life is horses. Nothing, I daresay, about this portrayal of a youthful Socrates in the *Parmenides* can give us confidence as to its historical accuracy.

The secondhand character of the memory of a Socrates made young in the *Parmenides* reminds us of one other memory of a young Socrates portrayed in the dialogues, in Plato's own memorial of Socrates. In this case, the interlocutor's memory inspires considerably more confidence: for the recollector is Socrates himself. As we have seen, in the *Symposium*, Socrates is portrayed as recalling his own instruction in eros as a young man by Diotima, the Mantinean priestess. Now Socrates, at least as remembered by Plato in the dialogues, has a prodigious memory, though he regularly apologizes for having a bad one. He apparently remembers, for example, all ten books of the *Republic*, and even if he only needs to remember the story for a day (the dialogue, recall, begins, "I went down yesterday to the Piraeus"), such a memory—such a *claim* to memory—is remarkable indeed. (Nothing in the dialogue, of course, gives us a standard to measure the accuracy of Socrates' memory. The *Republic* is, again, a *claim* to remembering: it is entirely compatible with the possibility that Socrates' regular self-assessment of having a bad memory is itself an accurate memory of his own memory!)

But does Socrates in his account in the *Symposium* actually *remember* Diotima and her teaching? Nothing in or out of the dialogue suggests that he does, and there is much to suggest that he does not. There is not a shred of evidence outside this dialogue of an historical figure, Diotima—and this from an author, Plato, who almost always employs historical personages as his characters. Moreover, recall that Diotima's teaching contains many references to things said by the previous speakers at the very party where Socrates tells the story that, if it really were an accurate memory by Socrates, the way in which Diotima, years ago when Socrates was young, prefigured the very teachings of the present speakers would be uncanny. When we add to this that Socrates is given to supporting his regular claim to have nothing positive to offer himself by attributing to others all the positive teachings he does present—others whose names he more often than not forgets—all this points to a conclusion more plausible than that Socrates remembers an historical Diotima: Socrates invents Diotima for his purposes at the party. Diotima is indeed "become new" (*neos*) in the speech of Socrates. Socrates' own remembrance of his youth in this dialogue is hardly dependable. And that dubious dependability is made even more unstable by the dramatic frame of the *Symposium*. Like the *Parmenides*, this account too, we recall, is a secondhand, or rather a thirdhand account. Aristodemus was present at the party and recounts it to Apollodorus who—after telling it to a certain Glaucon—finally relates the story to us, the readers for whom Plato writes.

One conclusion at least must be drawn from these two accounts of a Socrates "become young," a conclusion that I think could be generalized in the dialogues: when Plato raises the issue of memory in the dialogues, he almost always raises it *as problematized*. If we listen to the Second Letter, *every* dialogue exhibits a problematized memory—the memory of a Socrates self-consciously transformed by Plato. And within the dialogues, the problematization of memory is regularly deepened. In a culture still much more oriented toward an oral tradition—and so toward the importance of memory—than our own, Plato seems to teach already and always that memory is a *problem*. Including his own memory. Whatever memory is, it is not historically accurate. One might risk a generalization: the presence of memory in thinking is inherently destabilizing; it introduces an always problematic element into any thinking in which it inheres, which is to say, almost all thinking. We saw this dramatically at the beginning of the *Phaedrus*, for example, where Socrates found Phaedrus's memory of Lysias's speech notably undependable compared to its written version. And in the palinode, the problematic of memory became philosophically thematic, this time in terms of the question of recollection and the way in which the sight of mortal beauty "reminds" us of beauty itself. We shall have occasion to return to this when we turn to Socrates' critique of writing in the next chapter: the question of memory will be at the heart of the problematic of writing.

But as we have seen, Socrates is only rarely portrayed in the dialogues (however problematically) as young. In most dialogues he is much older and remarkably, in at least eight—that is, about a quarter of the dialogues—he is portrayed in his early seventies, within weeks of his death.[3] It would have been considerably less ironic and more straightforward if Plato had said that his was the tale of a Socrates "become old."

However, by most standards and especially by ancient Greek ones, Socrates is *never* portrayed as "beautiful" (*kalos*)—the second transformative quality of Socrates in the Platonic dialogues. Here too, on the standard translation, the irony is deep. Socrates become beautiful? Socrates, and this in a culture virtually obsessed with beauty, was notoriously ugly. His squat physique, bulgy eyes, and snub nose are probably the most recognized personal description of anyone in the history of philosophy. If one is to take seriously the notion that in the dialogues Socrates is "become beautiful," one can only wonder at what the historical figure must have looked like! But of course, we can plausibly interpret the "beauty" of Socrates as an inner, not a bodily beauty. As in Alcibiades' speech in the *Symposium*, where we recall that he proposes that Socrates is like the Silenus figures in Athens: ugly on the outside but with images of gods within. Indeed, from the *Symposium* to the *Lysis* to the *Theaetetus* to the closing lines of the *Phaedo* where he dies, Socrates is portrayed, often explicitly, as beautiful within.[4]

But if he has *become* beautiful in the dialogues, and that is taken to mean that he has been transformed with an *inner* beauty, what does that imply? Was

Socrates in the flesh perhaps not so beautiful of soul either? Is, then, the Socrates of the dialogues given an inner beauty that the historical Socrates did not have? One might support that supposition, cautiously, with a look at Xenophon's portrayal of Socrates, where most scholars have noted a much more pedestrian, doctrinaire Socrates than that of the Platonic dialogues. Not to mention the portrayal of Socrates in Aristophanes' *Clouds*, where he is portrayed as at least as ugly of soul as of body. If we accept, with all due caution, the implicit suggestion of the Second Letter that the Socrates of the Platonic dialogues is *become beautiful* of soul, the first question is: why would Plato do so? For one clear implication of this admission is that Plato is not so much *recording* the life and character of Socrates as *employing* (not to say *exploiting*) Socrates for his own philosophic ends. So once more, we must ask: what Platonic ends might be served by transforming Socrates into a man with such inner beauty as he exhibits in the dialogues but apparently or at least possibly not in person?

Before turning to this question we must note at least in passing a necessary qualification on the "inner beauty" of even the Platonic Socrates. While the dialogues I have mentioned do indeed portray him with a certain inner beauty, in other dialogues the quality of Socrates' soul is much more problematic. One can hardly imagine Thrasymachus, Protagoras, or Critias (among others) sharing the conviction that Socrates is a thinker of inner beauty. And we saw that even Alcibiades, who employs the Silenus image in his own very ambivalent praise of Socrates, goes on to characterize him as holding the humans he claims to love in contempt, and "playing" and "ironizing" with them all his life (*Symposium* 216e). Just as the ascription of youth to the Platonic Socrates had about it a certain irony, so with the notion of a Socrates endowed with inner beauty: the ascription is at least complicated, if not ironic. Nevertheless, even with this qualification, there is a certain inner beauty exhibited at least sometimes by the Socrates of the dialogues, and if that beauty is to an extent constructed by Plato, we still have to ask why.

He may have done it in part to present a certain idealized image of philosophy and the philosopher to a culture which, as the fate of the historical Socrates attests, was by no means fully persuaded of the beauty of philosophy. As I have argued elsewhere, part of Plato's intention in writing the dialogues he did was to preserve the very possibility of philosophy in a culture where philosophy was regarded by the spokesmen for political orthodoxy as at least as dangerous as it was attractive.[5] The fate of the historical Socrates in this regard must have been for Plato only the most recent and most poignant episode in a short but violent history of philosophers in ancient Greece, many of whom before Socrates were ostracized or worse. Plato had good reason to feel the need to *save philosophy* from the constraints of political orthodoxy—to argue that it was more a boon than a danger to the city—and to do so, he might well have presented an idealized, a "more beautiful" Socrates to the world.

But he also might have done so, in these always complicated dialogues, to raise the *question* of beauty: of inner and outer beauty, of the potential (but not always actual) beauty of philosophy, and of beauty itself. Perhaps the beauty of the Platonic dialogues and of the Socrates portrayed therein are intended as a replacement for the not-so-beautiful reality of the historical Socrates and of philosophy as it was experienced by the Greeks. Perhaps the transformed beauty of Socrates is but a piece of the transformed beauty of philosophy in the Platonic dialogues. Perhaps, just perhaps, the more "objective" memory of the historical Socrates would not have served to save philosophy, to preserve and encourage its very possibility. The dialogues would then be a portrayal not so much of how beautiful philosophy *is,* but instead how beautiful it *could be,* under certain circumstances. To make this plausible, one need only imagine the history of philosophy if Plato had followed his teacher and decided not to write, if all we had of the memory of Socrates were the writings of Xenophon and Aristophanes. Perhaps Plato had very good reasons to make Socrates "beautiful," to transform his memory.

But let us return to the crucial passage in the Second Letter on which we have been dwelling, for "young" and "beautiful" are not the only plausible translations of the Greeks words *neos kai kalos.* A Socrates "become young" could also be read as a Socrates "become new." On this reading it would be a *new* Socrates that we meet in the Platonic dialogues, one "new" presumably by virtue precisely of his *difference* from the historical Socrates known to the Greeks. We might say, of course, that *every* memory is "new" each time it is called forth: new insofar as it is a present memory, but new also insofar as it is a constructed memory. In this sense, no doubt, Xenophon's and Aristophanes' memories of Socrates are as "new" as Plato's. But the Second Letter suggests what is at least not admitted in the other two authors—that the newness of Socrates is a self-consciously constructed one, a matter of art, not the unconscious and inevitable workings of memory. Plato's reasons for presenting a new Socrates, his intentions in presenting this transformed Socrates, might be something like those I suggested a moment ago. The new Socrates of the dialogues might be necessary not to *present Plato's* philosophy—that is precisely what he denies he has done—but to preserve and encourage the very possibility of philosophy, then and now.

The case is similar with *kalos,* which typically means "beauty" but which can also take on the connotation of "nobility." Perhaps, then, the dialogues are a presentation of a Socrates become "*noble* and new." This would surely fit with the notion we discussed earlier, of an inner beauty in Socrates: inner beauty, and especially when applied to Greek males, often took on the sense of a certain nobility and dignity. Suppose, then, that the Socrates of the dialogues is one "become noble." If so, we certainly avoid the irony of the ascription of beauty to Socrates, but still, the same sorts of questions must be asked. What does it mean, after all, that Plato should write of a Socrates *become* noble? Again, it would seem to imply that the historical Socrates somehow lacked the noble quality that the Platonic Socrates sometimes (again not always) exhibits. And we could again cite Xenophon and especially Aristophanes for our initial evidence that not everyone found in the historical Socrates the undeniable nobility generally exhibited by the Platonic Socrates. Once again, I suggest, the reasons for Plato's doing so might be similar. In portraying a noble Socrates, at least a more noble Socrates, Plato raises for us the *question*—and we must not forget that it is indeed a question—of a possible nobility to philosophy and to a philosopher, of a noble philosophy that *might be,* could we even say, the nobility of a philosophy to come? In this sense, Plato might be not so much remembering Socrates as recollecting him, in the quasi-technical sense that that term is occasionally given within the dialogues, recollecting, that is, a Socrates that might function as a paradigm for the possibility of philosophy.

We can turn now to the Seventh Letter. If my suggestions regarding the Second Letter have any force, then there is less tension than is often supposed between the so-called "secret teaching" thesis of the Second Letter and the more elaborate and philosophically challenging claims about the limits of philosophic language in the Seventh. Before we turn to the section of the Seventh Letter which addresses the whole question of philosophic language and writing, we must again briefly remind ourselves of the Letter's dramatic context.

The Seventh Letter is addressed as follows: "Plato to the associates and comrades (*oikeiois te kai hetairois*) of Dion, fare well." R. G. Bury, however, in the introductory remarks to his Loeb edition, argues that although the Letter is in his view almost certainly genuine, it was probably intended not actually for the specific addressees, but as something like an "open" letter.[6] He observes that such a literary genre—a letter apparently addressed to individuals but in reality intended for a broad audience—was already a common one. Moreover, he adduces specific and at least plausible reasons why the conditions at the time of the Seventh Letter (353 BC) make it unlikely that it was really intended for these people: the long descriptions Plato gives of the situation in Sicily would hardly have been necessary for these addressees; the regnant Syracusan tyrant, Callippus (who had murdered Dion), would never have allowed the letter to be delivered in any case; and the more plausible point of the letter is for Plato to defend himself against various rumors and accusations then abroad *in Athens.* In addition, this hypothesis of a larger intended audience would make more plausible the otherwise extremely puzzling and long "philosophic digression" that begins at 342, to which we shall turn presently. In a straightforwardly "political" letter, why would Plato take the time to expand so richly on his philosophic understanding of the relation between language and knowledge? All of this, then, serves to support what I suggested in the introduction: we must consider that the Letters may have been intended for a wider audience.

In any case, and consistent with Bury's hypothesis, the Seventh Letter begins with an autobiographical account of Plato's commitment to involvement in politics. Plato reports that from his youth—in part, one imagines, because of his distinguished family—he more or less assumed that he would enter politics

(324c). This differs from another account of Plato's youth that makes him an aspiring poet who was turned from poetry by his encounter with Socrates. Though some, such as Edelstein,[7] take this difference as a contradiction and therefore as evidence of the inauthenticity of the Letter, this is hardly so. In democratic Athens, it would have been entirely possible for Plato to aspire both to public life *and* to an artistic career. More important is the lesson that Plato quickly learned from his observations regarding political life. Noting first the high promise of what became the tyranny of the Thirty—which included members of his own family—Plato reports his disillusionment that those who had promised justice brought only injustice and chaos (324d). This leads him, interestingly—in light of the several apparent criticisms of democracy in the dialogues—to a qualified praise of the democracy. "But as I watched them (the Thirty) they showed in a short time that the preceding constitution (i.e., the democracy) had been golden" (324d). Moreover, when the democrats took back control a year later, "in general those who returned from exile acted with great restraint" (325b), despite the fact that it was the democracy that put Socrates to death. Nevertheless, the upshot of these experiences was to lead Plato to the conclusion that the only hope for political justice would be that "either those who are sincerely and truly lovers of wisdom come into political power, or the rulers of cities, by some divine destiny, become really philosophic" (326b). Edelstein and many others take this as a clear reference to the famous "third wave" of the *Republic,* where it is also claimed that a condition for perfect justice in a city is that philosophers become rulers or rulers become philosophers. From which, I hasten to add, it surely does not follow that the draconian measures suggested in the *Republic* should be taken as serious proposals by Plato—much less that he was actually trying to install those measures in Syracuse. All of us can surely wish for wiser, more philosophic political leaders without espousing the extraordinary suggestions of that dialogue as practical policies.

Notwithstanding his growing reservations regarding the political situation, as Plato goes on to relate at length, his deep friendship with Dion led him over time to at least make an effort, at Dion's request, to come to Syracuse and try to educate the young tyrant Dionysus, Dion's nephew. Plato suggests that it was largely out of this friendship that he agreed to the attempt, fearing that he would be unjust to his friend should he decline. These efforts led to the three notorious trips to Sicily that Plato describes, the upshot of which, and in part which he tries to explain, was utter failure.

I need not for our purposes repeat the long description Plato gives of his involvement with Dionysus, the various intrigues in which he became involved, indeed, the danger to his own life that he incurred, except to note some of the more striking lessons that Plato draws from his experience. First, in contrast to the surface teaching of the *Republic*—and more in keeping with the general spirit of the *Laws*—Plato comes to hold that the only possible justice will be the rule of good laws, not of men. It is instructive that Plato, in a striking prefiguration of Hegel, interprets this subservience to good laws as *freedom*. He says to the associates and comrades to whom the Letter is ostensibly addressed: "after having cleansed her (Syracuse) of her servitude (under the tyrant, Dionysus) and put on her the garment of freedom," Dion "would have made every effort to adorn her citizens with the best and most suitable laws" (336a). It is especially important, he goes on to add, that the *victorious party* be the ones to make these good laws, and to make them with no more attention to their own interests than to those of the weaker parties. In an instructive passage that presages a more democratic emphasis on the importance of political reconciliation, Plato argues that an endless cycle of violence and revenge will continue until

> the party that has gained the victory in these battles and in the exiling and slaughtering of fellow citizens forgets its wrongs and ceases trying to wreak vengeance upon its enemies. If it controls itself and enacts laws for the common good, considering its own interests no more than those of the vanquished, the defeated party will be doubly constrained, by respect and by fear, to follow the laws—by fear because the other party has demonstrated its superior force, and by respect because it has shown that it is able and willing to conquer its desires and serve the law instead. (336e–337a; Glenn R. Morrow's translation)

He concludes: "If the victors show themselves more eager than the vanquished to obey the laws, then everything will be safe, happiness will abound, and all these evils will take their flight" (337c). What is striking about this proposal is what we might call its practical wisdom. There is nothing here of the extremism of the recommendations in the *Republic,* not to say that it would be easy to find political victors willing to act in this way. A look at the contemporary political world, with all its crises, suggests that these words could be recommended to political leaders today as much as ever.

A second striking position taken by Plato in the letter is his strong stand against the feasibility of violent revolution. No recommendations here about establishing a regime by getting rid of everyone over ten years of age, or other such draconian and manifestly impossible measures. Instead:

> This is the principle which a wise man must follow in his relations towards his own city. Let him warn her, if he thinks her constitution is corrupt and there is a prospect that his words will be listened to and not put him in danger of his life; but let him not use violence upon his fatherland to bring about a change of constitution. If what he thinks is best can only be accomplished by the exile and slaughter of men, let him keep his peace and pray for the welfare of himself and his city. (331c–d; Glenn R. Morrow's translation)

The contrast between the prudence of these teachings, which borders on pacifism, and the far more extreme positions of the *Republic* have led some, including Edelstein, to see them as further evidence of the inauthenticity of the

Seventh Letter. But that is only plausible on the hypothesis—against which I and many others have argued for years—that Socrates' extraordinary proposals in the *Republic* are intended as serious, practical recommendations for political life. Only then is there a conflict between the positions. Far more plausible, I suggest, would be to consider the two contexts. The Letter is portrayed as a set of practical proposals to practical-minded people. The *Republic,* by contrast, presents a "city in speech" in which we are regularly reminded that whether or not such a city is possible is not the issue. The Seventh Letter, then, gives us a glimpse of a Plato practicing the *phronesis* of a politically astute philosophical consciousness.

One final observation will lead us toward the crucial comments about writing and the philosophic digression. By the time of his second visit to Syracuse, Plato has a considerable and well-founded skepticism regarding the sincerity of Dionysus's interest in pursuing a philosophical education. So, as he describes it, he devises a test of Dionysus's sincerity—a test, he says, particularly appropriate for tyrants (340b). To wit, he takes the opportunity to speak with the tyrant about the philosophic life, emphasizing the depth of the commitment necessary, its difficulty, how much labor is involved (340c). The point of this is that a truly philosophic consciousness will welcome such a challenge, whereas an unphilosophical one will be put off by the daunting life described.

Dionysus fails the test. He claims that he already has sufficient knowledge of the subjects, and indeed, Plato later learns that the young tyrant has written a book in which he claims to know the teachings of Plato and even claims them as his own (341b). It is at this point that Plato begins his famous denial of the possibility of writing one's philosophy, and to this passage we can now turn. This denial is in two parts, and each is worth quoting and commenting upon. It begins as follows:

> I know that certain others have written on these same matters, but who they are, they themselves do not know. But this much I can certainly say about those who have written or who will write claiming knowledge about the subjects about which I am serious, whether they have heard it from me or from others or from their own discoveries; it is impossible, in my opinion, that they have learned anything at all about the subject. There does not exist, nor will there ever, any written work of my own on these things. For it cannot at all be put into words like other objects of learning, but only after a long period of dwelling together concerning the subject itself and living together with it, when, suddenly, like a light kindled by a leaping spark, it comes to be in the soul and at once becomes self-nourishing. (341b–c)

We note, first, Plato's chastisement of those, apparently like Dionysus, who claim to have written about Plato's philosophy or about philosophy itself for that matter. Within this passage there is again, as with the Second Letter, the explicit denial that Plato has written or will ever write his philosophy. In this case, however, there is not even a hint of a "secret teaching" that needs to be kept from anyone, whether because of danger to the speaker or to the hearer. This time—more explicitly than in the Second Letter but commensurate with the reading I have given of it—the impossibility of writing philosophy is a function of the nature of philosophy itself.

How could it be that philosophy "cannot be put into words like other objects of learning": *reton gar oudamos estin hos alla mathemata*? Surely if philosophy, if Plato's philosophy, were a set of doctrines—what we have come to call in our day "philosophical positions"—then it could be put into words just as mathematical, historical, or literary theories can be put into words. If Plato's philosophy were something like a "theory of Forms," a "metaphysics," or a particular moral, political, or aesthetic theory then it could be put into words. Indeed, such theories have been put into so many words so many times that it is now impossible for a person to read them all! At very least then, the first implication of this remarkable statement in the Seventh Letter is that Plato emphatically did *not* think of his philosophy as that set of formulated doctrines we call "Platonism." And it must be emphasized: this is not because no one has succeeded in stating them *properly* yet. No, it is rather because—in Plato's utterly plain language here—they cannot be put into words like other objects of learning. What can this mean?

This time, Plato gives us a crucial clue. Whatever the insights of philosophy are, they are garnered only after a long and sustained period of dwelling together with the matter. As we might say, somehow, the insights of philosophy must "grow" on one through long study. Plato uses two words in this sentence that strongly suggest that this process is dialogical or at least that it is between two people: *all' ek polles sunousias gignomenes peri to pragma auto kai tou suzen,* which I translate above as "a long period of dwelling together with the subject itself and of living together with it." The *sunousias* and *suzen* suggest so strongly the quality of doing something "together" that many translators simply render this as something like "after long-continued intercourse between teacher and pupil, in joint pursuit of the subject."[8] This is certainly plausible and perhaps the most plausible reading, especially given the context in which it is introduced—Plato's account of his failed instruction of Dionysus—though it must be said that the grammar does not strictly demand that the togetherness be of two people rather than the togetherness of the individual and the matter for thought. Nevertheless, both the immediate context and the spirit of the dialogues themselves lead us to the reading that Plato assumes that philosophy is something that must be *lived together,* and I join in accepting that reading.[9] At the same time—and this is what I tried to capture in my translation—there is sufficient ambiguity in the grammar of the sentence to suggest something like this: philosophy (at least Platonic philosophy) somehow requires a living together of thinkers with the matter for thought over a sustained period of time; a living together that, one way or another (whether of teacher and student or fellow-thinkers together) will be dialogical. Nevertheless, the ultimate "togetherness" implied is less the togetherness of two individuals than the togetherness of each *with the matter for thought.* This in turn implies a certain fading away, in the very dialogical encounter, of the "subjectivities" that dwell together with the matter for thought. That is, though a dialogical encounter between two or more individuals might be—and presumably will be—the *occasion* for the dwelling together of each with the matter for thought, it is the latter, the encounter with the matter for thought, that is at stake: this is the *telos* of the encounter. This issue, of the diminishing of the significance of subjectivities in the name of philosophy, in the very presence of one astonishingly dominant—not to say domineering—personality, that of the Platonic Socrates, will become an important theme for us as we eventually return to the *Phaedrus,* to the question of writing and of philosophical language itself. But not quite yet. Let us return to the passage from the Seventh Letter.

Plato's "philosophy," as it were, cannot be a set of doctrines and certainly not a "secret" doctrine. Whatever it is, it must be *lived,* and moreover, *lived together* (with the appropriate ambiguity inherent, as we have seen, in that phrase). We have to try to make sense of the profundity of this notion, so often reduced to the cliché that for Socrates and Plato "philosophy is a way of life." The Seventh Letter suggests that yes, philosophy *is* a way of life, but the question is: what does this mean? We take a small but important step in recognizing that it means that philosophy is *not* for these two thinkers a set of doctrines they espouse, Platonism notwithstanding. But we need to think in a more sustained way about this remarkable idea.

We get a clue, perhaps, from an aphorism of Heraclitus, one whose spirit seems to inform the Platonic dialogues. Fragment 112 reads: "*Sophrosyne* is the greatest virtue, and wisdom is speaking and acting the truth, paying heed to the nature of things": *Sophronein arete megiste, kai sophie alethea legein kai poiein kata physin epaiontas.* Let us dwell on this provocative saying for a while. We note, first, that Heraclitus joins together what Aristotle will later call a "practical" or "moral" virtue, *sophrosyne,* with the "intellectual" virtue of *sophia,* while indicating a certain hierarchy: *sophrosyne* is *the greatest* virtue—greater, by clear implication, than wisdom, if indeed Heraclitus was already thinking of wisdom as a "virtue." Even without looking ahead to Aristotle's division of virtues into intellectual and moral virtues, however, we note that *sophrosyne* is surely a virtue that has to do with *living* a certain way. The particular way of living that constitutes being *sophron,* of course, is given the most careful examination by Plato in his *Charmides.* There, it should be noted, all but one of the understandings of this virtue clearly indicate not just an articulated position but a way of living, whether it is "a kind of quietness," "modesty," "minding one's own business," or the Socratic version of self-knowledge. The one exception—and one that clearly fails—is Critias' attempt to turn *sophrosyne* into something that falls under the heading of what Aristotle will call "theoretical": "the *science* (*episteme*) of itself and of the other sciences and of the absence of science" (*Charmides* 166d ff.). The clear implication, then, both of Heraclitus's sentence and of Plato's dialogue, is that *sophrosyne*, this greatest of virtues, is a way of living.

But so is *sophia*, if we listen to Heraclitus! For wisdom, the sentence ends, is "speaking *and acting* the truth, paying heed to the nature of things." If Heraclitus had simply said, "wisdom is speaking the truth," it would have been instructive but not especially striking. What makes the sentence so striking is the assertion that wisdom, not in its obviously pragmatic (in the Greek sense) form of *phronesis* but wisdom precisely as *sophia*, is in part *acting* in a certain way. Indeed, not "in part" but entirely, since speaking is itself a mode of acting and living. As is his way, Heraclitus does not proceed to give us the recipe for this "wise speaking and acting" of the truth. But he says enough to establish for us, and apparently to establish for Plato, that wisdom, along with *sophrosyne*, is somehow a certain way of living, a certain dwelling-with, a dwelling-with *aletheia*. Perhaps, then, the dialogues are not, as he insists they are not, "Plato's philosophy," but rather an exhibition of that dwelling-with unhiddenness, sustained over a lifetime, that might be philosophy.

But in Plato's brief account in the Seventh Letter, philosophy is not only a sustained dwelling-with. That dwelling-with *leads* to something, leads to a certain "sudden" experience of a different sort. For presumably, the sustained dialogical dwelling-with is one of logos. Yet what this dialogical logos leads to Plato captures with his captivating Heraclitean metaphor of the flame: "suddenly, like a light kindled by a leaping spark, it comes to be in the soul and at once becomes self-nourishing." This is the description of the happening of philosophy in the soul after long preparation. Its "sudden" (*exaiphnes*) character recalls the use of the same word to characterize the culmination of a similarly long "dwelling together" described by Socrates' Diotima in the *Symposium*. This dwelling together, she says, must begin when one is young and be gradually led with the help of "beautiful *logoi*" through a progression of experiences and recognitions of beautiful objects until, at long last, but "suddenly," the aspirant gains an insight, literally a revelation, into "Beauty itself." And recall, Diotima explicitly describes this insight as *oude tis logos, oude tis episteme*: "neither some discursive account nor some demonstrable knowledge."

In the Seventh Letter, Plato offers two reasons why his understanding of philosophy cannot be written. First, because it is not a doctrine but a sustained *experience:* one of dwelling-with the matter for thought over a long period. To be sure, we may expect that this experience in question will be one imbued with logos; but just as surely the experience, as experience, cannot be *reduced* to the speech uttered in its light. Second, the culmination of this dwelling-with is itself a non-discursive experience: an instantaneous, noetic *happening* in which the philosophic spirit is born in the soul and becomes self-nourishing. It needs to be emphasized: it is *philosophy itself* that is born in this culminating noetic experience, not one particular philosophical insight or another. The consistency of this with the standpoints articulated in the three dialogues we have addressed is remarkable.

Plato finishes his statement about why he has not written his philosophy:

> And I know this, that writing or speaking about this would best be said by me. Moreover, if they are written badly, I would be not least pained. And if I thought that such things could be put in writing or speech adequately for the many, what nobler action could I have done in my life than that of writing what is of great benefit to mankind, and bringing to light the nature of things for all? But were I to try this it would not, I believe, be a good for mankind, except for some few who are able to discover the truth with a little instruction. As for the rest, some it would fill with a mistaken and unbecoming contempt, others with an exaggerated and foolish hope, as if they had learned something grand. (341d–e)

Plato offers what we can surmise is a justifiable confidence that were this lifelong dwelling together to be articulable in writing, he is the one who could best articulate it; and moreover, that were it done badly (recall Dionysus's fraudulent book), he would be most pained. And he adds: who would not desire, if it were possible, to benefit mankind by bringing the nature of things to light for all? (This suggests, incidentally, that universal enlightenment would be a worthy but impossible goal.) But, he concludes, if anyone did try to write the results of this lifetime of dwelling-with the experience of philosophy, its articulated version could only be damaging. One plausible way in which it could be misleading and falsely uplifting, commensurate with my reading of the Second Letter, is that it would give the impression—apparently an impression shared by Dionysus— that the results of this lifelong commitment are simple and easily understood "doctrines."

Once again, this leads us to a conclusion and raises a question. Whatever Plato's written dialogues are, they are *not* his "philosophy." But if so, what is it that the dialogues are trying to accomplish? If what is at stake with philosophy is the long *experience* of dwelling-with and the noetic, non-linguistic culmination of that dwelling, what might a writing *in the light of this* accomplish? Socrates, choosing not to write, might encourage this dwelling-with among those fortunate enough (if that is the right word) to spend the requisite time with him, as the young Plato apparently did. Plato, had he not written, might have encouraged the experience with those in the Academy with whom he engaged, and with others—Dionysus for example—whom he tried to encounter in a sustained way. But Plato failed with Dionysus; and the Platonic Socrates, truth to tell, more often than not fails with those whom he engages. Plato's admitted failure with Dionysus, and the regularly portrayed failure of Socrates to do so in the dialogues (one thinks of his attempted engagements with Charmides, Critias, Alcibiades, Euthyphro, and quite especially Hippias and Phaedrus) testify to the difficulty of even such a personal, sustained dwelling-with. If even the lived experience is so precarious, so likely to fail, what can the writing of it do? On the other hand, is there no writing that might at least try to *imitate* and at the same time *invite* such a dwelling? That, I suggest, is what the dialogues are an effort to do. There is no incompatibility, then, nor even a tension between the dialogues that are Plato's and his denials in the Second and Seventh Letters that he has written his philosophy. The dialogues *are not* Plato's philosophy. Their purpose is altogether different: to limn the possibility of philosophy, to limn it through mimetic portrayal, to limn and invite the possibility of that life of dwelling-with and its culminating experiences. To that end, Plato wrote.

What, then, are we to take from Plato's dialogues, if not his philosophy? If we are not to read them by taking the adequacy of their philosophic arguments or positions as our measure—as we do with works by writers with very different conceptions of philosophy—what measure are we to employ? If, as I suggest, they are written as mimetic invitations to philosophy—efforts to start us on that longer road, the dwelling-with over years that culminates in the inspiration to philosophic living—then the proper measure of their success may be just that. Do they invite us, encourage us, seduce us, into that life and that mode of dwelling? (Even as Socrates tried with Phaedrus in the palinode?) The regular failure of Socrates within the dialogues, as well as Plato's own failure that he describes in these Letters, attests that Plato is by no means optimistic that we, "the many," will usually take up the invitation. But just as surely—and as surely as Socrates tried again and again, almost quixotically, as surely as Plato tried three times in Syracuse—he considers it worth the risk of writing.

However, Plato does not leave the matter at the few sentences I have quoted from the Seventh Letter so far. He now goes into his famous and extended "philosophic digression," to which we can now turn. As we do so, however, we must pay the closest attention to the reasons why he does so. The matter he has just discussed, the impossibility of writing philosophy, needs expansion and clarification. The discussion to come, then, is an expansion and clarification of *this* issue: the impossibility of putting philosophy adequately into words. We must understand and assess this famous digression on the question of knowledge primarily in terms of the issue that leads to it, the impossibility of writing one's philosophy. Clearly, Plato assumes that most Greeks would think of philosophy as something that *could* be written, even as most of us today would. He understands that the denial of that possibility needs considerable clarification. Let us turn to that expansion and clarification.

Plato's first statement, on which he expands, delineates five things involved in knowledge. He at first summarizes what—he indicates—he has said before but bears repeating: "There is for each of the beings three things that are necessary if knowledge (*epistemen*) of it is to be acquired; the knowledge itself is the fourth. As a fifth one must posit (*tithenai dei*) what is itself knowable and true (*gnoston te kai alethes*). First of these is the name (*onoma*), second the logos, third the image (*eidolon*), fourth the knowledge (*episteme*)" (342b).

As an example which he says can be applied to all of these, Plato uses the circle, which has the name (*kuklos*), the logos, in this case a definition, "the figure whose extremities are everywhere equally distant from its center," which, perplexingly, Plato attributes to not one but three possible objects—"round," "circumference," and "circle"—and the image, which is drawn and rubbed out without affecting the circle itself. But now, in place of the simple "knowledge" (*episteme*) as the fourth, Plato expands significantly:

> Fourth comes knowledge (*episteme*), thinking (*nous*), and true opinion (*alethes doxa*) regarding these things. And these must be posited as forming a single whole, which is not in words (*phonais*) nor in bodily shapes but in souls. Whereby it is clear that it differs both from the nature of the circle itself and from the three previously mentioned. Of these, thinking (*nous*) is nearest the fifth in kinship and likeness, and the others are further away. (342c)

The fourth is in fact threefold. Knowledge—presumably knowledge in general—is somehow composed of these three: *episteme* itself, *nous,* and true opinion. The suggestion invokes any number of discussions in various dialogues. One thinks of the characterization of knowledge (*episteme*) in the *Theaetetus* as "true opinion with a logos" (201d ff.). The role of *nous* in knowledge in turn invokes the several discussions we have already examined of non-discursive, noetic insight into forms (or, as in the *Phaedrus*, "the beings"). For the reason that *nous* is "closer to the fifth" than the others, even than *episteme* itself, is presumably precisely because of its non-discursive character. We should also note the striking fact that the fifth is not here named either "idea" or "form," but only "the knowable and true."

But now, and especially for the themes to which the present study is devoted, things get exceedingly complex. First, Plato generalizes the applicability of this "fivefold" to seemingly all knowledge: to all figures, to color; to the good, the beautiful, and the just; to body in general and the elements; to all living things and qualities of souls, all ethical actions and all passions (342d). Second, adequate knowledge of the fivefold's fifth is impossible without each of the preceding four: "Unless one somehow grasps the four of these, he will never acquire full knowledge of the fifth" (342e). So on the one hand, a necessary condition for adequate knowledge of virtually anything, at least of that knowledge that is called *episteme,* is that one "somehow" (*pos*)—and the reason for this vagueness will become immediately apparent—grasp (*labe*) the four. But on the other hand, and immediately in the next sentence, we are told that such full (*teleos*) knowledge of the fifth will inevitably be impossible "because of the weakness of logos."

> These four, moreover, because of the weakness of language (*dia to ton logon asthenes*), are just as much concerned with making clear the particular quality of each object as the being of it (*to poion ti peri hekaston deloun e to on hekastou*). On this account, no sensible man will dare to posit his thoughts in it, especially in a form which is unchangeable (*ametakineton*) such as is the case with what is written. (343a)

Hans-Georg Gadamer is right to emphasize what too few notice here, that on the question of knowledge language is a classic double-edged sword.[10] On the one hand, human knowledge absolutely depends on language, in which, in one way or another, the four are all involved. On the other, language is inherently weak, defective, finite. The strong suggestion in this Letter is that the epistemic enterprise, inescapably involved with language, *must* be limited in its adequacy, and limited precisely because of the nature of language.

It is crucial to understand here what is being denied and what is not being denied. First, there can be no question, as it were, of skipping over language and its limitations—that is, skipping over the first four, and leaping to pure noetic insight into the beings themselves. That, as the *Phaedrus* teaches us, would be the activity of a god. As human, we *must*, Plato tells us, go thorough the four, and therefore prepare for what noetic insights we might gain through language. And that in turn means that we are necessarily subject, in our efforts to know, to the limits of language. Our knowledge, therefore, will be necessarily finite.

But finite knowledge remains *knowledge*. The statement encourages us: careful employing of the four *will lead us* to insight into the fifth, into beings themselves. It is just that those insights, that knowledge, will always be limited; as future thinkers will say, it will never be absolute. I note again the striking consistency with what is said in the *Phaedrus* and *Symposium*.

Just what are the particular limitations of knowledge limned in this Letter? There seem to be several. On the one hand, language seems involved in a certain paradox. The words we use are not fixed or stable. In addition, they have about them a certain arbitrariness. They can never attain, therefore, to the stability of the beings themselves. On the other hand, our possible efforts to stabilize those words by *writing* them exacerbates the problem rather than alleviates it, for once written, the words lose the flexibility they preserve in dialogical speech. So whether we, as Plato seems to suggest here in Socratic fashion, limit our speech to the most flexible speech, dialogical speech among fellow lovers of wisdom; or whether, foolishly like Dionysus, we attempt to stabilize them by writing them down, we remain within one or another of the limits of language. If we have language, we are in this paradox.

Moreover, the particular limit of language to which Plato here alludes is that, bound up with words, images, and so with phenomena, words never quite articulate with precision the beings themselves: they refer, always and necessarily, in part to the specific qualities of this or that; they inevitably refer, one might say, to phenomenal particulars and not exclusively to the things themselves. But again, it is not as if we might avoid this limitation by ceasing to speak. It is only language that gives us what access we have to being.[11] There can be no question here of the repudiation of language in favor of a life of silent, mystical vision.

Another point must be emphasized here. This is a limitation on absolute knowledge, not a limitation on philosophy. We must not confuse the reasons offered earlier in the passage as to why one cannot write one's *philosophy* with the reasons offered here as to why *knowledge* (*episteme*) will inevitably be limited. This needs to be clarified. It seems to me that the critique of philosophic writing developed here, in the Second Letter, and (as we shall soon see) in the *Phaedrus*, is embedded in a larger critique of the *limits of logos*. The two are connected in complicated ways, but they are not identical. The limits of language being described in the philosophic digression—limits having to do with the arbitrary character of words, their inherent instability, and their inevitable connection to the particularity of phenomena—are limits on the "perfection" (*teleos*) of our possible knowledge. Writing exacerbates this by imposing a no less arbitrary stability of its own. All language, including certainly but not limited to philosophic language, is subject to these limitations. That writing exacerbates the problem should teach us, Plato says, not to try to write our deepest thoughts (343a). But the limits on *philosophic* writing are not quite the same and, if not exclusive to philosophy, are at least more specific: philosophy is not a set of doctrines that might in principle be articulated. It is an *experience,* one that takes long sustenance, and what it gives rise to, hopefully and eventually, is not a particular "science" (*episteme*) but the "sudden" and self-sustaining birth of philosophy itself. So, yes, philosophic language and philosophic writing have the necessary limitations of any speaking and writing, but they have further, one might say deeper ones as well.

Throughout the rest of the "digression," Plato reiterates and thereby emphasizes the weakness of the four ingredients to knowing: names, *logoi,* images, and knowledge itself. He notes at 343b that "countless words" (*murios de logos*) could be added regarding each of the four, "how unclear" (*hos asaphes*) they are. At 343d he reminds us yet again of how the problem with our efforts at knowledge is less the soul than "the nature of the four, each of which is by nature defective (*pephukuia phaulos*)." That not only the first three (names, *logoi,* and images) are defective but, as he repeats, all four, calls for further reflection. This fourth is initially referred to, simply, as "knowledge itself" (*episteme*); but it is then expanded to "*episteme, nous,* and *alethes doxa*" (342c). That this threefold—dependent as it is on names, *logoi,* and images—will necessarily be "weak" or "defective," suggests something crucial about Plato's thinking, especially by contrast to Aristotle. For Aristotle, in his famous account of the modes of *aletheuein* in book 6 of the *Nicomachean Ethics*, delineates, among the others, *episteme and nous* as "not admitting of being false."[12] Plato's view seems at once less optimistic and more complex: as part of "the four," *episteme, nous,* and *alethes doxa* are *also* "weak" and "defective." That is, as I put it earlier, they are *finite.* Our *episteme and even our nous* are sufficiently dependent on language to share in the finitude conferred by it. We have already seen this view confirmed in the *Phaedrus:* we mortals get "glimpses" of the beings, not the full contemplative examination of the gods.

But—and here again the complexity comes to the fore—*they are still epi-*

steme and *nous,* that is, they are still modes of knowing and insight. Plato, unlike Aristotle, does not seem to demand of these two modes of knowing that they be infallible. They can be, they are, fallible, *but are still knowing and insight.* We should perhaps say, they are *human* knowing and *human* insight. This fallibility means that there will always be an element of aporia in our claims to knowledge and insight; and so, if we understand ourselves, the *stance of questioning* that the dialogues exhibit so well will always be necessary.

Plato brings the "philosophic digression" to a close by drawing together, to be sure in a cryptic way, the theme that led to the digression—his warning against the possibility of writing one's philosophy—and the larger theme of the digression itself—the limits of language and of our possible knowledge deriving from it. He does so by reminding us, at 343e, that through the use of these instruments, it will "barely" (*mogis*) be possible for knowledge to be engendered in the soul—and now only in a "naturally good" (*eu pephukoti*) soul. Those not so endowed cannot be made to understand. He expands: "so no one who is not naturally inclined and akin to justice (*ton dikaion*) and the other noble qualities (*ta kala*), even though he may be quick at learning and remembering this and that and other things, nor anyone who, though akin to nobility (*suggeneis*), is slow at learning and forgetful, will ever attain the truth that is possible concerning virtue nor of vice either" (344a–b). We note the striking reference to *ta kala:* the worthy qualities are somehow "beautiful" or "noble." What we call "natural intelligence" and a good memory is not sufficient for philosophic insight. One needs as well the proper character. How is that character to be endowed? The most plausible reference for this is surely the "long period of dwelling together" that Plato had earlier suggested was the condition for the sudden birth in the soul of philosophic being. At very least, it is that sustained period of dwelling-with that will lead us to discover whether we have the requisite character. Moreover, as we now see, the real issue at stake in the quest for knowledge and the discussion of its necessary finitude is not so much knowledge of things such as circles (however important such knowledge may be as a propaedeutic), but the acquisition of that knowledge that constitutes virtue: "speaking and acting the truth" according to the nature of things. What is at stake in the philosophic quest, then, more than anything else, is justice and the other virtues, that is, *living* in a certain way.

This conclusion is also strikingly consistent with a passage we have already examined in the *Symposium.* I refer to the culminating insight into "Beauty itself" portrayed in the famous "ascent passage" of that dialogue—the insight toward which Diotima tries, without much confidence, to lead the young Socrates. There, recall, she tells Socrates that the final insight into Beauty itself is unlike the various stages along the way up the ascent, each of which is accomplished discursively—accompanied, that is, by "beautiful speeches." The final revelation is *oude tis logos, oude tis episteme:* "neither some discursive account nor some demonstrative knowledge." But strikingly, Diotima says that if one should ever attain this final insight into Beauty itself, they would "nearly" (*skedon*) be at the end of their quest (*Symposium* 211c). We raised the question, why "nearly"? Once one achieves an insight into a given form, is one not (by the measure of a certain "Platonism") *at* the end, not "near" it? No, as Diotima explains, for the real "end" is not this insight but what she says will follow from it: "not images of virtue but true virtue" (212a). The real point of philosophical insight, even of the highest philosophical insight, then, is a certain way of living—living in virtue. Consistent with the teaching of the Seventh Letter, the *Symposium* teaches us that a long period of instruction is necessary; that even then the outcome is by no means certain; that, if it comes, the non-discursive noetic insight into formal structure will come suddenly; and that the ultimate import of that insight is not, strictly, "knowledge" in some abstract sense but virtuous living.

We are nearing the point where we can return to the *Phaedrus* to see how the issues we have been addressing get played out toward the end of that dialogue. In preparation, let us note two more features of Plato's remarks as he ends his digression and draws what he takes to be the appropriate conclusions. First, Plato draws the now-obvious conclusion that if Dionysus did indeed claim to put the insights of Platonic philosophy into writing, he was utterly wrong to do so. It is certainly not necessary to write them, Plato emphasizes (in what seems a clear reference to an important point in the *Phaedrus*'s critique of writing) as aids to remembering (*hypomnematon charin*), "for they are contained in the shortest (*brachutatois*) of formulations" (344e).

We hear the theme of simplicity sounded again. On the one hand, for the reasons given, words are inadequate to express the real "truths" of philosophic living. On the other, if and when they *are* put into words, they will seem utterly simple. We face a complicated situation here: on the one hand, the deepest insights of philosophy cannot be put into words because they are *too complicated* to be adequately comprehended (in the literal sense) in language, since they are, as we have seen, about a certain experience or way of living. On the other hand, they are *too simple*, in that when we do attempt as best we can to put them into words, they will appear utterly banal. Perhaps we could say that they will appear too simple if put *in words* because their complexity, their profundity, is not a complexity and profundity of linguistic formulation, but the complexity and profundity of *living philosophically*.

Second, Plato's general conclusion to the digression is short and blunt:

> In sum, our conclusion must be that whenever one sees a man's written compositions—whether they be the laws of a legislator or anything else in any other form—these are not his most serious works, if indeed that writer himself is serious. Rather, these works abide in the most noble and beautiful place (*en chora te kalliste*) he possesses. If, however, these really are his serious concerns and he put them into writing, then it is not "the gods" but mortals who "have utterly ruined his senses." (344c–d)

Then what are the Platonic dialogues? For Plato, surely, regards himself as a serious man. We can note first that neither here nor anywhere in the Second or Seventh Letter does Plato say that one should never write. Rather, he has denied that the deepest truths of philosophy can be adequately put into words, and here we see him insist that the "most serious" (*spoudaiotata*) concerns will not be put into writing. In neither case is there a blanket denial that a serious man might write. One might well write, indeed, about all but the "most serious" things. The suggestions I made earlier regarding the written dialogues, I submit, continue to be plausible. They do not contain Plato's philosophy—which, once more, cannot be put adequately into words. Plato's philosophy is indeed, one can surmise, Plato's "most serious" concern, and he has not been so senseless as to claim to put that adequately into words. The dialogues do something else; something very serious, we can imagine Plato believing, though not the most serious. They are written to put those readers so disposed by nature on that "longer road," the long dwelling together that might lead them to the sudden revelation of the philosophical life. The guiding question to be asked of the dialogues, if something like this is so, would not be: what is Plato's philosophy here? But rather: do the dialogues lead us enduringly into philosophic living? Or again: how should they be read that they might be allowed to do so? Or, once more, and joining together our reflections on the Second Letter with those on the Seventh: how might a transformed memory of Socrates lead us toward such a life? We are ready to return to the *Phaedrus,* and to the culmination of Plato's critique of logos and of philosophic writing.

FIVE

The Critique of Rhetoric and Writing in the *Phaedrus*

In a clear prefiguration of the Kantian notion of critique, the *Phaedrus* could be said to be in some measure a critique of logos. We have already seen certain aspects of that critique played out in the palinode. It will now be completed in the critique of rhetoric and writing that constitutes almost the entire second half of the *Phaedrus*. But first, we must understand how and why the dialogue switches at the end of the palinode—to the great puzzlement and consternation of many interpreters—from the rich discussion of eros and beauty to rhetoric and writing. The reason, in a word, is Phaedrus (though Phaedrus and his limitation will be seen to represent something important). To see this, let us return to the point in the dialogue where we left off, to the conclusion of the palinode where Socrates prays, among other things, that Phaedrus turn to philosophy (257a–b).

Nearly everyone who reads the *Phaedrus*, it seems, is deeply moved by the palinode that Socrates gives, rich as it is in discussions of soul, immortality, divine madness (and in particular eros), of beauty, the nature of insight and the possible knowledge we might have. Nearly everyone, but with one most notable exception: Phaedrus himself. Phaedrus, at the end of Socrates' palinode, is stunningly—one might say appallingly—unmoved by its content. He is impressed *only* by its superior rhetoric, as if he did not even hear the content of the speech and surely was not moved to *thinking* by it. Here is how he responds to that remarkable speech of Socrates:

I join with you in that prayer, Socrates, if this will really be better for us. But for some time now I have been astonished by your speech, considering how much more beautifully you turned this speech than the first one. It actually made me anxious lest Lysias seem second-rate by comparison—if, that is, he even wanted to match your speech with one of his own. In fact, my astonishing man, one of those public figures in the city was recently haranguing him for this very thing, throughout his speech referring to him as a "speechwriter." So out of love of honor, he might refrain from writing for us. (258c)

Phaedrus has heard only the rhetoric of this magnificent speech. He has heard nothing of its content, a content that has moved so many of us for centuries. One can only imagine what Socrates is thinking as he listens to this reaction to his remarkable palinode. He has, manifestly, tried to move Phaedrus past his fascination with rhetoric, oblivious to its content, by presenting a speech that might move him to philosophic thinking. As his ending prayer explicitly requested, Socrates hoped by the palinode to move Phaedrus toward philosophy: that the boy would "devote his life simply toward eros with wisdom-loving logos": *haplos pros Erota meta philosophon logon.* He learns immediately in Phaedrus's reaction that he has failed. But Socrates—as we know from these Platonic remembrances, the dialogues—is persistent to the point of being quixotic. He will make one more try, this time by appealing to the only thing that genuinely captures Phaedrus's rather limited passion: rhetoric. So Socrates turns with Phaedrus to the topic that he knows Phaedrus will listen to, and the rest of the dialogue will dwell on the question of rhetoric. It is noteworthy and perhaps not accidental that most of this second half of the dialogue—with the important exception of the last few pages where the myth of Theuth is introduced—has not drawn much philosophic attention or caused much excitement. One might well ask: how many people have, with Phaedrus himself, found the speeches on eros and the palinode *less* stimulating and provocative than the discussion of rhetoric that leads from the end of the palinode to the closing discussion of writing? And how many have been as stimulated as Phaedrus is by the passage from 266d to 267e, where Socrates parodies the rhetoric of rhetoric with a catalogue of some eighteen "parts" of a well-constructed speech, from the "preface" to the "recapitulation"? Indeed, who *wants* to be like Phaedrus? Or has Plato presented Phaedrus this way because philosophy must recognize that Phaedruses are everywhere? All those calling themselves philosophers who think that the "argument" is everything—that the "philosophy" in any text, any speech, any discussion is contained in the arguments, narrowly construed? Is Plato suggesting, perhaps, that we must remember Phaedrus and the problem of Phaedrus because we meet Phaedrus every day and always will? That each of us, moved by the logos of philosophy, is ever in danger of becoming Phaedrus ourselves? As long as the distinction between philosophy and sophistry is blurred, as long as philosophy remains in danger of falling into sophistry? Perhaps one need not "analyze the arguments" of the section on rhetoric in detail to learn the lesson that Plato may be teaching us.

And, given our topic, we shall not do so except to note that throughout his discussion of rhetoric we see Socrates making one more attempt to woo Phaedrus from rhetoric to philosophy, and to do this precisely within a discussion of rhetoric. He develops what is (to Phaedrus) the striking thesis that to be a good rhetorician, it is not sufficient to know the truths of the art of rhetoric: one must know the truths regarding the matters at stake (justice, beauty, love) and must also know the truths of the human soul (differing kinds of soul and what will move each kind). Socrates thus tries to move Phaedrus from rhetoric to philosophy by making the distinction between rhetoric and philosophy disappear—by turning what we may call "true" rhetoric into philosophy itself. Philosophy, one must emphasize, and not wisdom. For the ideal of true rhetoric that Socrates has set out—knowing not just the art of making speeches but knowing as well the objects about which one might speak (the beings) and the souls of all humans to which one might speak—is manifestly an impossible task, as Phaedrus himself recognizes: "That's said very beautifully, it seems to me, Socrates, if only anyone could do it" (274a). Socrates replies with the well-known recognition of the worthiness of a philosophy founded in aporia, but this time stated explicitly in terms of the issue of beauty: "And yet even in striving for the beautiful there is beauty, and also in suffering whatever it is that one suffers along the way": *Alla kai epicheirounti toi tois kalois kalon kai paschein ho to an to xumbe pathein.*

Socrates' response is thought-provoking in its joining of beauty and suffering.[1] What is the connection he sees, or wants us to see, between beauty and suffering? The palinode has made this clear already with regard to the beauty of a beloved: the lover indeed suffers mightily to withstand the demands of desire (the black horse) in order to attain to philosophic friendship. This is a reflection of an "earlier" suffering (in mythological time) that we underwent as we tried to struggle our way up to get a glimpse of beauty itself and the other beings. But here in Socrates' remark, he reminds us of the explicit tie of these sufferings with the stance of philosophy itself. *Philosophy* will involve a certain suffering (recall Plato's "test" of Dionysus): the suffering of aporia, of recognizing that we do not know what we need to know, and of striving for knowledge. Yes, suffering can indeed be part of the experience of the beautiful, indeed, part of the experience of a beautiful life. Perhaps Socrates is alluding to Plato's "test" with regard to Phaedrus's own possibility of philosophical living. Phaedrus, obviously, is not one to suffer overmuch.

Does Plato have Socrates succeed in this last attempt to accomplish with Phaedrus what we have seen that Plato seeks to accomplish in all his writing? Does he move Phaedrus toward philosophy? That Phaedrus ends the dialogue by acceding to all of Socrates' questions leads many to think so. But I am less sanguine. I cite here only two incidents of the concluding lines of the dialogue that make me skeptical. First, at 277b–c, after Socrates has developed his account of the myth of Theuth which we shall take up in detail in a moment, Socrates asks Phaedrus to remember the account they have given of "true" rhetoric, of what would make rhetoric truly an art: "But, I'd say, we have shown with due measure what is made with art and what is not." Phaedrus, alas, does not remember! "It seemed so at the time, but remind me again, how it went," he replies. And Socrates must recapitulate the lesson about matching, with knowledge, the speech to the character of the listener. Even in the discussion of rhetoric, it seems, Phaedrus remembers only the rhetoric, and forgets the content. Is this the response of one whose soul has been turned to philosophy?

Second, at the very end of the dialogue (278e—the dialogue ends at 279c), Socrates recalls for Phaedrus the just-completed discussion regarding writing, where it was determined—in agreement with the two Letters we have addressed —that one cannot and should not put one's serious thoughts into writing but only one's play, "as reminders," and asks Phaedrus to remind Lysias of "these things." Phaedrus's response is not (as one might hope and expect of a now philosophically inclined soul) to make sure that he has understood, or to indicate just what he plans to say to Lysias, or even to affirm that he will do so. Instead, Phaedrus asks what *Socrates* will say to *his* companion (Isocrates, we learn, is who is meant)—as if what he has just said to Phaedrus were not revealing enough! I take it as a sign of his recognition of failure with regard to Phaedrus, then, that in Socrates' final prayer he does not, as he did at the end of his palinode, include the welfare of Phaedrus. (He prayed there, recall, that Phaedrus would turn to philosophy.) In this last prayer, Socrates prays only for himself: "Dear Pan, and you other gods who dwell here, grant that I become beautiful within, and that my worldly belongings be in accord with my inner self. May I consider the wise man rich, and have only as much gold as a *sophron* man can carry and use." Exactly in accord with Plato's account in the Second Letter that his writings are of "a Socrates become beautiful," Socrates here prays that he may "become beautiful within" (*kalo genesthai t'andothen*—279b). Phaedrus, to be sure, asks that the prayer apply to him as well, but given what we have seen in the dialogue and what we know of Phaedrus's future conduct (his involvements with the scandals especially), we can surely understand Socrates' curt reply: "Let's go."

Let us return, though, to the concluding section of the discussion of rhetoric that takes up most of the second half of the dialogue, to the point where, at 274b–c, Socrates completes the discussion of the *giving* of speeches and turns to the question of writing, where the question of memory again becomes crucial. Socrates begins, as is his wont, not by developing his own understanding but by claiming to remember what he has heard about writing. He proceeds to tell the story of Theuth and Thamus. It is worth noting as we turn to it that Socrates does not have a written copy of the myth, but remembers it.

The story that Socrates claims to have heard (*ekousa*—274c) is the now well-known and often written-on story of Theuth and Thamus. Both are "gods," even if, as it seems, finite ones. Theuth is portrayed as a god beneficent to humans, in certain ways parallel to Prometheus, as many have noted. He develops many arts (number, calculation, geometry, astronomy, draughts, dice—274d), apparently with an eye to distributing them to humans. However, Theuth, like Prometheus, apparently does not have the authority to distribute these gifts on his own. They must first receive the imprimatur of the god-king Thamus, who proceeds, almost in a Socratic fashion, to question Theuth and ask him to defend the benefits of each art. Thamus then judges which are truly worthy and beneficial for humans and which are not.

One of Theuth's inventions—the one very much at stake here, the one signaled by Socrates as "especially" important—is "letters" (*grammata*). When the time comes, Theuth must defend the benefits of letters. He lists two: letters will be an aid to memory and to wisdom. Here is the way he defends his invention: "This branch of learning (*to mathema*), O king, will make the Egyptians wiser (*sophoterous*) and improve their memory (*mnemonikoterous*). The drug (*pharmakon*) for memory and wisdom (*mnemes te gar kai sophias*) has been discovered" (274e).

Thamus will reject both claims, but we must note several things about Theuth's defense of letters. First, we should take note of the two words employed for "memory": *mnemonikoterous* and *mnemes*. In a moment, Thamus will reject this claim by distinguishing "memory" from "reminding." Here is his critique:

> And now you, father of these letters, have in your fondness for them said what is the opposite of their real effect. For this will produce a forgetting in the souls of those who learn these letters as they fail to exercise their memory (*mnemes ameletesia*), because those who put trust in writing recollect (*anamimneskomenous*) from the outside with foreign signs, rather than from themselves recollecting from within by themselves. You have not discovered a drug (*pharmakon*) for memory (*mnemes*) but for reminding (*hypomneseos*). (275a)

Perhaps we should be cautious about accepting Thamus's critique at face value—this critique of one god by another. On the question of memory, it depends on the distinction between recollection (various forms of *anamnesis*) and memory (*mnemes*), which are desirable, and reminding (forms of *hypomnesis*), which is somehow of lesser worth though perhaps not quite useless. The force of this criticism is not obvious. After all, what else could Theuth have meant in his claim that letters will be an aid to memory than that, precisely when our memory fails, letters—texts that we can read—will *remind us* of what we once knew, or perhaps once read, and have forgotten? In addition, letters might plausibly be said to aid our memory precisely when we are trying to memorize, as Phaedrus does with the written text of Lysias at the beginning of the dialogue. When we are having difficulty memorizing something, being able to refer to the written text will indeed help us by *reminding us* of what we are trying to memorize. What, then, is so inferior about reminding?

In any case, the tone of this criticism, coupled with the criticism of the claim that letters will enhance wisdom, suggest that Thamus, on this basis, will *reject* this invention of Theuth's, though he does not quite explicitly say so. Letters will not help but detract from memory or recollection; they will only serve as "re-minders," which presumably are somehow of far less value.

In addition to the reservations about this critique I have mentioned, we should note that it is in clear tension as well with what Socrates has said in his palinode. There, to the contrary, Socrates *included* reminding (*hypomnesis*—the very word Thamus uses above) with memory (*mnesis*) and recollection (*ana-mnesis*) as precisely the experience that will give rise, if anything can, to our recognition[2] of beauty itself and the other beings. The passage is worth quoting again. The context, recall, is a discussion of how the things we experience on earth, such as mortal beauty, can "remind" human, embodied souls of their "prior" experience of beauty itself in the hyper-ouranian place.

> This is because only a soul which has seen the truth can enter into our human form: for a human being must understand what is said (*legomenon*) in reference to form, that which, going from a plurality of perceptions is drawn together by reason-ing (*logismo*) into a single essence. This process occurs by recollecting (*anamnesis*) those things which our soul once saw when traveling in the company of a god, looking down at those things which we now say exist, and lifting up its head to see what really is. As is just, only the *dianoia* of a lover of wisdom grows wings. For thought is always, according to her capability through memory (*mneme*), near to those things, and by this nearness a god is divine. And only a man who correctly handles such reminders (*hypomnemasin*) and is perpetually initiated into those perfect mysteries, is complete. (249c)

Here, in this earlier account, Socrates not only does not criticize reminding (*hypomnesis*), he emphasizes its crucial role in our possible knowledge of the beings. For it is precisely the ability of our experience of mortal things here on earth to *remind us* of what we once knew as we followed our god that enables us to know what we might come to know. Here, reminding is virtually tantamount to *recollection itself.* And if knowing—or perhaps better, knowledgeable thinking —is remembering or recollecting, does this not begin to approach the view that *thinking is itself remembering*? One is reminded here of Heideggerian *Andenken*. If Socrates in fact accepts Thamus's critique, then ironically he *fails to remember* what he said earlier, fails to remember the crucial and altogether positive signifi-cance he gave to reminding.

We are in the presence of a Platonic provocation. Which are we to accept as the more plausible: the positive statement of the crucial importance of remem-bering or reminding in the palinode, or Thamus's critique of it toward the end of the dialogue? I have already suggested some considerations why Thamus's critique of reminding is not especially plausible on the face of it. Surely Socrates' positive use of reminding in the palinode is more forceful. But that is not to say that Thamus's critique has no point at all—and indeed, as he expands on the myth, Socrates at least gives the impression that he agrees with this critique. But it is important to recognize that even to the extent that he agrees with it, he softens it considerably. Let us see how.

As we noted above, Thamus's objections give the strong impression that he therefore rejects the invention of writing, rejects Theuth's request that it be distributed to human kind. If so, it would seem that Theuth gave it anyway, for we humans surely have writing. This puts Theuth even more in a position analogous with Prometheus, as one who not only gave gifts to humankind but defied other gods in order to do so. Socrates, to be sure, does not make this explicit, but perhaps he does so implicitly in the way he develops his apparent acceptance of Thamus's critique. For Socrates does not take it as justifying that writing be abolished, disallowed, or even not done. The conclusion toward which he moves regarding the question of memory and writing is only that we should recognize that *all writing can do* is remind us of what we know. He puts it in these words:

> So the person who thinks he is leaving behind an art in written form and the person who receives it thinking that there will be something clear and secure in these written forms would be exceedingly simpleminded and truly ignorant of Ammon's (that is, Thamus's) prophecy, if he thinks that *written speeches are anything more than reminders* (*hypomnesai*) for a person already in the know about the things written down. (275c–d; my emphasis)

Socrates' softening of the criticism, then, is that we should not *reject* writing on the grounds that it only is an aid to reminding, but simply understand that this is as much as it can do—"remind" us of what we somehow know in our souls. Despite the somewhat dismissive rhetoric of Socrates' words, is his point not similar to the one he made in the palinode about reminding? And to the one that Plato made in the Seventh Letter, that written texts will not *be knowledge,* at least, not knowledge of philosophy or the highest things, but that writing *can* have the positive effect of aiding us in our recollection? Indeed, as Socrates a bit later summarizes, writing should not be avoided but should become precisely the *play* of philosophers. The philosopher will

> sow his gardens of written words, it seems, in the joy of play (*paidias charin*) and he will write, whenever he does write, to build up a treasure trove of reminders (*hypomnemata*) both for himself in case he reaches forgetful old age and for all who walk down the same path, and he'll take pleasure watching the tender shoots in the garden grow. But when others indulge themselves in other kinds of play, finding pleasure in drinking parties and whatever is related to these, he, it seems, instead of this kind of play will engage in the play I just mentioned. (276d)

Far from disparaging writing because it only helps us with reminders, as Thamus's critique had intimated, Socrates here comes close to *recommending* writing as the play of philosophers, but a serious play, in that it has a most helpful function: to remind us of the possibility of knowledge, of the possibility of philosophy. Might not the dialogues, these reminders of Socrates, be just this, not Plato's philosophy but his philosophic play, written to remind us "who walk down the same path" of the possibility of philosophy?

But let us return to Theuth's defense of his invention of writing and Thamus's critique of it, for it is not just its value as an aid to memory that Theuth asserts and Thamus denies. Theuth also claims that writing will "make the Egyptians wiser" (274e).

Thamus's critique is that writing will give us "an apparent, not a true wisdom (*sophias . . . doxan, ouk aletheian*). For they have heard much from you without real teaching, and they will appear rich in knowledge when for the most part there's an absence of knowledge, and they will be difficult to be with, since they appear wise rather than really being wise" (275b). Socrates does not explicitly elaborate on this critique, but his development of the theme, to which we shall turn presently, that it is not written texts but that which is "written in the soul," as a result of dialogical conversation that is the source of what real knowledge there can be, of the "serious" matters for thinking, perhaps hints at his response to it. For under what conditions would Thamus's critique be true, that written words would give us an apparent wisdom, not a true one, and would instill in the reader a false sense of being wiser than he or she is? Perhaps the obvious answer would be, it would be apparent wisdom if we *took what is written to be real knowledge,* that is, if we *forget* that writing can only be a *reminder* of the true wisdom, the true matter for thought. On the other hand, if we *remember* what writing can and cannot do—remember in particular that writing can at best help us remember—then presumably we would not fall prey to the "apparent wisdom" that writing risks, the belief that in writing or reading, we attain true knowledge of the highest. This is thoroughly consistent, we can note, with Plato's remarks in the Seventh Letter that philosophy cannot be put into words like other studies, and that consequently, he has not been so foolish as to try to write his philosophy.

Theuth's defense of writing contains another curious element. In claiming that writing will "make the Egyptians wiser and will improve their memory," Theuth adds, "the drug (*pharmakon*) for memory and wisdom has been discovered" (274e). In this very formulation, the ambiguity on which Thamus will base his critique is already contained. Theuth, presumably, believes that writing will be a "drug" in the curative or restorative sense—that it will aid, enhance, our memory and our wisdom. But Thamus reads it as the opposite—that writing will be a drug in the sense of a suppressant and depressant, even a poison, to memory and wisdom.

Much has been written, of course, about the question of the *pharmakon*, particularly in the light of Derrida's groundbreaking essay.[3] It is important to note that the ambiguity present in this discussion regarding the positive and negative connotations of *pharmakon* have been present from the beginning of the dialogue, when Socrates first uses the term. He introduces it at 229c, in the midst of explaining to Phaedrus the mythological significance of the place where they are about to sit down and talk, and why he refuses to engage in the "demythologization" then prevalent among the sophisticated. The relevant myth has to do with the maiden Orithuia, who was seized by Boreas the wind at that spot. In a passing observation that would be insignificant were in not for the subsequent employment of the term in the dialogue, Socrates mentions that Orithuia was "playing with Pharmaceia" (229d). And a moment later, at 230d, referring to his "sickness for speeches" (228b) and his willingness to follow Phaedrus anywhere at the promise of hearing Lysias's speech (227d), Socrates comments to Phaedrus: "you seem to have discovered a drug (*pharmakon*) to entice me into walking outside the city." Socrates' use of *pharmakon* here is multiply ambiguous. If, as Socrates and Phaedrus seemed to agree early in the dialogue, getting outside the city occasionally is a healthy thing (that is why, at the beginning, Socrates finds Phaedrus walking outside the walls—227a), then the speech that will lead Socrates here is a drug in the sense of a curative that will restore him—cure and restore him, that is, from his self-induced confinement to the things of the city. But how might a speech such as Lysias's restore Socrates? If indeed Socrates has, as he earlier admits, a "sickness for speeches" (*to nosounti peri logon*—228c), then perhaps the "cure" offered by Lysias's speech will derive from the imperative for critique to which the speech moves Socrates, as well as the curative palinode that he is led to give. On the other hand, is the speech that Phaedrus holds a drug in the sense of a drugging enticement that will bring Socrates out of the city in spite of his conviction that it is in the city that he belongs (230d)? That is, is it a drug in the negative sense? Is Socrates here already limning the negative character of written speeches? Or is not Plato the provocateur inviting us to think of all these possible readings—in *his* writing?

Who then could suppose that in these multiple instances of multiple meanings Plato was not fully aware of the ambiguity he was putting into play? That he was not doing so precisely to invite us to wonder about the curative *and* poisonous power of writing and of logos? That he was not putting this ambiguity into play (in the play of his own writing) in order to provoke us to think about the misleading nature of writing, its false claim to wisdom, and its value as a playful reminder, and so an invitation, to the longer road?

Socrates, in his development of Thamus's criticisms of writing, now develops further arguments beyond Thamus's two regarding memory and wisdom —further limitations of writing—and he does so in order to draw the strong contrast between writing and personal dialogue. To do so, he first adds two new problems with writing. First, once written and sent beyond their "father" (the author), written words cannot answer questions put to them, but can only repeat themselves endlessly. Second, once written and beyond its father, a written text can be read by anyone and will say the same to anyone, and thus, unlike a live speaker, "has no idea to whom it should speak and before whom it should remain silent" (275d–e).

Thamus's objections pertained directly to letters and did not draw the explicit contrast to oral speech, much less to dialogue. In his development here, Socrates moves to a defense of his own apparent decision not to write by explicitly referring to the inferiority of writing to oral conversation on these two grounds: the inability of writing to engage in question and answer and so to defend itself, and its lack of ability to discriminate regarding its audience. His own objections seem to have more force than those presented by Thamus. Two people in oral dialogue do have the advantage of give and take, of question and answer, of objection and defense, that a written text does not typically have by itself. And it is true enough that a written text can be read by anyone who obtains it, and cannot of itself nuance what it says to accord with the individual reader's character, limitations, and abilities.

Notice, however, that Plato does not put into the mouth of Socrates the strongest possible contrast he might have drawn. Socrates might, surely, have drawn an almost absolute contrast between writing and oral speech—a contrast that presumably would have been more accessible in a culture that still (perhaps) remembered a time without writing, a time of the hegemony of orality. The contrast then would have been simply between writing and orality: oral speech and speeches that are remembered and recalled from time to time (as the rhapsodes did with Homer and Hesiod). But that is not quite the contrast that Plato has Socrates draw. Instead, Socrates formulates the distinction as one between speech *written in manuscript* (of whatever sort) and *another kind of writing:* things "written in the soul." The moment at which the distinction is drawn needs to be quoted:

> SOCRATES: But let's consider a different kind of speech, a legitimate brother of that one, and ask how it comes into being and how it is by nature better and more capable.
> PHAEDRUS: What is this, and how do you mean that it comes into being?
> SOCRATES: One that is written (*graphetai*) with knowledge in the soul of one who understands; this is able to defend itself and it knows when and to whom it should speak, and when and to whom it shouldn't.
> PHAEDRUS: You are referring to the speech of a person who knows, a speech living and ensouled (*zonta kai empsychon*), the written version of which would justly be called an image. (276a)

Somewhat curiously, it would seem, Plato has Socrates contrast not pure oral speech and written text but *two kinds of writing:* that written in a text and that written in the soul. To be sure, the clear referent of soul-writing seems to be oral speech and dialogue, and Phaedrus in his last reply clearly takes it that way, describing the "written version" as an "image" (*eidolon*). But why does Plato have Socrates refer to oral speech as a mode of writing? Its effect, at least, is the one which Derrida emphasizes so strongly: it makes *all* speech a modality of writing and so gives writing a primacy, in the end, over speech. The *différance* of the apparently intended distinction between oral speech and writing is that all speech is, one way or the other, a mode of writing—and we are on the way to grammatology.

We may pass over at least one problem with this reading, that if oral speech is "writing in the soul," it is—and this would be a mystery indeed—a writing that is "alive and ensouled"; and thus would still meet the objections that Socrates has against what I suppose we would have to call "written writing." More importantly, Socrates immediately moves to a different metaphor to make the point that he is apparently really driving at, the metaphor of planting seeds in one "garden" or another.

> And tell me this. Would a farmer with half a brain sow seeds in all seriousness—if he cared for his seeds and wanted them to become fruitful—in the summer in the gardens of Adonis, and would he rejoice seeing them bloom beautifully in eight days? Or, whenever he did this kind of farming, would he do it for the joy of play and Adonis's festival? But when he farms seriously—employing his art, and sowing in proper soil—he would be pleased with what he sowed when the things he planted attained perfection in the eighth month. (276b)

The real import of the distinction Socrates is drawing is that instilling philosophic knowledge in the soul cannot be accomplished by the "quick fix" of writing: "read this and then you'll know." Rather, it can happen only over a long period of time, of question and answer, objection and reply. It can happen, that is, only after that "long period of dwelling together" of which the Seventh Letter speaks so vividly. On this, apparently, the Platonic Socrates and Plato himself agree entirely.

So we have five objections given to writing: two by Thamus, regarding memory and wisdom; and three by Socrates, regarding the inability of writing to answer objections, discriminate its audience, and endure the sustained dwelling-with that might be the occasion for philosophy coming to be in the soul. It is at least possible, then, that here Plato is recalling the very reasons Socrates may have articulated and on the basis of which he chose not to write—perhaps even on the basis of which he discouraged the young Plato, one clearly given to writing, from doing so.

Before we turn to that large issue, however, let us return once more to the myth Socrates tells, this time to dwell on Phaedrus's response to it. In a way similar to his response to Socrates' palinode, Phaedrus responds to Socrates' myth of Theuth and Thamus without the slightest hint of a fascination or even interest in its substance. Rather, he responds with skepticism that Socrates has really "heard" the myth (274c) and the suspicion that he made it up himself, that is, that Socrates is the true author of the myth. This occasions a thought-provoking reply from Socrates, one that articulates an oft-expressed view of Socrates in other dialogues. Here is the exchange at the end of Socrates' initial recounting of the myth:

PHAEDRUS: Socrates, how easily you construct speeches (*logous*) about Egypt or any other place you want.
SOCRATES: But my friend, those at Zeus's sanctuary at Dodona claim that the speeches of oak trees were the first prophetic words. Because people back then weren't wise the

way you young are today, it was enough for them in their simplemindedness to listen to an oak or a rock so long as it spoke the truth. *But perhaps it makes a difference to you who is speaking and where he comes from. Why don't you consider this alone, whether it is as they say or not?*

PHAEDRUS: You're right to rebuke me; about letters it does seem to me to be just as the Theban king says it is. (275b–c; my emphasis)

We should note two things in passing before turning to the substance of Socrates' reply. First, Phaedrus characterizes Socrates' myth as a *speech* (*logous*) and not a myth. Early in the dialogue, discussing the stories about the location where they sit, Phaedrus expressed skepticism about myths, a skepticism in which Socrates refused to participate (229c–e). Perhaps we see a hint here as to why he is so unresponsive to Socrates' palinode, whose central feature, one might say, is the myth of the charioteer/horses. In any case, in this present response, we perhaps see again Phaedrus's lack of enthusiasm for myth: what he hears in Socrates' words is a *speech,* not a myth. Second, in his response, Socrates appeals to the notion of prophecy coming from an oak tree. He seems in the course of the dialogue to have modified his own earlier skepticism regarding the ability of trees to teach us anything! Recall that early in the dialogue Socrates explained his reluctance to leave the city for the country: "I'm in love with learning. Country places and trees do not wish to teach me anything, but human beings in the city do" (230d).[4] One more Platonic provocation!

But the issue on which we must concentrate is the substance of Socrates' response to Phaedrus's skepticism. That substance, as the sentences I emphasized indicate, is that the issue should not be who says what or even whether it is a human being who says it. The issue is the matter for thought, whether what is said is true or not. As he so often affirms in the dialogues, Socrates wants very much that the issue be the matter for thought, not what we today would call the "egos" of those involved in the discussion. The *Charmides* is one of those dialogues, and a brief look at it will be instructive both to see the view that Socrates expresses and to begin to see the problem with it that Plato allows to emerge. In the *Charmides,* when Critias expresses pique at being refuted by Socrates, especially in front of his nephew Charmides and the crowd present, Socrates responds in essentially the same vein as here in the *Phaedrus:* what counts is not who is refuted and who refutes, but the matter for thought. "Be courageous then, my friend, and answer the question as it seems best to you, paying no attention to whether it is Critias or Socrates who is being refuted. Instead, give your attention to the argument (*logos*) itself to see what the result of its investigation will be" (*Charmides* 166e). In passages such as these, Socrates makes an extremely important point about the character of thinking, especially in a culture which placed such high importance on the *agon,* the contest (as Nietzsche is so fond of emphasizing), and where the sophists had virtually succeeded in turning this agonistic tendency into the measure of thinking: thinking too is a contest, in which one participant wins, the other loses. (A look at much of contemporary philosophy indicates that this attitude regarding philosophic thinking has not exactly withered away.) Socrates recognizes, it seems, the inadequacy of this subjectivist, egocentric, and contestual model of philosophy or thinking. The matter for thought is the issue—not individual egos, not who said what and not even, as the *Phaedrus* passage we are discussing indicates, whether the thought comes from a human being. It is as if the Platonic Socrates prefigures, in his voice at least, the emphasis rightly placed in our own time on the need to overcome the metaphysics of subjectivity if we are to attain to thinking.

The problem is, Plato does not usually portray Socrates as achieving this goal of the overcoming of subjectivity in fact. Indeed, in the very dialogue where Socrates expresses his worthy exhortation to Critias—only a few pages earlier, in the midst of Critias' attempt to defend the view that *sophrosyne* is "the doing of good actions"—Critias tries to get the assent of his respondent in making a point, as Socrates himself so often does. The exchange goes as follows:

> SOCRATES: And the man who performs evil actions is not *sophron,* but the man who performs good ones?
> CRITIAS: Doesn't it seem so to you, my friend?
> SOCRATES: Never mind that, I said, we are not investigating what I think but rather what you now say. (163e)

Socrates may understand in principle that dialogical thinking should transcend a contest of egos, but Plato rarely allows him to achieve it in the event. More often than not Socrates' famous procedure of *elenchus* turns precisely into such a contest, one which Socrates usually wins—at least rhetorically, on the face of it. When he engages in discussion with sophists, this is even more obvious: these discussions almost always turn into contests, and contests in which Socrates is not always a generous victor. In the *Protagoras,* Socrates pushes Protagoras almost to the point of cruelty on claims which he has already refuted; and in the *Republic,* Plato portrays him in his refutation of Thrasymachus as embarrassing the sophist to the point where he turns red. No—the Platonic Socrates is hardly a master at suppressing his own agonistic ego, even if he realizes that this is what should be done.

This issue is made more complicated still by the insistence—by Socrates in the dialogues and by Plato in the Seventh Letter—that there is an irreducibly *personal* quality to philosophy. Recall Plato's emphasis in the Seventh Letter that philosophy only can arise out of a long period of *personal* dwelling with the matter for thought. And Socrates, in the *Apology,* defends his conviction that philosophy has fundamentally to do, after all, with *self*-knowledge (a conviction reiterated explicitly at *Phaedrus* 229e), and that "the unexamined life is not a worthy life for a human being" (*Apology* 38a). But perhaps the most poignant moment of this complication is in the contrast between the *Theaetetus* and the *Sophist.* These dialogues are dramatically set one day apart, and in them a young and extremely talented Theaetetus experiences two utterly different forms of interrogation. In *Theaetetus,* Socrates engages in a deeply *personal* questioning of Theaetetus' convictions and of his willingness to sustain such intense interrogation right from the beginning, where Socrates introduces the famous midwife image as the model for his questioning. In striking contrast, the next day, the youth is questioned by the Eleatic Stranger. In the latter's development of his method of diaresis, it is made clear from the beginning and throughout that, as we might now say, the questioning is "nothing personal." Indeed, the Stranger at first asks for *anyone* as an interlocutor—anyone who is pliable and will not give him trouble (*Sophist* 217d ff.)—and the questions he asks do not penetrate Theaetetus's views but for the most part only gain his assent to points which the Stranger himself has made. He seems to accomplish, in the event, something of the overcoming of subjectivity that Socrates espouses but rarely achieves— though in reality the Stranger overcomes only the subjectivity of the *other*.

But do we really want to give up the ineluctably personal character of philosophic thinking in the name of overcoming subjectivity and the egotism of the contest? Or more positively: how can a thinking be deeply personal, as Socrates and Plato insist, yet also overcome the egotism that will always inhibit us from turning truly to the matter for thought? This, I suggest, is the problematic (and provocation) present in the contrast between Socrates' oft-repeated conviction regarding the importance of overcoming egotism, the difficulty of actually accomplishing it, and at the same time the deeply personal character of philosophy. The dialogues give us an unmatched presentation of the problem. They do not show a Socrates who resolves it. Does Plato? We here broach the question of Platonic anonymity.

For one thing is clear: Plato never includes his own person in the dialogues, he never puts into play therein a character named Plato who speaks. As a consequence, Plato himself never authorizes us to call what is said in the dialogues "Plato's philosophy." And this means that the authorial subject—the authority named Plato—is suppressed, even if he does not disappear completely. That is, there can be no question in the dialogues of a subjective individual, Plato, telling us what we should believe, making statements that we need either agree or disagree with it. By writing the dialogues in the way he does, Plato puts himself as an individual significantly out of play.

What he puts into play, however, is the matter for thought. He puts into play situations, predicaments, and a virtual horde of individual psyches who face up to and respond to their situations in myriad ways. One of them—an important one, to be sure—is a character named Socrates. Many take this character as speaking for Plato. But not once does Plato suggest that we do so—not in his dialogues, and certainly not in his Letters, where he speaks to us in his own name, as author. Thus, however many characters are introduced into the dialogues, however many "theories" are posited, however many ideas are expressed, just whose they are is always already shot through with ambiguity. To be sure, Plato the writer puts them in his dialogues—but as his own, as belonging to his peculiar subjectivity? Not at all. The remarkable consequence of this, I suggest, is that in the Platonic dialogues the thinking, the matter for thought, can never be reduced definitively to that of a single individual. The views expressed in the dialogues by a certain Parmenides are already those of a double—the Platonic Parmenides; Thrasymachus's views are those of the Platonic Thrasymachus; and decisively, Socrates' are those of the Platonic Socrates. "What are called mine," writes Plato, "are those of a Socrates become young and beautiful." Our perhaps natural or perhaps culturally and historically biased inclination to fix a given view, idea, or thought as that of a certain individual, this or that subjectivity, is always destabilized in the dialogues. Is this destabilization of the metaphysics of subjectivity not intended to invite us instead to the matter for thought? Socrates is portrayed in the dialogues as recognizing the need to overcome this meta-physics, but is also shown to be unable consistently to do so. Was it Plato who was able to succeed in doing so by writing as he did? If so, in this sense at least, one might call into question Heidegger's conviction that Socrates (and was he thinking of the historical Socrates or the Platonic Socrates?) was "the purest thinker of the west."

Let us return, then, to the end of the *Phaedrus,* and to the criticism Socrates gives of writing. Are these the very reasons why Socrates did not write? Is Plato's memory of Socrates accurate on this point? We do not know. What we do know is that these are the reasons *Plato gives us* as to why Socrates did not write. So if Socrates had other reasons why he did not write, we do not know them. But the situation then is immediately more complicated. For these reasons not to write are *written* in Plato's dialogue, the *Phaedrus,* one of some thirty-five dialogues that Plato wrote, some of them very long. What Plato is really asking us to consider, then, are the reasons given not to write in the light of Socrates' appar-ent decision not to do so and of *Plato's decision to write anyway.*

If we assume that Socrates did not write for the reasons he gives, how are we to understand the Platonic decision to write—but to write dialogues? If Plato had chosen, in spite of these arguments, to write treatises—to write a treatise, as Dionysus apparently did, claiming to assert his philosophy—we would have to say then quite simply that Socrates accepted the arguments against writing but Plato rejected them. But that Plato wrote not treatises but dialogues—not to mention what he says in the Second and Seventh Letters—complicates things yet again. It may be that Plato indeed felt the effect of the arguments he puts into the mouth of his Socrates, but thought that in the dialogue form he had discovered a mode of writing that would enable him to *take the risk* of writing, despite the qualified efficacy of these arguments. Let us look, then, at the extent to which the dialogue form, coupled with what Plato himself says in the Letters, might re-spond to the legitimate objections to writing presented in the *Phaedrus.*

We have already noted the general point that Socrates, in his elaboration of Thamus's objections, significantly softens their force. Socrates, that is, does not issue a blanket repudiation of writing, even if he himself does not write. Instead, he warns that no one who understands will try to express *their most serious thoughts* in writing, but will reserve them for oral conversations. Still further, he quietly *affirms* a certain writing *in the light* of philosophy: a writing that would be the *play* of philosophic souls, and a writing, he adds, that might serve as reminders of the real matter for thought.

If we think explicitly about the first objection, that writing will not aid our memories but serve only as "reminders," we can note several things. First, as we saw, this objection is already destabilized by Socrates' own affirmation of such "reminders" in his palinode. But what about the dialogues themselves? Might they, too, serve as just the sort of reminders of which Socrates speaks more positively? Might they serve, not as reminders of "Plato's philosophy"—for this is denied both in the Seventh Letter and the *Phaedrus*—but as reminders of what we might name the *call of philosophy*, the call to that sustained dwelling together that Plato intimates in his Letters? And as a measure of their success, we need only ask: how many, over the centuries, have been called to philosophy—called, and then reminded again and again—by the Platonic dialogues?

Theuth's second claim in behalf of writing and Thamus's second objection concern wisdom: Theuth claims writing will be a "drug" for wisdom, Thamus claims it will generate only a false impression of wisdom. Do the writings called Platonic dialogues generate a false claim to wisdom—indeed, a claim to wisdom at all? To be sure, many characters *within* the dialogues make claims to wisdom, the sophists who appear there most of all but not only the sophists. However, those claims are regularly *called into question* by the famed Socratic *elenchus*, not to mention by the events of the dialogues themselves. The philosophic stance exhibited paradigmatically by Socrates—and in an even deeper sense by the dialogues themselves—is, as I have previously argued, not a set of claims to wisdom but instead a stance of questioning, a stance of aporia. Read in this way, we may ask: has there been in the history of philosophy a more sustained warning against the claims to wisdom that *writing* might engender, than the Platonic dialogues?

Let us turn to the three objections that Socrates adds to Thamus's two: written texts cannot answer questions, they cannot discriminate before whom to speak and before whom to remain silent, and they cannot by themselves sustain the long dwelling together that philosophy would require. Consider the context in which the first of these would have force: I write a certain claim to wisdom in a text, that is, I assert what I call "my philosophic position." You, the reader, have questions of that position—perhaps skeptical questions, perhaps questions of understanding. You read my text again. You get the same claim, repeated. The text cannot answer questions, as Socrates says. But are the dialogues susceptible to this objection? The very claims made *within* the dialogues are not left alone, but are rather called into question, sometimes by Socrates with his *elenchus*, sometimes by what happens within the dialogue itself (as when Socrates first praises the function of "reminding," then constructs a myth that criticizes "mere" reminding). The dialogues, that is, far from not being able to answer questions, *begin the questioning,* begin a questioning that a reader, if he or she happens to be philosophical, can continue. That questioning, again, thus invites the reader into thinking; it does not tell the reader what to think.

The situation is similar with Socrates' second objection, that writing cannot tell before whom to speak and before whom to remain silent. That objection would seem to have force for a writing that asserts theses: the theses are asserted for any reader, of any sort, to read. But how does it stand with the dialogues? First of all, in the sense of asserting theses, Plato is *always* silent in the dialogues as Socrates only sometimes is (e.g., for long sections of the *Timaeus, Sophist,* and *Statesman*). Lest we miss this, Plato writes his own name into the dialogues three times: twice in the *Apology,* where he does not speak, and once in the *Phaedo,* where he is named as being *absent.* (On the other hand, the *Phaedrus* has Socrates and Phaedrus sitting under a "Plato tree" [*platonos*—230b].) Moreover, Plato gives us an exhibition within his written dialogues of the kinds of conditions under which one might speak and remain silent, as well as how to speak to whom, by allowing us to watch Socrates from dialogue to dialogue: we notice the very different ways in which he speaks to different souls, and notice as well before whom he occasionally remains silent (the Eleatic Stranger, for example). And in yet another sense, the dialogues pass over the horizon of the objection by issuing not theses or claims, but an invitation to hear the call of philosophy. That invitation, to be sure, is extended to anyone who will hear, and so perhaps to no one. The dialogues, as much as any written texts in philosophy, would then be written "for everyone and no one."

Socrates' final objection to writing, developed in terms of his contrast between the "garden of Adonis" and the more serious gardens of the serious farmer, is that it purports to be in a sense a "quick fix"—to give us in one unit what we need to know about a given topic—whereas what is needed for philosophy is that long period of dwelling together adumbrated in the Seventh Letter and surely exhibited by Socrates in his own life. Here too, as I hope is now obvious, the dialogues offer us no such quick fix. We call some dialogues, those that end with the question at issue still explicitly unanswered, "aporia dialogues," or sometimes, "Socratic dialogues," but in truth, all the dialogues in the end are aporetic: they raise more questions than they answer, and most importantly of all, they *leave us* with questions. Moreover, in portraying the life of Socrates—in memorializing that life—they give us an image, a *mimesis,* of what such a sustained life of dwelling might look like. To be sure, they are not that life itself; the dialogues *are writing,* and as such cannot themselves *be* the philosophical life to which they invite us. They themselves are not and cannot be the sustained dwelling together in question; but they are wonderfully vivid reminders to us of what such a life might be.

Nothing that I have said in this discussion is meant to suggest that Plato *solved the problem* of writing, in the sense of showing that the objections he himself raises against writing have no force, or that he had in any case answered those objections definitively. Rather, all I suggest is that Plato thought he had discovered in the dialogue form a mode of writing that would enable him to *take the risk* of writing, despite the qualified efficacy of the objections against it. The way in which the Platonic dialogues over the centuries have been transformed into supposed vehicles for the transmission of a set of doctrines we now call "Platonism" is ample testimony that the risk of writing remains real and is very great. If Plato thought that he had "solved" the problem of writing with the dialogue form, the history of the interpretation of his texts has surely shown him to be very, very wrong. Writing, even writing dialogues, was and is a risk indeed. Plato thought it was a risk worth taking, to extend the invitation to thinking to what would be anonymous readers—and Socrates apparently thought it was not.

Socrates, if we take the word of the Platonic dialogues, issued this invitation to almost everyone he met—indeed, took it as his calling to issue this invitation. Plato, we might assume, continued to issue the invitation to those who engaged with him in his Academy. But here the two figures part ways. For Socrates apparently felt no responsibility to issue the invitation to any whom he could not engage personally. To be sure, as the *Apology* so poignantly exhibits, Socrates took with utter seriousness his responsibility to invite those he spoke with into thinking, into the "examined life." He took it as a command from the god, and what could be more serious than that? In the end, we could say that he took on that responsibility even at the risk of his own life, and so he took on that responsibility courageously.

Still, it remains that he apparently did not feel the responsibility to issue his call beyond those with whom he could speak, and we can imagine how this may have begun to trouble a Plato who also, surely, issued this call to members of the Academy, to Dion, and to Dionysus. He must have felt his responsibility with special force in a time and a city where, he thought—as evidenced by Socrates' fate—philosophy was very much at risk. But Plato, we might suppose, felt this responsibility even more widely. He felt a responsibility to issue a call even to those with whom he could not speak, despite his own conviction that it was in the end only through personal encounter that such a call could be sustained. Perhaps he sought to meet this responsibility by writing—and writing in such a way as to issue the invitation in an incomparable way. Perhaps, then, Plato felt the *responsibility* to write, despite the risks of writing that he understood so well. But did he then hold Socrates responsible for *not writing*?

In the *Symposium*, we have seen that Plato has Alcibiades issue perhaps the harshest criticism of Socrates in all the dialogues, a criticism embedded in a speech of praise. Alcibiades accuses Socrates of being ironic in his oft-affirmed love of the young men with whom he spoke and engaged, including Alcibiades himself. Socrates' purported love is ironic, Alcibiades insists, masking what is in fact *contempt* for humans and all we hold dear. Instead, he concludes, Socrates *plays games* with human beings and does so ironically (216d–e). Nothing that we know about Alcibiades suggests that we need take his complaint against Socrates as objectively valid, but neither can we merely dismiss it. Given the way Socrates treats the sophists; given the way he treats Charmides, Critias, or Alcibiades; given the way he treats his wife, Xanthippe, on the day of his death; and given Diotima's perhaps justified skepticism as to whether Socrates will ever understand the "higher mysteries" of love (210a): might it not be that there is a certain point to Alcibiades' charge, and that Plato has not written these accusations simply for the reader to dismiss them? Might there be some point, then, to the charge that Socrates, for all his greatness, did not love human beings enough? That he did not love them enough, for example, to write?

Writing, then—a certain kind of writing, the writing of the dialogues— would be a gift, a beautiful gift: a gift of the love of human being and the love of philosophy. It is not, it must be emphasized, that writing is somehow *as such* a gift; or rather, if all writing is a gift, then no doubt most of it is a gift within an economy of transaction about which Derrida has written so well. I write a treatise; it is my gift to the reader. But in return, I get fame (or notoriety), tenure, promotion, even wealth, or the ego-satisfaction of being a "writer." But Plato clearly did not write within such an economy. There was no money in writing in ancient Athens—he did not need the money in any case—and there was nothing for him to be promoted to. We could conceive, only vaguely given his culture, that he wrote in part for "fame," for the "immortality" that Diotima says is the only immortality we can have, but even that must be qualified. Homer and Hesiod were the most famous Greeks, but they were participants in an oral, not a written, tradition.

But the writing of the dialogues, if what I have said has worth, is a gift within a very different economy, if it can be called an economy at all. For as Plato himself insists, and as we have seen, he did not write in a genre whose purpose was to expound a "philosophy" by which its author might become famous. Instead, the dialogues offer a gift which needs the response of the reader for its fulfillment. This is a response in a double sense: it also confers a *responsibility* on the reader, appeals to his or her freedom. Jean-Paul Sartre captures this set of relations very well in his *What Is Literature?* Writing, Sartre argues, is a gift to the reader but at the same time an appeal to their freedom and a conferring of responsibility: to respond to the author's freedom with their own freedom. Writing is thus a "pact of generosity between author and reader."[5] However, in the case of the dialogues, if the reader accepts the invitation—if the call to philosophy is heard—nothing is given back to Plato. As the gift of an invitation, without the egoism of the presentation of authorial doctrines, do not the dialogues broach for us the question of the pure gift?

I have tried to suggest in these reflections that Plato wrote his dialogues as "reminders" (*hypomnemasin*) to us—and perhaps to himself—not in the sense which Thamus disparages as "mere" reminders (275a), but in the sense in which

Socrates employs the term in his palinode (249d): as mortal events, mortal things, mortal acts that "remind" us, enable us to recall, the beings themselves. This would suggest that the dialogues are written to recall for us the matter for thought, the ultimate matter for thought, which Plato himself tells us in the Seventh Letter is a dwelling together with what must be thought which might lead, "like a flame kindled by a leaping spark," to a self-sustaining philosophical existence. The dialogues, then, are intended—in the absence of Plato himself and Socrates himself—to be the leaping spark that might inspire us to philosophy. Plato, it seems, felt a responsibility which his own teacher, Socrates, apparently did not: to remind us *in his absence* of the possibility of philosophic existence, of its possible (but only possible) beauty, and to invite us to this existence. He did this by writing. And I think it is fair to say that, over the centuries, no writings have been more successful at this particular aim, no works more beautiful reminders of the possibility of philosophy.

This means, as Plato himself insisted in both his Second and Seventh Letters, that the dialogues are *not* "Plato's philosophy." They are not because they cannot be so—because, as Plato insists: "Philosophy cannot be put into words like other subjects" (*Letters* 341c). As his Socrates tells us in the *Apology* and exhibits throughout the dialogues, and as Plato himself insists in the Seventh Letter, philosophy is a mode of *living*. To speak properly then—and in a sense which we should call "Platonic"—one should not speak, strictly, of "philosophy," nor of "my philosophy," much less of "Plato's philosophy." One should speak rather of "philosophical existence." And it is as a reminder of the possibility of a philosophical existence that might constitute "walking in beauty" that the dialogues are written, as Plato's gift to us, playfully.

But surely, it will be objected, philosophical existence will have something to do with holding certain views on important questions, and rejecting other views! Of course it will. But the dialogues remind us as well, by the persistently interrogative stance the Platonic Socrates maintains therein, that it is the stance of questioning—the *life* of questioning—that is more fundamental than the attractiveness of any of the possible answers. Questioning, it must then be said, comes *before* any possible answers occur to us and is the only genuinely philosophical *response* to the answers that so occur. And questioning, to say it once more, is a mode of existence, a mode of living.

Meanwhile, it might be supposed, the character of philosophy has changed radically in its history. During that history it certainly came to be that philosophers other than Plato *had* "philosophies," philosophical positions and doctrines, and certainly seemed to claim to *write them down*. For we surely have, do we not, Descartes's philosophy, Spinoza's philosophy, Kant's philosophy, Hegel's philosophy?

And what of us? Virtually all of us today who call ourselves philosophers write, and I suppose we would claim in some sense to write "philosophically." But on reflection, who among us would be so daring as to say that what they write is their "philosophy"? For my part, I surely would not indulge in the fantasy that in this book I have written "my philosophy." Do any of us really believe any more that one's "philosophy" can actually be written? Would it not be more accurate to say of most of us that we write—to use once again a metaphor ubiquitous in the dialogues—"in the light" of philosophy? In this, perhaps we have remembered Plato. And are our own writings, then, not also in a sense recollections—*reminders* of philosophy? And so *not* philosophy itself? Perhaps this is what we have learned—what we have recalled, at long last, from Plato and from his dialogues. In this sense, and in this sense only, might we want to call ourselves, in his memory . . . Platonists?

Notes

Introduction

1. The famous passage toward the end of the *Republic* where Socrates hints that those over the age of ten must be gotten rid of in order for the *Kallipolis* to be established might be thought to broach the issue of genocide, but not strictly, since presumably there would be a host of youth left over to be retrained.

2. Indeed, suggests Nietzsche, even for Socrates. See *The Birth of Tragedy,* where he speaks of "aesthetic Socratism" as embodying the conviction that "to be beautiful everything must be intelligible" (Nietzsche 1967, 83–84). Nietzsche continues this conviction to the end: in *Twilight of the Idols,* speaking of Socrates' famed ugliness, he comments, "But ugliness, in itself an objection, is among the Greeks almost a refutation" (Nietzsche 1982b, 474).

3. See Edelstein 1966.

4. Edelstein 1966, 73ff.

5. Reported to me by Stanley Rosen. Strauss expressed this in seminars, but apparently not in his published writing.

6. I am thinking particularly of Jacques Derrida's questioning of the status of the "author" Plato in his "Plato's Pharmacy." See Derrida 1981, esp. 129–130.

1. The Question of Beauty in the *Hippias Major*

1. I elaborate on the significance of this dramatic situation in *The Virtue of Philosophy: An Interpretation of Plato's Charmides.* See Hyland 1981, chaps. 1–2.

2. Nails 2002, 13–14. This volume, *The People of Plato: A Prosopography of Plato and the Other Socratics,* is an excellent source for information of this sort.

3. I translate literally but awkwardly to bring out that *kalos* is Socrates' first word in response.

4. In addition, at 284a (twice) and at 285c, superlative forms of *kallistos*, "most beautiful" or "best," are employed.

5. In addition, Aristophanes' *Clouds*, first performed in 423 BC, portrayed Socrates as ugly in soul as well as in body. Socrates' notorious ugliness is particularly noteworthy in a culture as obsessed with beauty as the Greeks.

6. This issue gets complicated in Kant by his regular emphasis on the core status of the beauty of *nature*. This Platonic-Kantian contrast is obviously a topic for a subsequent book, but for an excellent discussion both of the Kantian formulation of this issue and its modern consequences—e.g., "beauty (or its primary instance, art)"—see Bernstein 1992.

7. A different but related issue: for the Greeks—and this would have to be addressed eventually—even though beauty is not located "originally" in art, it remains that beauty is a virtual requirement for good art. Yet for modernity, which locates the origin of beauty in art, gradually but surely (as in contemporary art) beauty becomes an entirely *contingent* feature of good art.

8. See *Theaetetus* 152d ff.

9. Martin Heidegger's classic formulation of this claim (not, however, with regard to Plato) is in *The Origins of a Work of Art*. See Heidegger 1971, 81.

10. One cannot read this passage without being reminded of Zarathustra's famous formulation of beauty in part 2 of *Thus Spoke Zarathustra*, in the section titled "On those who are sublime": "When power becomes gracious and descends into the visible, such descent I call beauty. And there is no one from whom I want beauty as much as from you who are powerful." (See Nietzsche 1982a.) It should also be noted that Hippias's immediate response to Socrates' suggestion is to remove it from the abstract (the beautiful is power) to the particular: in *politics*, he replies, it is especially beautiful to be powerful in one's city, and ugly to be powerless (*Hippias Major* 296a).

11. Made even more provocative if joined with the claim of the Eleatic Stranger that *Being* is power (*Sophist* 247e). Thinking through the consequences of a position that suggests that Being is power and that such power is what *beauty* is would take us through virtually the entire history of philosophy on the topic.

12. This step itself is even more problematic with the Greek *aition* than the English "cause," for which the very notion of a "self-cause" would at least be a complication here.

13. To be sure, for entirely different reasons, the Socrates of the *Republic* will agree that strictly, the beautiful is not the cause of the good, *because the good is the cause of the beautiful*. (See *Republic* 505a ff.) This possibility, of course, is ignored in the *Hippias Major*.

14. Though this does not stop either Hippias or Socrates from continuing to use forms of the term "beauty" in their own exchanges in perfectly coherently ways. See *Hippias Major* 297c, 297d.

15. One of my readers notes that there is much more to be said about definition, and indeed about the definitions of this dialogue. He is surely correct on both counts. There is a vast and important literature on the issue of definition in the dialogues, and my brief study here of the definitions of the *Hippias Major* makes no claim to comprehensiveness whatsoever. Were this a book on this dialogue, each definition—not to mention the issue of definition per se—would require much closer attention. The point of this brief examination is to concentrate on one aspect of the issue of definition in the dialogue: the meaning and significance of the *failure* to adequately define *to kalon*. I hope I have said enough to bring out that significance.

16. See Plato 1983. The translator is Paul Woodruff.

2. The Question of Beauty in the *Symposium*

1. In both dialogues this general sense is qualified and complicated. Virtually every speaker in the *Symposium*, in the midst of praising eros, indicates his awareness that eros also has its dangers; and in the *Republic*, despite the relentless criticism of eros, it becomes clear that philosophy, and so the philosophic rulers on whom the city will depend, are impossible without eros. Stanley Rosen sheds light on this complicated situation in his recent *Plato's Republic: A Study*. See Rosen 2005.

2. Agathon immediately signals his real interest in Aristodemus's presence, however: "How is it you did not bring Socrates?" (*Symposium* 174e). If Tonto shows up at the party, the Lone Ranger cannot be far behind!

3. Too briefly: Phaedrus will present a utilitarian or self-interest position; Pausanias the position of sophistic relativism; Eryximachus the scientific account; Aristophanes the standpoint of religion; Agathon that of poetry; and Socrates, in a way highly qualified by the introduction of the priestess Diotima, the philosophic account.

4. Phaedrus almost surely knows this. At the beginning of his speech, in support of his contention that eros is among the oldest of the gods, he quotes a line from Hesiod (*Theogony* 116ff.). However, he stops the sentence at the first mention of eros as among the "first" of the gods who came to be, neglecting to complete Hesiod's sentence, which continues: "and Eros, handsomest among all the immortals, who breaks the limbs' strength, who in all gods, in all human beings, overpowers the intelligence in their breast, and all their shrewd planning" (my trans.). Phaedrus probably leaves out this part of the sentence, which clearly points out the dangers of eros, because he is supposedly giving an encomium, a speech of praise. He also may want to hide the real implications of his speech from his lover, Eryximachus, who is present.

5. In the *Phaedrus*, Socrates will try to show Phaedrus that the beloved, too, falls in love, at least in the highest love affairs, the "Zeus friendships." See *Phaedrus* 255d ff.

6. My reading of Phaedrus's speech and indeed of all the speeches is deeply indebted to Stanley Rosen, who long ago was my dissertation advisor in my first effort to understand this dialogue, and who subsequently published what remains the most thorough study of the *Symposium*. See Rosen 1968.

7. There is a very limited case that could be made for Pausanias's claim, given the cultural conditions at the time. Since women were not, by and large, educated nor did they partake in public life, it might have at least been more plausible then to associate love of men with love of the mind, since the issue of intelligence rarely arose with women. But there are obvious exceptions: Aspasia, for example, and most pointedly, the soon-to-be-introduced Diotima. Not to mention the strong portrayal of women in several of Aristophanes' plays, as well as Sophocles' Antigone.

8. One might here translate alternatively something like "neither noble nor disgraceful." I continue to translate forms of *kalos* as "beautiful" to preserve the continuity.

9. Even as Alcibiades later confesses he tried unsuccessfully to do with Socrates!

10. It will remain for Agathon to join these together, and he will do so precisely with the issue of beauty.

11. Though it might be noted that some representatives of his standpoint today are still trying to fulfill his project.

12. Culminating, perhaps, in the remark of A. E. Taylor that the fact that Plato put the speech in the mouth of the comic poet "should, of course, have proved to an intelligent reader that the whole tale of the bi-sexual creatures is a piece of gracious Pantagruelism, and that Plato's serious purpose must be looked for elsewhere" (Taylor 1956, 209, cf. 219).

13. Socrates throughout the *Clouds,* and Agathon in the *Thesmophoriazusae,* where he is mocked for his excessive effeminacy.

14. In his plays, homosexuals are almost always portrayed in a disreputable light, and Socrates, in the *Clouds,* is chastised in part for transforming the gods into principles of physics: clouds, thunder, etc.

15. We shall need to recall this later when we note a similar situation in the *Phaedrus.* After Socrates develops his remarkable account of the charioteer and the two horses, an account that *seemed* to be an account of the *soul,* he comments that "the whole speech so far has been about the fourth kind of madness" (249d): i.e., about eros! Socrates, as we shall see, would thus seem to agree with Aristophanes that an adequate account of eros is tantamount to an account of human nature.

16. The popular criticism of "Plato's" account of eros, that it is not reciprocal, is thus purchased only by ignoring Aristophanes' teaching. This, however, is easily accomplished by wrongly confining the "Platonic teaching" on eros in the *Symposium* to what Diotima says.

17. It is also possible that Plato is here quietly criticizing Aristophanes: if, as he has him say, homosexual orientation is "by nature," why in his plays should he be so harsh on them for a standpoint which they do not choose, which is not a "life-style choice"?

18. Indeed, Agathon says, eros "despises old age" and wants nothing to do with it. One can only imagine how Agathon's older lover, Pausanias, feels about this opening—not to mention Agathon's flirtation at the beginning with Socrates, and his subsequent flirtations with Socrates and Alcibiades. At the very end of the dialogue (223b), all conversation ends because "someone" has left the party and left the door open. Since all the other named participants are subsequently mentioned as still present, the party pooper is almost certainly Pausanias, who presumably left in a huff.

19. It is instructive that at the end of Socrates' speech, everyone *except Aristophanes* applauds!

20. One version of this recognition, of course, is Aristotle's famous claim that human being is the *zoon politikon,* the "political animal."

21. I have tried to elucidate the details of the argument here and elsewhere in the dialogues in Hyland 1968: "*Eros, Epithumia,* and *Philia* in Plato." Among the important issues raised in the present argument is that of the complicated connection between eros and *epithumia,* love and desire. To summarize my claims in that article: though eros and *epithumia* often overlap (as in the present passage), the two are distinguished by the presence of reason in eros, whereas *epithumia* is literally "without reason." The difference between eros and *philia,* on the other hand, is one of degree—the degree of reason in the particular experience.

22. *Timaeus* 37d.

23. Although some have argued that Diotima must be an historical figure, the strong consensus among scholars, with which I agree, is that she is the Platonic Socrates' invention. Two strands of evidence strike me as crucial here. First, there is not a single reference outside of this dialogue to a figure from Mantinea named Diotima, and if indeed, as Socrates says, she held back the plague, there surely would be external evidence for her existence. Second, her speech is so full of implicit references to and incorporations of the earlier speeches that were it really the accurate portrayal of a teaching long ago, the parallels with the previous speeches would be positively uncanny.

24. Aristophanes, appropriately enough, is the only speaker in the *Symposium* not involved erotically with someone else present. The various relationships are complex and would need to be analyzed carefully.

25. Plato has nevertheless been chastised by some interpreters for not literally introducing a real woman into the discussion, but instead having Diotima be made present through the voice of the male Socrates. Diotima, and so feminine experience, is thus "appropriated" by a still male experience, we are told. This strikes me as demanding too much from an already revolutionary thinker for his time. Still, if Diogenes Laertius is to be believed, Plato reserved the *actual* introduction of woman into male intellectual company for his Academy, where, Diogenes tells us, he introduced two women, Lasthenea of Mantinea (!) and Axiothea of Phlius, into the discussions, apparently having them disguise themselves in men's clothes! See Diogenes Laertius 1853, 129.

26. Because it does not bear directly on the question of beauty, I will not engage here in such a secular reformulation of this mythical passage. Let me just say, however, that I believe such a reformulation would have everything to do with the relation between "forms" and "phenomena," here presented not as a "dualism" but rather as triadic: they are joined together by the daimon eros.

27. Though it should be noted that even the "adult" Socrates seems exceedingly interested in the parenthood of the young men with whom he engages.

28. Freud's notorious "penis envy" notwithstanding!

29. Aristotle asserts almost exactly the same thing in book 1 of the *Nicomachean Ethics.*

30. See Hans-Georg Gadamer's intriguing suggestion of the relation: the good is the beautiful as it is manifested in the harmony of things (Gadamer 1991, 209; cf. Gadamer 1986, 115). The issue of this relation is underlined by Diotima at 205e, when she clearly "corrects" Aristophanes' claim that love is of our other half and our desire to be whole. Love, she insists, is of the good—not the half or the whole—and people will even cut off parts of themselves if only they think it will do them some good. Earlier, we noted that beauty was missing from Aristophanes' speech. So too, Diotima here reminds us, was the good.

31. Particularly when one reads the *Symposium* with regard to the question of beauty, one sees what an utterly frustrating dialogue it can be. That issue after issue is raised but not developed in this dialogue, but then developed more fully in the *Phaedrus,* is in my opinion the best evidence that, dramatically and pedagogically, the *Symposium* must be read as prior and a propaedeutic to the *Phaedrus.*

32. Irigaray correctly observes that it is noteworthy that Socrates seems oblivious to the creative dimension of eros in its connection to beauty. See Irigaray 1984, 25.

33. I first developed the basic account to follow in Hyland 2005: "*Oude tis logos, oude tis episteme:* The Hermeneutics of Beauty."

34. *Phaedo* 64a ff.

35. *Phaedrus* 247c ff.

36. This might be seen as a preparation for Aristotle's later characterization of happiness as activity in accordance with human excellence in the *Nicomachean Ethics.*

37. As Alcibiades tells it, this seems a general reaction to Socrates' *sophrosyne.* His other examples of Socrates' exhibition of this virtue are his ability to withstand cold while on military campaigns, and his staying up all night thinking about something (*Symposium* 220c–d). In both instances, the reaction of onlookers was amazement at Socrates' *sophrosyne* tempered by the sense that he was exhibiting contempt for those present who were not so self-controlled.

38. And apparently more generally: in the beginning of the *Charmides* (155d), Socrates gets a glimpse inside the cloak of the also strikingly beautiful Charmides and claims to be "inflamed with passion" (*ephlegomen*). That passion is extraordinarily short-

lived, however: Socrates gets control of himself in virtually a second and proceeds to dialogue with Charmides—about *sophrosyne*!

3. The Question of Beauty in the *Phaedrus*

1. One dimension of this is also that, in a culture still more orally oriented than our own, Phaedrus seems not very adept at memorization—which is why he wants to practice on Socrates. This may be one of the intellectual limitations of Phaedrus, to which we shall have occasion to turn presently.

2. If one adds the more "dramatic" elements of critique—Socrates' criticism of Phaedrus for hiding the written text under his cloak, and his criticism of those "rationalists" who insist on demythologizing mythical accounts such as the tale of Pharmaceia that is associated with the locale at which the discussion takes place—one could say that the *Phaedrus* is one of the most persistently critical of all the dialogues, one especially attuned to the limits of language, and indeed, of human possibility.

3. This is obviously bizarre: who has ever given—or received—a speech of seduction that began, "let's begin by defining our terms"? On the other hand, if you're trying to seduce Phaedrus . . .

4. The entire list of levels at 248d is as follows: (1) philosophers, lovers of beauty, followers of the Muses, and lovers have seen the most of "the beings"; (2) a law-abiding king or military commander; (3) a politician, manager, or businessman; (4) athletes who love exercise or those who heal the body; (5) those devoted to prophecy or the mysteries; (6) poets or other imitative artists; (7) artisans or farmers; (8) sophists or demagogues; and (9), at the lowest, tyrants.

5. Nietzsche 1982a, 153.

6. I have argued for just such an interpretation in Hyland 1981.

7. Cf. *Republic* 377a: "Don't you understand, I said, that first we tell myths to children? And surely they are as a whole false, but there is also truth in them."

8. E.g., William Cobb in his mostly solid translation in *Plato's Erotic Dialogues*. See Plato 1993, 103.

9. This is Charles Griswold's interpretation in his *Self-Knowledge in Plato's Phaedrus*. (See Griswold 1986, 82ff.) I find his reading to be by far the most plausible.

10. All the talk about the movement of the heavens, etc., would be evidence for this reading. This understanding of the exhibition reminds us that it reads almost as a prototype of what will be Aristotle's "proof" for God as the unmoved mover in *Physics* book 8 and *Metaphysics* book 12. The crucial difference will be that Aristotle will limit the possibility of self-motion, which he understands as moving without being moved, to one "soul" (if one can even call it that), the unmoved mover, whereas this exhibition seems to attribute it to "all soul," whatever that means.

11. Heraclitus, fragment 115.

12. There is thus an obvious parallel (though not an identity) between this image and the triadic soul of the *Republic*, where, once again, the reasoning part of the soul serves the double function of guiding and controlling the other parts and knowing (or seeing) the forms.

13. Since this constitutes a virtual denial of personal immortality, those who construe the earlier "exhibition" of the immortality of soul as referring to individual souls typically mistranslate this sentence. Cobb, for example, translates: "We are unable to give an account of an immortal being" (Plato 1993, 104). The sentence also destabilizes the

very story Socrates is telling: the very image he is presenting is "constructed" from the image of our own selves, and we cannot know the gods adequately, even though this very account presents an image of the gods.

14. Curiously, we are told that Hestia stays home (247a). That would presumably make the other eleven be Zeus, Hera, Apollo, Artemis, Ares, Hephaestus, Demeter, Poseidon, Aphrodite, Hermes, and Athena.

15. If there are differences in the characters of the gods which lead to different experiences of the beings, no indication is given that these differences are discussed among the gods. To the contrary, the implication is that they all experience exactly the same thing: complete, adequate noetic vision of the beings.

16. I first attempted to make some sense of this complicated human situation in Hyland 1981. See esp. chap. 3.

17. For a fascinating discussion of this passage which I think is very compatible with my reading, see Carson 1998, 155–167. It should be noted that the playful etymology does not comprise a *complete* understanding of eros (how could it?), since as we saw above, the charioteer and the two horses, as well as the wings, are implicated in the soul's self-motion and so are dimensions of eros.

18. This is, to say the least, a curious image to employ if one's intent is to denigrate the body. For an oyster is hardly "imprisoned" in its shell! The shell is its home, the source of its protection against predators. Is that the proper relation of body to soul? The body as the protector of the soul, whose being and logos is the self-motion of eros? Are we to understand this strongly contrasting image in the manner of a Derridean *différance*? Or is Plato trying to tell us something?

19. Could it have been for this reason in part that Plato, playfully, chose as Socrates' interlocutor and the title of this dialogue, "Phaedrus," which means "shining one" in Greek?

20. One of the many indications that this is a specifically philosophic friendship.

21. A *certain* Hegelianism, by no means the only or the most plausible one, but a widespread one nevertheless.

22. *Republic* 505a ff.

4. The Second and Seventh Letters

1. Derrida plays on this situation insightfully in Derrida 1987.

2. Heidegger, "Out of the Experience of Thinking." See Heidegger 1971, 7.

3. In dramatic order: *Theaetetus, Euthyphro, Sophist, Statesman, Apology, Crito, Phaedo.* It is likely as well that the *Cratylus* belongs in this group, not to mention the "unwritten" *Philosopher.*

4. The *Theaetetus* addresses this issue dramatically by portraying the young Theaetetus as almost as ugly as Socrates, yet as emerging as "truly beautiful," that is, as having a beautiful soul.

5. Hyland 2004, 90ff.

6. See especially Bury's general introduction to the Letters (Plato 1989, 385–392) and introduction to the Seventh Letter (463–475).

7. Edelstein 1966, 6ff.

8. Glenn Morrow's translation. See Plato 1997, 1659 (341c–d).

9. The "philosophical friendships" of the palinode we have just studied, as well as Socrates' regular philosophical conduct, support this reading as well.

10. In his essay, "Dialectic and Sophism in Plato's *Seventh Letter*." See Gadamer 1980, 104, 105, 112, 120, 121, 122.

11. There is no better example in modern philosophy of one who wrestled throughout his philosophic life with this issue than Martin Heidegger, who tried again and yet again to find the right language to "say" what he wanted to say—to say the question of Being.

12. Aristotle 2003, 1139b17.

5. The Critique of Rhetoric and Writing in the *Phaedrus*

1. *Paschein* and *pathein* both mean "suffering," though this rendering is at the strong end of their shades of meaning. They can have milder meanings, even to the point of something like "experience" or "undergoing." In this passage, I agree with almost all translators in rendering them "suffering."

2. Note that the English noun already includes a reference to memory.

3. "Plato's Pharmacy," in Derrida 1981.

4. A third consideration I note only as a puzzle: why does Phaedrus refer to the story as one about "the Theban king"? Socrates mentioned only in passing that the Upper Kingdom of Egypt, where the myth takes place, is called by the Greeks "Egyptian Thebes" (274d).

5. Sartre 1962, 55. For writing as a gift, cf. 53, 62; for the conferring of responsibility and the appeal to freedom, cf. 46–47, 64–65.

Bibliography

Aristophanes. 1912. *The Eleven Comedies*. Anonymous trans. New York: Tudor.

Aristotle. 2003. *Nicomachean Ethics*. Trans. A. Rackham. Cambridge, Mass.: Harvard University Press.

Bernstein, Jay. 1992. *The Fate of Art: Aesthetic Alienation from Kant to Derrida and Adorno*. University Park: Pennsylvania State University Press.

Carson, Anne. 1998. *Eros the Bittersweet*. Princeton: Princeton University Press.

Derrida, Jacques. 1981. *Dissemination*. Trans. Barbara Johnson. Chicago: University of Chicago Press.

———. 1987. *The Postcard: From Plato to Freud and Beyond*. Trans. Alan Bass. Chicago: University of Chicago Press.

Diogenes Laertius. 1853. *Lives of the Philosophers*. London: H. G. Bohn.

Edelstein, Ludwig. 1966. *Plato's Seventh Letter*. Leiden: E. J. Brill.

Gadamer, Hans-Georg. 1980. *Dialogue and Dialectic: Eight Hermeneutical Studies on Plato*. Trans. P. Christopher Smith. New Haven: Yale University Press.

———. 1986. *The Idea of the Good in Platonic-Aristotelian Philosophy*. Trans. P. Christopher Smith. New Haven: Yale Univerity Press.

———. 1991. *Plato's Dialectical Ethics: Phenomenological Interpretations Relating to the Philebus*. Trans. Robert Wallace. New Haven: Yale University Press.

Griswold, Charles. 1986. *Self-Knowledge in Plato's Phaedrus*. New Haven: Yale University Press.

Heidegger, Martin. 1971. *Poetry, Language, Thought*. Trans. Alfred Hofstadtler. New York: Harper & Row.

Hyland, Drew. 1968. "*Eros, Epithumia*, and *Philia* in Plato." *Phronesis* 13:1. 32–46.

———. 1981. *The Virtue of Philosophy: An Interpretation of Plato's Charmides*. Athens: Ohio University Press.

———. 2004. *Questioning Platonism: Continental Interpretations of Plato*. Albany: State University of New York Press.

———. 2005. "*Oude tis logos, oude tis episteme:* The Hermeneutics of Beauty." *Internationales Jahrbuch fur Hermeneutik*, vol. 4. Mohr Siebeck. 9–26.

Irigaray, Luce. 1984. *An Ethics of Sexual Difference.* Trans. Carolyn Burke and Gillian Gill. Ithaca: Cornell University Press.

Nails, Debra. 2002. *The People of Plato: A Prosopography of Plato and the Other Socratics.* Indianapolis: Hackett.

Nietzsche, Friedrich. 1967. *The Birth of Tragedy and The Case of Wagner.* Trans. Walter Kaufmann. New York: Vintage.

——. 1982a. *Thus Spoke Zarathustra.* In *The Portable Nietzsche.* Trans. Walter Kaufmann. New York: Penguin.

——. 1982b. *Twilight of the Idols.* In *The Portable Nietzsche.* Trans. Walter Kaufmann. New York: Penguin.

Plato. 1958. *Platonis Opera,* vols. 1–5. Ed. John Burnet. Oxford: Clarendon.

——. 1983. *Two Comic Dialogues: Ion and Hippias Major.* Trans. Paul Woodruff. Indianapolis: Hackett.

——. 1989. *Plato IX: Timaeus, Critias, Cleitophon, Menexenus, Epistles.* Trans. R. G. Bury. Cambridge, Mass.: Harvard University Press.

——. 1993. *Symposium and Phaedrus: Plato's Erotic Dialogues.* Trans. William Cobb. Albany: State University of New York Press.

——. 1997. *Plato: Complete Works.* Ed. John Cooper. Indianapolis: Hackett.

Rosen, Stanley. 1968. *Plato's Symposium.* New Haven: Yale University Press.

——. 2005. *Plato's Republic: A Study.* New Haven: Yale University Press.

Sartre, Jean-Paul. 1962. *Literature and Existentialism.* Trans. Bernard Frechtman. New York: Citadel.

Taylor, A. E. 1956. *Plato: The Man and His Work.* New York: Meridian.

Index

kalos, 28–29, 32, 99
Kant, Immanuel, 115, 134, 138n6
knowledge: absolute, 110–111; components of, 108–112; definition of, 13–14; finite, 88–89, 109, 111; power and, 35
kuklos, 108

laws, 101–102
Letters, Second and Seventh, the: authorship, 91, 102–103; dwelling-with in, 106; enigma in, 92–94; on inner beauty, 97–99; on philosophy as a way of living, 105–106; Plato's philosophy in, 107–108, 134–135; recipients, 92–93; Socrates' youth portrayed in, 95–97; structure of, 100–101; subjectivity of philosophy in, 127–129; on virtue, 113; on written texts, 94, 103–104, 106–107, 121, 129–132
logos, 4, 59, 68, 77, 79, 80, 108–109; finite knowledge and, 88–89, 109, 111; *Phaedrus* as a critique of, 115
love. *See* eros
Lysias, 66–70, 97
Lysis, 9, 61, 97

medicine, 35–36, 122–123
memory versus recollection, 118–124
metaphysics, 46
myths, 122–123, 126

nature, beauty of, 65–66
nature of the soul, 142n13
Nicomachean Ethics, 47, 111
Nietzsche, Friedrich, 72, 126, 137n2
noetic experience, 106–107
nomoi, 33
non-discursive dimension of beauty, 4, 17–18, 56–57, 82, 87–88
non-lovers, 66, 68; transformed to concealed lovers, 69

onoma, 108
oral speech, 123–126
origins of eros, 47–48

parentage of eros, 47–48
Parmenides, 95–96

Pausanias, 31–35
pederasty, 32–33
perfection, 79
Phaedrus, 14, 25, 44, 57, 58, 97, 105, 110, 113; beauty as experience and being in, 81–85; beauty defined in, 5; beauty of nature in, 65–66; contrast between writing and oral speech in, 124–126; as a critique of logos, 115; cynicism toward love in, 69–71; dialogues in, 2, 68–69; on divine madness, 69–73; focal dialogue of, 3; the gods and heavens in, 74–79, 84–85, 111; on immortality, 73–74; love as irrational in, 69–73; on nature of the soul, 74–81; non-discursive dimension of beauty in, 82, 87–88; on reincarnation, 77–79; setting of, 64–65; Socrates' rhetoric in, 115–118; on virtue, 84
pharmakon, 122–123
philosophic relationships, 85–87
philosophy: of beauty, 89–90; of Plato, 107–108, 113–114, 130, 134–135; rhetoric and, 117–118; subjectivity of, 127–129; as a way of life, 105–106, 113–114, 134; written, 94, 103–104, 106–107, 118, 134–135
physical appearance of Socrates, 13, 61, 97, 138n5
physical beauty, 36–37, 52–54, 60
Plato, 27, 28, 36, 67; authenticity of authorship by, 5, 91, 102–103; hatred of art, 50, 78; on knowledge, 108–112; on laws, 101–102; non-discursive element in writings of, 90; philosophy of, 107–108, 113–114, 130; poetry and, 60; on politics, 100–102; teaching by, 92–95, 102–103; written philosophy of, 94, 103–104, 106–107
Platonism, 52–53, 55, 58–59, 105, 113
politics, 100–102
Poros/Metis, 47–48
power, beauty as, 22, 82–83, 138n10
prattein, 32
Protagorean relativism, 31–32

recollection versus memory, 118–124
reincarnation, 77–79
relativism, 76, 84–85; Protagorean, 31–32

DREW A. HYLAND is Charles A. Dana Professor of Philosophy at
Trinity College. He is editor (with John Panteleimon Manoussakis) of
Heidegger and the Greeks (Indiana University Press, 2006).